———⌇⦂⦂⦂⦂⦂⦂———

Reconsidering
No Man Knows My History

Fawn M. Brodie and Joseph Smith
in Retrospect

Fawn McKay Brodie, 1966, at her home in Palisades, California.
Utah State Historical Society. All rights reserved. Used by permission.

Reconsidering
No Man Knows My History

Fawn M. Brodie and Joseph Smith
in Retrospect

Edited by
NEWELL G. BRINGHURST

UTAH STATE UNIVERSITY PRESS
Logan, Utah
1996

To
W. Turrentine Jackson
and to the memory of
A. Russell Mortensen
two mentors who greatly influenced my fondness for
American Western history
and to
Lois Cooper Allen
a nurturing aunt and empathetic friend

Copyright © 1996 Utah State University Press
All rights reserved

Utah State University Press
Logan, Utah 84322-7800

Typography by WolfPack

The paper in this book is acid free.

Library of Congress Cataloging-in-Publication Data

Reconsidering No man knows my history : Fawn M. Brodie and Joseph
    Smith in retrospect / edited by Newell G. Bringhurst.
      p. cm.
    Includes bibliographical references and index.
    ISBN 0-87421-214-6 (paper)
    ISBN 0-87421-205-7 (cloth)
    1. Brodie, Fawn McKay, 1915– No man knows my history. 2. Smith,
Joseph, 1805–1844. 3. Church of Jesus Christ of Latter-Day Saints—
Presidents—Biography. 4. Mormon Church—Presidents—Biography.
5. Mormons—United States—Biography. I. Bringhurst, Newell G.
BX8695.S6B738 1996
289.3'092—dc20   96-25261
                                                              CIP

Contents

Foreword
The Example of Fawn McKay Brodie: A Tribute

William Mulder

Fawn McKay Brodie and I were strict contemporaries: We were born in the same year; we met on several occasions; we corresponded; and once, in June 1978, we shared the same platform with the distinguished Black historian John Hope Franklin at a Phi Beta Kappa ceremony.

The Papers of Fawn McKay Brodie, officially so called, which now form part of the special collections at the University of Utah, occupy twenty-five linear feet of shelf space in the Marriott Library. The records of her final work, the Nixon biography, alone fill twenty-nine boxes, evidence of what she called, in the middle of the project, "the enormous swamp known as the Nixon literature. It is like the great swamp of the upper Nile known as the Sudd, which blocked navigation on that river for centuries, and still does. I don't know," she said, "whether I'll ever find my way through the accumulated vegetation in the river of Nixon's life." She did find her way through, as we know, and completed her book one month before she died of what one of her sons has described as a "horribly rapacious" cancer in January 1981. It was her last testament in a life-long scholarly obsession with sifting truth from the lies we tell, consciously or unconsciously, when we manipulate the past. To browse among the Brodie papers is to trace the intellectual journey of one of the notable women of our time.

We catch glimpses of that journey in reminiscences now part of the University of Utah's collective memoirs published as *Remembering* (1981); in the interviews and correspondence, the notes, records, articles, and reviews that comprise the Brodie collection; and finally in the major biographies themselves, the published results of all that research: *No Man Knows My History: The Life of Joseph Smith, the Mormon Prophet* (1945), *Thaddeus Stevens, Scourge of the South* (1959), *The Devil Drives: The Life of Sir Richard Burton* (1967), *Thomas Jefferson: An Intimate History* (1974), and *Richard Nixon: The Shaping of His Character* (1981). In these we may perceive Fawn's preoccupation with truth and lying, and we detect a pattern of love and envy, attraction and aversion, admiration for and bafflement about the public figures (all of them male, incidentally) she chose to write about. We detect that she had very positive feelings toward Stevens (like him, she felt herself a scourge), toward Jefferson (who nevertheless lived a lie), and toward Burton (whose fascination for Fawn grew out of her editing *The City of the Saints*); ambivalent feelings toward Joseph Smith (by whom she felt betrayed); and finally loathing for Nixon (whose life at one point she called "an obscenity"). Each book began with puzzling questions she felt simply had to be answered, paradoxes that had to be resolved; and each book proved to be controversial because in each Fawn had to take courageous risks. Her husband, Bernard Brodie, a distinguished political scientist at the University of California at Los Angeles (UCLA), with whom during a year in Paris she wrote a history of weaponry, *From Cross-Bow to H-Bomb*, and who also died of cancer just two years before her own death, used to say of her, "History is alive with mysteries, and Fawn is always in busy pursuit of the answers."

In the Brodie papers we can also chronicle her courageous confrontation with a series of establishments: the family, which objected to her marrying a Jew (and at the same time her husband's family objected to his marrying a Mormon); the Mormon establishment, which excommunicated her for heresy; the historical establishment, which, for her suspect method of psychobiography, denied her tenure at UCLA until the chancellor reversed the decision; and, within that establishment, the "Jefferson establishment," which called her "intimate history" of him "dirty graffiti on his statue" and led to a memorable debate between Fawn and Gary Wills of the *New York Review of Books*, her high executioner, at the Kennedy Center in Washington, D.C., in 1975. For the record, Fawn's excommunication did *not* come at her own request, as has been widely believed: when the missionaries arrived with the summons to the bishop's court in Cambridge, Massachusetts, to answer charges of heresy and to defend herself against excommunication, she did not go, "cheerfully admitting my heresy to one and all," as she recounts the episode in a letter to me, "but went off to the hospital instead," to give birth to her second son.

We catch glimpses of her intellectual growth from her reminiscences, as mentioned before, about her undergraduate days at then Weber College and the University of Utah and her graduate studies at the University of Chicago, where she met her husband and married him on the same day she received her master's degree, at twenty-one. Fawn received her B.A. degree in English from the University of Utah at the age of eighteen, in 1934, a Depression year, when she and an older sister shared an apartment a half mile below campus, where her father, she remembered, would visit them once or twice a week carrying an "ancient brown leather satchel" filled with food from the family farm in Huntsville. "The largesse," she explained, "came not out of our abundance but out of our poverty." She remembered her two years at the university, years when, among other things, she learned "the beauty of a properly constructed sentence," as marked by a "humbling anonymity and a slow maturing. . . . I have no recollection at this point," she said, "of deciding formally that a search for truth was more exciting than composing a legal brief" (she was on the debate team); "my affection for history came much later." She developed a taste for Russian novels and for Shakespeare. "Lear captured me most," she said, "Lear, who mistreated the daughter who loved him best. I wept not at Hamlet's dying, but at Cordelia's. . . . The incredible richness of the literature upon which I was nourished," she remembered, "served permanently to alter my parochial perspectives about the nature of society and man. . . . There was a smashing of icons within those walls, but I did not hear the noise until later. It all happened very quietly."

Since those days Fawn's career, as the record shows, was marked by honors and acrimony in about equal measure. She came to know more notoriety than anonymity, scorned in some quarters, celebrated in others. She was one of ten women honored by the *Los Angeles Times* in 1975 as women of "distinguished accomplishment." Meanwhile she had had to fight a bitter battle for recognition within her own profession. Colleagues who came to Fawn's defense during the controversy over her promotion from senior lecturer to professor with tenure at UCLA in 1971 (a controversy her supporters called an "outrage," "a politicization," a "scandal," "a petty ordeal by a clutch of little vipers") called for an objective criterion that would be free of "preconceptions stipulating the kind of methodology that *ought* to be used in the study of history." They found her work "meticulously researched, responsive to the secondary literature on every problem she considered, beautifully written, and always original in conceptualization and execution." "It is of course biographical," wrote one, "and biography itself is considered oftentimes by the successive avant-gardes of the profession to be a second form of historiography, but it remains as the staple of historical studies, as fashion after fashion passes; and no one does it better than Fawn." "The history she writes," asserted another, "is truly so very good, from the scholarly, literary, and the creative standpoints, that it is difficult to conceive of serious reservations against her full membership in the department." Fawn's advocates took issue with those critics who took one or two passages of her work out of context, "which conveys a distorted impression of thinness and superficiality, when a coming to grips with the fullness of her documentation and the integrated richness of her work would easily correct these distortions. . . . Mrs. Brodie's scholarship has a thrust to it that constitutes one of the most important commentaries and correctives to American history and culture in our time. She focuses," he said, "on the American need to sterilize and disembody our national heroes, as if they had neither senses nor passions. She returns to them their sexuality, their ambivalences, and their human vitality."

Sterling McMurrin, in a tribute in *Dialogue* at her death, appreciates Fawn's method of *Verstehen*, of empathetic understanding, of probing the inner life, but finds it fraught with possibilities for error. As far as her life of Joseph Smith is concerned, he quips, "A part of the trouble is that most devout Mormons do not want the 'intimate' life of their prophet investigated and publicized and they are not comfortable with efforts to examine his 'inner' life."

Fawn, who called herself "an accidental historian," acknowledged that "the writing of biography that tries to explain motivation and character is an act of very great arrogance. . . . If the story is of such consequence to me," she once asked, "why am I not a novelist?" She gave her own answer, insisting on important distinctions between the novelist and the biographer: "The novelist distorts freely, willingly, of necessity, for the sake of art. . . . The biographer cannot distort the truth without guilt. So he tells the truth as best he can." The biographer is, she said, echoing the British critic Desmond McCarthy, "the artist on oath. . . . To tell the whole truth . . . as best one can . . . is a major obligation and is the reason historians make such a fetish of footnotes. . . . Footnotes are our tracks backward into the primary documents. . . . The novelist covers his tracks for the sake of art; the biographer must expose his tracks if he is to remain professional."

Fawn used to tell her students that "the writing of a biography is very like making a mosaic. It is not a jigsaw, where there are an exact number of precut pieces, which, when put together, make the photographic likeness. The biographer works with millions of small pieces of historical evidence, some of them fraudulent, out of which he selects some, and builds a mosaic which he hopes is close to the essential man or woman. But the biographer," she reminded them, "does not create the mosaic pieces. If he invents a single conversation he has become a novelist. The good biographer, like the good novelist, selects what Virginia Woolf calls 'the fertile fact,' the fact that reveals character rather than event. Here the two artists are united in intent. For it is the mystery of character above all that is the magical lure of biography."

Fawn Brodie, who once observed that Russian historians have to "sanctify the past," knew as well as anyone that we can, and do, manipulate the past. "The way a person brought up in this area [Mormon country] chooses to reckon with the past," she said, "either to wrestle with it, to abominate it, to submit to it, or to adore it and try to convert others to its overwhelming significance—has major consequences for his life." In her acceptance speech, which she called her "two-and-a-half-minute talk," on being named a fellow of the Utah State Historical Society in 1967, Fawn applauded the "climate of liberation" she felt was developing in the region. Her work and her life have contributed to a climate of liberation not only in a region but in a whole profession. We can be glad that at the age of nine, when a poem of Fawn's first appeared in a children's magazine, she found it "an unspeakable thrill" to see her name in print. Her name in print has thrilled us many times over, and we are thrilled to honor her with this publication.

Acknowledgments

I am extremely grateful to a number of individuals whose help, influence, and inspiration facilitated publication of this book. This volume would not have been possible without the contributions of William Mulder, Marvin S. Hill, Mario S. De Pillis, Lavina Fielding Anderson, Todd Compton, and Roger D. Launius, whose varied, insightful, and sometimes provocative perspectives on Fawn M. Brodie and her *No Man Knows My History* are represented in this collection of essays. A special debt of appreciation is owed to the Utah Endowment for the Humanities, which financed and sponsored a one-day symposium in August 1995 at which five of the seven essays were initially presented. Also sponsoring and providing support for that symposium were the University of Utah and the Sunstone Foundation. Linda King Newell, William Mulder, and Nina Anderson were extremely helpful in encouraging me during a particularly difficult period to push ahead and complete this work. Of indirect but significant influence was Thomas G. Alexander, whose earlier work *Great Basin Kingdom Revisited: Contemporary Perspectives* (1991) served as an inspiration and a "role model" for this volume. Finally, I am particularly appreciative of John R. Alley and the capable staff at Utah State University Press, whose encouragement and editorial skills made the publication of this volume a reality.

Introduction

NEWELL G. BRINGHURST

Alfred A. Knopf first published Fawn M. Brodie's *No Man Knows My History: The Life of Joseph Smith, the Mormon Prophet* in November 1945. Over the next twenty-five years, this work went through eight printings. In 1971, it was revised and enlarged into a second edition. This revised edition, in turn, has gone through a dozen printings and is still in print.

The obvious question is: Why has *No Man Knows My History* retained sufficient appeal to remain in print over the course of the past half century? This feat is even more remarkable given the publication of several subsequent biographies on Joseph Smith.[1] There are several possible explanations. First, *No Man Knows My History* quickly established itself as an extremely controversial work, evident from the time of the book's initial publication. An early reviewer, Herbert O. Brayer, writing in the *Mississippi Valley Historical Review*, sagaciously predicted that Brodie's biography would "probably be one of the most highly praised as well as highly condemned works of 1945."[2] This was certainly the case as *No Man Knows My History* enjoyed favorable reviews, particularly in the eastern press and from non-Mormon professionals in the field of American history. But at the same time the book was roundly condemned by critics within the Mormon church in Utah and from within the smaller, midwestern-based Reorganized Church of Jesus Christ of Latter Day Saints.[3] The book's author, Fawn Brodie, found herself the focal point of official Mormon denunciation, culminating in her formal excommunication from

1

the Church of Jesus Christ of Latter-day Saints in June 1946. The Mormon church summons issued in connection with this action charged Brodie with apostasy: "You assert matters as truths which deny the divine origin of the Book of Mormon, the restoration of the Priesthood and of Christ's Church through the instrumentality of the Prophet Joseph Smith, contrary to the beliefs, doctrines and teachings of the Church."[4] The publicity generated by this drastic action further fueled the controversy around *No Man Knows My History,* which has continued to the present.

A second factor promoting continuing interest in Brodie's biography is that the book is well written and relatively easy to read. "Gracefully written with a compelling momentum" that sets it apart from earlier accounts, "Brodie's Joseph Smith is interesting, a flesh-and-blood person with whom one can have sympathy," concedes Latter-day Saint scholar and former assistant Mormon church historian Davis Bitton.[5] A third factor that quickly established the popularity of *No Man Knows My History* is its engaging methodological approach. Specifically, Mormonism's founder is placed within an analytical framework "explicitly psychoanalytical," setting it apart from other biographies of Joseph Smith as well as from studies on various other Mormon leaders.[6]

A fourth reason for continuing interest in Brodie's biography is its unquestioned status as a seminal work. In the words of Brigham Young University archivist David J. Whittaker, *No Man Knows My History* stands as "a watershed in Mormon biography," setting "the agenda for a new generation of studies on Mormons."[7] Or as Brigham Young University Professor Emeritus Marvin S. Hill has noted, *No Man Knows My History* "quickly became the standard life of Joseph Smith and the most influential book on early Mormonism."[8]

The seven essays in this volume consider *No Man Knows My History* from contrasting contemporary perspectives. Five of the seven, based on original research and published here for the first time, were originally presented in conjunction with the August 1995 symposium held in Salt Lake City under the joint sponsorship of the Utah Endowment of the Humanities and the

University of Utah to mark the fiftieth anniversary of the publication of *No Man Knows My History*. The two remaining essays, which also focus on Brodie's seminal biography, were previously published in two scholarly journals, namely the *Utah Historical Quarterly* and *Church History*.

The first essay, entitled "A Biography of the Biography: The Research and Writing of Fawn Brodie's *No Man Knows My History*," gives a historical overview of the manner and rationale in which Brodie's biography was conceived, researched, and written over the seven years that it took to complete it.

The second essay is entitled "Applause, Attack, and Ambivalence: Varied Responses to Fawn M. Brodie's *No Man Knows My History*." Originally published in 1989 in the *Utah Historical Quarterly*, this essay considers the differing reactions to Brodie's seminal work immediately following its initial publication and continuing to the present.

The third essay, entitled "Secular or Sectarian History? A Critique of *No Man Knows My History*," was written by Marvin S. Hill, professor emeritus at Brigham Young University. This essay originally appeared in *Church History* in 1974, following publication of *No Man Knows My History* in its second, enlarged edition. Hill's review was immediately acknowledged as the most complete and careful analysis of *No Man Knows My History*—a status that it continues to enjoy. This essay is indicative of Professor Hill's status as the foremost living expert on the life and times of Joseph Smith, having spent many years collecting various historical and primary source materials for what was to be his own book-length biography on the Mormon leader. Marvin Hill, however, did not complete his biography, turning the task over to his sister, Donna.[9]

The fourth essay, entitled "Fawn McKay Brodie at the Intersection of Secularism and Personal Alienation" and written by Mario S. De Pillis, former president of the Mormon History Association and professor emeritus at the University of Massachusetts, considers *No Man Knows My History* within the context of the larger American society of the early to mid-twentieth century. De Pillis argues that Fawn Brodie in writing *No Man*

Knows My History was greatly influenced by an American society going through two major sets of changes. These involved "first, a secularist rebellion of the intellectuals characterized by cynicism and the debunking of patriotism and religious belief, and, second, a widespread indifference to religion that has left the period 1929 to 1959 a historiographical black hole in the history of American religion."

Approaching Brodie's biography from a somewhat different perspective is Lavina Fielding Anderson, widely noted scholar of Mormon studies and editor of the *Journal of Mormon History*, in the fifth essay, entitled "Literary Style in *No Man Knows My History*: An Analysis." Anderson carefully describes Brodie's skillful use of various "literary devices," which allowed Brodie to produce "an absorbing, easily comprehensible narrative" outlining the events in Joseph Smith's life "swiftly and effectively." But Anderson also argues that "nearly all of" Brodie's literary devices "are the tools of *fictional* effect. Thus, to the extent that they are successful as literary devices, they simultaneously undercut the *historical* effect" of the biography itself.

The sixth essay deals with yet another facet of *No Man Knows My History*, specifically Brodie's treatment of the extremely controversial topic of polygamy. "Fawn Brodie on Joseph Smith's Plural Wives and Polygamy: A Critical View," written by Todd Compton, is based on years of careful, thorough research. Compton, who holds a Ph.D. in classics from the University of California at Los Angeles, concedes Brodie to be "the only scholar . . . who has produced a footnoted list of Joseph Smith's wives with small biographies" of them. But Compton critiques Brodie's list of the forty-eight women allegedly married to the Mormon leader, asserting that it is "not [completely] reliable" because it contains the names of women *never* married to the Mormon prophet. Nevertheless, this list, according to Compton, represents a "valuable first attempt" to identify and quantify Smith's wives. Compton also criticizes Brodie for being too "reductionist" in interpreting "Joseph's polygamy as derived entirely or chiefly from his pronounced sexual appetites."

The seventh and final essay, "From Old to New Mormon History: Fawn Brodie and the Scholarly Analysis of Mormon Culture" is by Roger D. Launius, chief historian for the National Aeronautics and Space Administration, former president of the Mormon History Association, and a prolific writer on varied aspects of Mormonism's past. In his provocative and stimulating essay, Launius assesses "the degree to which Mormon historiography has been shaped by the long shadow" of *No Man Knows My History*. "In many ways" this work "was a seminal study that served as a transition point between" the so-called "old and . . . new Mormon history." Equally noteworthy, Launius makes some provocative, penetrating observations and suggestions concerning the best course for future scholarship on Joseph Smith and early Mormon history.

In general, the contrasting perspectives presented in these essays point up the intense controversy, both past and present, generated by *No Man Knows My History*. But these essays also make clear the profound impact that Brodie's biography has had on the nature and content of Mormon historical scholarship over the course of the past fifty years—an influence that continues to the present.

Notes

1. These include five book-length biographies on Joseph Smith, specifically Carl Carmer, *The Farm Boy and the Angel* (Garden City, New York: Doubleday, 1970); Donna Hill, *Joseph Smith: The First Mormon* (Garden City, New York: Doubleday, 1977); Francis M. Gibbons, *Joseph Smith: Martyr, Prophet of God* (Salt Lake City: Deseret Book, 1977); Richard L. Bushman, *Joseph Smith and the Beginnings of Mormonism* (Urbana: University of Illinois Press, 1984); and Maurice L. Draper, *The Founding Prophet: An Administrative Biography of Joseph Smith, Jr.* (Independence: Herald House, 1990).
2. *Mississippi Valley Historical Review* (March 1946): 601–3.
3. For two overviews of the varied responses to Brodie's biography see Newell G. Bringhurst, "Applause, Attack, and Ambivalence: Varied Responses to Fawn M. Brodie's *No Man Knows My History, Utah Historical Quarterly* 57 (winter 1989): 46–63, reprinted in this volume, and Newell G. Bringhurst,

"The 'Renegade' and the 'Reorganites': Fawn M. Brodie and Her Varied Encounters with the Reorganized Church of Jesus Christ of Latter Day Saints," *The John Whitmer Historical Association Journal* 12 (1992): 16–30.

4.   William H. Reeder to Fawn M. Brodie, May 23, 1946. Copy in Fawn M. Brodie Papers, Special Collections, Marriott Library, University of Utah, Salt Lake City.

5.   Davis Bitton, "Mormon Biography," *Biography: An Interdisciplinary Quarterly* 4, no. 1 (winter 1981): 4–5.

6.   This according to Ronald W. Walker in "The Challenge and Craft of Mormon Biography," *BYU Studies* 22 (spring 1982): 189.

7.   David J. Whittaker, "The Heritage and Tasks of Mormon Biography," in *Supporting Saints: Life Stories of Nineteenth-Century Mormons*, by Donald J. Cannon and David J. Whittaker (Provo, Utah: BYU Religious Studies Center, 1982), 10.

8.   Marvin S. Hill, "Secular or Sectarian History? A Critique of *No Man Knows My History*," *Church History* 43 (March 1974), 78.

9.   Donna Hill's work was published in 1977 under the title *Joseph Smith: The First Mormon*.

1

A Biography of the Biography
The Research and Writing of
No Man Knows My History

Newell G. Bringhurst

Fawn Brodie did not originally set out to write a biography of Joseph Smith per se. Instead, she explained years later that when a study of the anthropology of American Indians convinced her that they were of Mongoloid rather than Hebraic origin, she wanted to satisfy herself by exploring "how the *Book of Mormon* came to be written."[1] Also prompting her were questions posed by her husband Bernard, "totally new to the Mormon scene and very fascinated by it."[2] But as Brodie got into her research, she found there was "no good biography of Joseph Smith" and thus undertook the task herself. A third factor, according to Brodie, was that "the whole problem of [Smith's] credibility . . . was crying out for some explanation." Brodie characterized her effort as compelling detective work: "It was fantastic! I was gripped by it."[3]

Finally, and perhaps most important, a compelling set of personal concerns motivated Brodie. The author candidly confessed that her study of Smith did for her "what an autobiographical novel usually does for the young novelist" in that "there was a compulsion to self-expression . . . as well as a compulsion to liberate [herself] wholly from Mormonism, and perhaps also certain family relationships."[4] In other words, as Brodie's good friend and mentor, Dale L. Morgan noted this work served as "a kind of a catharsis."[5] Or as Brodie herself told her favorite uncle, Dean

7

Brimhall, some years later, her work on Joseph Smith represented a desperate effort to come to terms with her childhood.[6]

Brodie began her research in 1938, while working in the University of Chicago library, following the completion of her master's degree in English. Her position at Chicago's Harper Library gave her access to various books and historical materials. She later recalled, "Every book I asked for was there, including crucial books by Ethan Smith and Elias Boudinot and others, who believed that the American Indians had been descended from the Lost Tribes of Israel."[7] Harper Library's great collection on the history of upstate and western New York enabled Brodie to learn about the mound builder Indians and about the "Antimasonic excitement" that swept the area in 1827, when the Book of Mormon was being written. Also available were the sermons of the evangelist preachers of the 1820s in the Palmyra area. Through these materials, Brodie learned about "millennialism and the health food passions that would later spark such religious leaders as William Miller, founder of the Seventh Day Adventist church, and Mary Baker Eddy, founder of Christian Science."[8]

In June 1939, Brodie shared her findings with Dean R. Brimhall. "Most of my spare time this past year," she told Brimhall, "I have spent analyzing the *Book of Mormon* & United Order. . . . I have had the most fun with the *Book of Mormon* & was able to trace almost every idea in it right down to Ontario Co. New York 1827 [including] the lost tribe theory, the exterminated race theory, anti-Masonry, anti-Catholicism—the whole gamut of sectarian religious controversy."[9]

Brodie then revealed to Brimhall her ultimate goal: "I hope sometime to be able to turn out a genuinely scholarly biography. . . . I've been wanting to tell someone besides [husband] Bernard what I'm doing," explaining, "I can't, of course, confide in my family." She then asked her uncle: "I hope sometime that you'll have the time to look over some of the research I've been doing on Joseph Smith. I think your own analysis is sane & judicious, perhaps because it conforms with my own."[10]

In the fall of 1939, Fawn Brodie overcame her initial reluctance concerning immediate family, sharing the results of her research with her younger brother, Thomas B. McKay. After returning from a Mormon mission to Germany, he enrolled as an undergraduate student at the University of Chicago. He lived near his sister Fawn, which enabled him to interact with her as she pushed ahead with her research.[11]

Thomas was bright and inquisitive, taking an interest in what Fawn was doing. In fact, he looked at many of the very same materials on Joseph Smith and Mormon origins. This generated great discussions on much of the material that went into the biography, with Fawn and Thomas differing sharply in their views. Thomas recalled, "I would look at it from the aspect of one who is thoroughly convinced that Joseph Smith was a prophet" whereas Fawn looked at the same information from the perspective of one thoroughly "convinced that he was not a prophet."

Fawn Brodie was particularly bothered by disclosures of Smith's early activities as a money-digger, telling her brother that the Lord would never have permitted Smith to take part in such activity "if he was going to be the Lord's prophet." Whereas Thomas asserted that Mormonism's founder "was a very poor youth" engaging in money-digging as a means to generate revenue for his financially impoverished family, noting that at that early date, Smith had not yet "proclaimed himself the prophet." Money-digging, he added, "was a very respected profession" at that time. Such arguments notwithstanding Thomas recalled: "Neither did [Fawn] change my mind nor did I change hers."[12]

More significant was the input that Fawn received from her husband throughout the course of her research and writing. Bernard acted as a "sounding board" for the author's ideas and evaluated her written presentation. Fawn praised her husband as "immensely helpful" in acting as a most valuable critic in evaluating her research with a detachment she could never have and she called him "a first rate literary critic besides."[13] Bernard, moreover, exerted a moderating influence on the author relative to her overall evaluation of Joseph Smith. Brodie confessed that her work would have been a harsher indictment of Joseph Smith had it not been for Bernard's influence: "I was angered by the obvious nature of the fraud in his writing of the *Book of Mormon* . . . [but Bernard] kept urging me to look at the man's genius, to explain his successes, and to make sure that the reader understood why so many people loved him and believed in him. If there is real compassion for Joseph Smith in the book," Brodie confessed, "and I believe there is, it is more the result of the influence of my husband than anyone else."[14]

The help and encouragement of Bernard notwithstanding, Fawn Brodie's main concern was not Joseph Smith during the three years from mid-1939 to late 1942. The Brodies focused first and foremost on completion of Bernard's own graduate studies at the University of Chicago. He received his doctorate in international relations in 1940. And then the Brodies moved two times, first to Princeton, New Jersey, in 1940; and then, a year later, to Hanover, New Hampshire, and Dartmouth College as Bernard sought a suitable academic position.[15] In addition, by late 1942, Fawn devoted much of her time and energy to the care of her first child, Richard McKay Brodie, born November 7, 1942. Also during this period, she concentrated her major literary efforts outside of Mormon history. Influenced by the prevailing environment of patriotism and service generated by World War II, Brodie felt compelled to contribute her literary talents. Accordingly she collected material for and wrote the introductions for two wartime pamphlets. The first, *Our Far Eastern Record*, was published in early 1942, and the second, which appeared later that same year, was entitled *Peace Aims and Post-War Planning: A Bibliography*.[16]

In a June 1942 letter to her uncle Dean Brimhall, Brodie wrote that work on these two pamphlets had forced her to "neglect" the Mormon leader for "several months," confessing "neither job has been in the least creative, but they somehow seemed more pertinent to 1942 than hunting up data on what happened in Nauvoo in 1842. . . . Of course I never really lose interest in church history." She then told her uncle that she had written a 300-page manuscript on Joseph Smith, characterizing it as a "very crude first draft, and far from finished . . . I shall probably be hacking away at it for the rest of the Summer and longer."[17]

Brodie also described her research on Joseph Smith's 1826 trial for "crystal-gazing," noting discovery of "the old court record" in which "one fellow testified that Smith, 'laid a book upon a white cloth, and proposed looking through another stone which was white and transparent, held the stone to the candle, turned his back to the book, and read.'" Brodie then noted that "the jump from this to translating the plates with a blanket stretched across the room is not a big one, I think." She concluded, "Well, it's all very absorbing, and sometimes depressing. [Smith's] career continues to astonish me—as does the stubborn survival of the church."[18]

Five months later, in November 1942, Brodie updated her uncle, once more requesting his help in reading and evaluating what she had written on Joseph Smith thus far. "The more I work with the man," she added, "the more of a challenge he becomes."[19]

In early 1943, Brodie, with her partially completed 300-page manuscript in hand, approached Datus Smith, the editor at Princeton University Press concerning publication. But Smith, after reading the manuscript, felt that Brodie's biography should be published by a nonacademic press because of its controversial approach combined with the topic's potential for commercial success. Thus he encouraged her to apply for an Alfred A. Knopf Literary Fellowship.[20]

Following Datus Smith's advice Brodie applied for a Knopf fellowship in February 1943. As part of her application, she submitted the "first seven chapters, about 45,000 words," covering "the period from [Smith's] birth to 1831."[21] In her letter of application, Brodie characterized Joseph Smith as "one of the most elusive and controversial figures in American history." She justified her topic in the following terms: "I believe that the book will have a peculiar timeliness, not because his life exactly parallels

that of any modern dictator, nor on the other hand, because persecution of the Mormons is at all comparable to that of the Jews
in this century; but rather because the book is the story of a challenge to certain enduring values which are a part of the American heritage. Both the guilt and the honor lie at times with the
Mormons, at times with the 'Gentiles,' depending upon the issue
at stake."[22]

Brodie asserted that she was not trying to "reinterpret" the
Mormon leader in the light of the twentieth century but "endeav-
oring to write accurate history, to reconstruct [Smith's] life from
the basis of a myriad of scattered documents." "My ambition," she
continued, "is not to produce a fictionalized biography," adding
that "where so much controversy is rampant, one needs documentation—not imaginary conversations." She then concluded: "I
believe that I am singularly well-equipped to do this study, for I
know the Mormon point of view intimately, having been reared
in the bosom of the church until I was twenty. Since then I have
achieved an attitude of complete objectivity toward Mormon
dogma. . . . My point of view has been shaped by the facts, not by
any predilection for or prejudice against the Mormons."[23]

In late May 1943, Fawn Brodie received the good news that
her application was judged the best out of a total of forty-four
entries submitted. One of the Knopf judges, M. Rugoff described
Brodie's work as a "model of intellectual sobriety and lucidity" but
conceded that it was not a "definitive" work. "A definitive biography of [any] religious leader," he wrote "would certainly be a
contradiction of terms." At the same time, Rugoff, with some
irony, noted that while Brodie had been "brought up a Mormon,"
she had "left the fold far behind." Nevertheless, the author's presentation was "perspicuous, balanced, thought through, astrin-
gently sane" with a narrative that "moves with unbroken
smoothness" and "reads surely and swiftly." Overall, Rugoff found:
"Brodie's portrait of Smith . . . [is] a very convincing one, for
although [Brodie is] aware of such special interpretations as those
supplied by psychoanalysis, economic determinism, religious
bigotry, worship and straight debunking, she steers a path that is

not so much a mean between these as [something] simply better than any of them alone."[24] In conclusion Rugoff stated that the author's presentation "should satisfy the scholar, impress the layman and absorb both."[25] The fellowship itself carried a stipend of $2,500.[26]

In the meantime, the Brodies had moved from Hanover, New Hampshire, to Washington, D.C. Bernard had joined the United States Navy in late 1942 and upon being commissioned a lieutenant was assigned to the Office of the Chief of Naval Operations.[27] As Fawn returned to the Joseph Smith biography, she worried about the Mormon community's reaction, not just to her receiving the Alfred A. Knopf Literary Fellowship, but to the projected biography itself. Brodie expressed deep anxieties in writing her father and mother about her award. She cautioned her parents "not to advertise to anyone" that she had received the fellowship, noting that it would "be announced in the papers anyway." As for the biography itself, she warned it "is likely to get a good bit of hostile criticism from the authorities of the [Mormon] Church" because she planned to present "certain things which [she felt] should be included to tell the whole story."

"You will probably be criticized for having raised a wayward daughter," she told her parents. "When someone mentions [the biography], you'd better say, 'Well, I don't know what the girl is up to. It's all her own doing you know, and she's always been inclined to be a little headstrong,' or something like that."[28] She then thanked her parents for bringing her up "to revere the truth, which is the noblest ideal a parent can instill in his children," adding: "The fact that we come out on somewhat different roads is certainly no reflection on you."[29]

Brodie's worries concerning her parents were compounded by the elevation of her father within the Mormon church hierarchy to the position of an assistant to the Quorum of the Twelve, the church's governing council, some two years earlier, in April 1941.[30] Sensitive to her father's position, Fawn confessed to her parents that winning the fellowship suddenly made her realize "the responsibility of writing about such an influential and con-troversial figure as the Prophet." She added,."I am really a little scared, and only hope I can do justice to the magnitude of the task."[31]

Extensive media publicity relative to Brodie's award was not long in coming. An official press release issued by Alfred A. Knopf in late May 1943 was printed in newspapers throughout the country. It quoted Brodie extensively: "Anyone who grows up with a Mormon background cannot escape" Joseph Smith. "He is the first cause—the explanation for Mormon country—the reason for one's being born at all. . . . I seem always to have known him, like Santa Claus and God. His influence permeates the state of Utah." She further admitted: "I found nothing quite so baffling and elusive as the character of Joseph Smith." More-over, she explained: "The more I read about him the more I wanted to understand why the same man could have inspired such fanatical adoration in his followers and such venomous hatred in his opponents. . . . the sheer drama of the man's life held me spellbound . . . I found that Mormon historians had so deified their prophet that they had robbed him of the healthy, earthy qualities which endeared him to his people. The old anti-Mormon diatribes, on the other hand, gave Satan the whole credit for his success. Both biases blinded their authors to one of the most exciting and fabulous success stories in Ameri-can history."[32]

Meanwhile, Brodie pushed ahead with her writing and research. Although she had completed seven chapters, taking her account of Joseph Smith to 1831, and had collected enough material to write up the story of the Mormon leader's experiences in Ohio and Missouri up to 1839, there remained research to be done on the crucial Nauvoo period, including Smith's introduc-tion of polygamy and the critical events leading up to his violent death in June 1844. "The book is still in a very formative stage," she told her parents in May 1943.[33] "I have an immense amount of research to do, to say nothing of the sheer labor of writing and rewriting."[34] She then conceded: "I . . . don't know quite where I will stand at the end of it. . . . But I am fascinated by the subject matter."[35]

Brodie also confessed to her parents: "Writing for me comes very hard and very slowly. I have to sweat over every line."[36] Her task was even more challenging in light of her ever-present responsibilities as a housewife and mother, all of which compelled her to carefully organize her time. She described her routine to a newspaper reporter as follows: "Four hours a day for the book, and the rest of the time for my 6 month old son."[37]

Brodie's research took her to the Library of Congress, located in Washington, D.C., close to her home. She also examined relevant materials in other libraries, thanks to money received from her Knopf fellowship. She traveled to the New York Public Library, which contained "one of the three great collections on Mormon history." Particularly useful was a file of newspaper clippings on the Mormons in Missouri and Illinois, which saved her many hours of work, as she later recalled. She also visited the New York State Library in Albany, where she was able to read "the newspapers Joseph Smith had read as a youth in Palmyra." Contained therein were "articles relating to the Moundbuilder Indians, and to the theory that they were descended from the Lost Tribes of Israel." Brodie also visited Kirtland, Ohio, where she found "invaluable material" on Joseph Smith's legal difficulties "in a neighboring courthouse."[38]

More significant was Brodie's visit to Salt Lake City during the summer of 1943 to do research and to consult personally with her family. Particularly concerned about the sensitive position of her father as a high Mormon official or "general authority," Fawn told him frankly that her account of Joseph Smith "would probably be an embarrassment to him" but that she "would not submit it for Church censorship." She even offered to publish under a pseudonym, if he wanted her to. But her father told her, "Absolutely not."[39]

While in Salt Lake, Brodie also visited the Mormon Church Library-Archives. But she quickly found access to research materials very restricted. She later recalled, "I learned very quickly that almost everyone is barred from its gates" with "a rule . . . in force forbidding anyone access . . . who is not completely without guile." Brodie attributed her own access to the fact that she was introduced as "Brother McKay's daughter," which made her feel "as guilty as hell."[40] She pursued her research but was initially very discreet: "I was scrupulously careful not to ask for anything remotely anti-Mormon." She spent most of her time going through two early Mormon newspapers published in Nauvoo, *The Wasp* and the *Nauvoo Neighbor*, which she characterized as "rich" with information.[41]

Near the end of her visit, Brodie summoned enough courage to ask Assistant Church Historian A. William Lund for permission to examine manuscript material, in particular Joseph Smith's diary in his own handwriting—a 93-page account.[42] Lund then referred Brodie to Apostle Joseph Fielding Smith as the only person who could grant such permission, acting in his capacity as official Mormon church historian. In meeting with Smith, Brodie told the Mormon apostle "quite frankly" that she "was trying to write scholarly and accurate history, to avoid sensationalizing and fictionalizing of any sort." She clearly stated that she was working on her own and without her father's blessing. Brodie characterized Smith's reaction to her own frankness as "most unfriendly." But Brodie pushed ahead, questioning Smith "about source materials in regard to polygamy in Nauvoo." According to Brodie, this high Mormon official gave her some rather astonishing answers. Among other things, he noted, "There are things in this library we don't let anyone see." He also told her that "a revelation on polygamy came as early as 1831 but has never been printed because it would be misinterpreted by the bulk of the church members."[43]

Word of Brodie's frank discussion with Joseph Fielding Smith quickly got back to her uncle David O. McKay, who in response "came storming up" to the Thomas E. McKay residence in Salt Lake City, where Fawn was staying. In an encounter, characterized by Brodie as "painful in the extreme," David O. McKay refused to hear her point of view. He "forbade" her from

going "back to the library since [her] presence was an embarrassment to him, and since he wasn't going to permit anyone to use
the library who would distort the truth." But later that very same
day, he sent Fawn what she described as a "formal little note"
granting her permission to use the library in view of her
expressed desire "to learn more about the Prophet Joseph."[44]

Brodie, however, rejected the offer in light of the earlier
confrontation. She spent the remainder of her Utah visit "reading in the University of Utah and Utah State Historical Society
libraries."[45]

After leaving Utah, Brodie traveled to Independence, Missouri, where she spent ten days in the library of the Reorganized
Church of Jesus Christ of Latter Day Saints. Her treatment by
the individuals in charge there contrasted sharply with that of
Utah Mormon officials in Salt Lake City. She later recalled, "I
was treated with every courtesy I could have wished for." Former
RLDS Church Historian S. A. Burgess, although semi-retired,
was still serving as a staff member in the church historian's office.
Burgess, according to Brodie, opened the library vault, bringing
out "piles of material" without her even asking for it: "I saw a
good many original letters, the photostatic copy of the Book of
Mormon manuscript, the original manuscript for the Inspired
Translation of the Bible, the Hyrum Page seer stone, several of
Joseph Smith's own books, and a good deal of printed material."[46]

While in Independence, Brodie also had the opportunity to
meet several of the Reorganization's "first family"—the direct
descendents of Joseph Smith. These included the Mormon
prophet's two grandsons, Frederick Smith, then-president of the
RLDS church, and his younger brother, Israel Smith, a high
RLDS official who would eventually succeed to the RLDS presidency upon Frederick's death. Brodie's impressions of the Smiths
were mixed. On the one hand, she came away with a very deep
conviction "that the Utah Church benefited enormously by losing the Joseph Smith heirs." Condescendingly, she noted: "They
are interesting, intelligent people, with a good deal of social presence, but they are such typical American bourgeois businessmen

that the thought of a halo above any one of them is immediately incongruous. After conversing with Frederick and Israel, his brother, I felt that neither deifies his grandfather to nearly the extent that the average Utah Mormon does. They are inclined to be a little apologetic, and they are definitely on the defensive."[47]

Brodie, however, in a later account, recalled Israel Smith in somewhat more positive terms as "a thoughtful man and a scholar, well-acquainted with Ethan Smith's *View of the Hebrews*," which she had come to view as an important source of the ideas in the Book of Mormon. She also argued with him about the evidence of polygamy in the early days of the Mormon church, and he admitted quietly, "There were indeed strange things going on at Nauvoo."[48] In further describing Israel Smith, Brodie noted: "I was struck by his resemblance to his grandfather, not so much a physical thing as a kind of halo of opportunism that shone over his head. He is nobody's fool, believe me, but like Joseph [Smith] he lets things slip now and then, as in his statement to me that he wouldn't admit it publically but there were some very strange things going on in Nauvoo. He's cagey and he's thoughtful, and I'm certain his revelations come from somewhere in his cerebrum rather than his viscera, where every respectably meaningful revelation ought to come from anyhow."[49]

In general, Brodie's research trip to Utah and Missouri had been profitable. Upon her return to Washington, D.C., the fledgling author felt that she now had enough material "to write the story of the incredible Nauvoo period." But at the same time, she did concede that a real "definitive study" could "be written only by someone" granted access to certain restricted manuscripts in the Mormon Church Library-Archives; in particular, those of Willard Richards, Wilford Woodruff, William Clayton, and especially Joseph Smith.[50]

As Brodie pushed ahead with the writing of her biography, she secured the services of Dale L. Morgan, whose role was absolutely crucial in its completion. Morgan was born in 1915, like Brodie, and like her he had attended and graduated from the

University of Utah. Despite his deep fascination with Mormonism's past, Morgan likewise was not an active, practicing Latter-day Saint. Although completely deaf from the effects of meningitis suffered at age fourteen, Morgan, by 1943, had already established himself as a respected scholar of western history. Working for the Utah Works Progress Administration on its Historical Records Survey, he had risen to the important position of supervisor of the Utah Writers' Project in 1940. He had numerous publications to his credit, including two major books, *Utah: A Guide to the State* (1941) and *The Humboldt: Highroad of the West* (1943). With the outbreak of World War II, Morgan moved to Washington, D.C., to assume a position with the Office of Price Administration.[51]

Almost from the moment of their first meeting in the summer of 1943, Brodie and Morgan became fast friends. More important, Morgan became a virtual mentor to the fledgling author, assuming the role of chief critic. Brodie later noted that Morgan's "indefatigable scholarship in Mormon history" served as "an added spur" to her own.[52] Morgan quickly demonstrated his skills in thoroughly critiquing a preliminary draft of Brodie's manuscript consisting of ten chapters, taking the story of Joseph Smith and the Mormons up through their expulsion from Jackson County, Missouri, and to the Zion's Camp army's subsequent march from Ohio to Missouri. This was, in fact, the same manuscript that Brodie had submitted to Alfred A. Knopf, winning for her the 1943 Knopf literary award.

With abrupt frankness, Morgan told Brodie, "This draft of your book is not, properly speaking, a biography of Smith [but rather] a history" of the Mormon leader. He pointed out the preliminary nature of her writing and research: "You are articulating the skeleton, primarily; you are crystallizing your own individual conception of the main facts of Joseph Smith's life, establishing a rationale by which you can come to grips with him as a human being." He found the manuscript was over simplified in its point of view and continued, "You are positive beyond what the facts will support when all the obscure lights and shadows of those facts are closely examined." He then stated: "Your own point of view, as set forth in this manuscript, is much too hard and fast, to my way of thinking, it is too coldly logical in its conception of Joseph's mind and the developments of his character. Your view of him is all hard edges, without any of those blurrings which are more difficult to cope with but which constitutes a man in the round . . . I am particularly struck with the assumption your MS makes that Joseph was a self-conscious imposter."

Morgan confessed that he himself was not at the point that he could "make any final judgements" about the Mormon leader. But he was willing to say, "Regardless of how he got started with the Mormon affair, he came to believe absolutely in what he was doing; his sincerity can hardly be challenged. I think he had an extreme capacity for fantasy, and ultimately the fantasy may have become more real to him than reality itself, to the point that it displaced reality." Pursuing this point, Morgan pointed to a revealing confession made by Brodie sometime earlier, whereby she had admitted to Morgan that "Joseph was more of a man than [she had] made him out to be." What she had presented "was too much in the vein of 'I expose.'"

Morgan told Brodie that the chapters she had shown him rested pretty heavily on the authority of Eber D. Howe's famous anti-Mormon exposé *Mormonism Unvailed*, published in 1834. He also felt that Brodie's "hard and fast" conceptualization affected her use of factual information. He noted, "Your chain of reasoning looks logical, but it is attended by a string of ifs all along the line (precisely as with the orthodox Mormon reasoning), and the probability of error increases as the chain of reasoning lengthens." He urged the author to "exhibit a good deal of humility with respect to the facts." In conclusion, he recommended that the final manuscript "be so written that Mormon, anti-Mormon, and non-Mormon alike can go to the biography and read in it with agreement—disagreeing often in detail, perhaps, but observing that you have noted the points of disagreement and that while you set forth your point of view, you do not have Absolute Truth by the tail."[53]

In overall terms, Morgan was much more incisive and penetrating in his critique than Alfred A. Knopf had been in judging and awarding Brodie her fellowship earlier that year for the very same manuscript. The difference was that Morgan knew Mormon history and Knopf did not. But at the same time, Morgan tempered his criticism stating, "I congratulate you on a research job which has all the earmarks of being a landmark in Mormon history" and adding that reading her manuscript gave him "a notable sense of fellowship" with what she had been doing.[54]

In response to Dale Morgan's suggestions, Brodie spend the next several months, from late 1943 until mid-1944, revising her first ten chapters. In addition, she wrote up the story of Joseph Smith's experiences in Ohio, his difficulties in Missouri culminating in his own imprisonment and expulsion of his followers from that state, plus Smith's varied activities during the all-important Nauvoo period.

As Brodie pushed ahead with her manuscript, she received significant help from several other scholars, all of whom lived in Utah and were, in contrast to Brodie, active, practicing Latter-day Saints. But, like Brodie, these individuals were part of Mormondom's so-called lost generation, fascinated by certain controversial aspects of Mormonism's past and willing to examine these in a critical, dispassionate light.[55]

One such scholar was Vesta Crawford, a Utah-based poet and writer, whose own research focused on Emma Smith, the first wife of the Mormon prophet.[56] Thus Crawford, like Brodie, was interested in Joseph Smith's practice of plural marriage. But unlike Brodie, Crawford remained close to the Mormon church and, in fact, was editorial secretary and later associate editor of the *Relief Society Magazine*, an official church publication for and by women.[57] Crawford, nevertheless, was most helpful, sharing with Brodie "the results of her [own] research" on the Mormon prophet's wives.[58] Crawford "uncovered some very interesting items," according to Brodie, "and gave me a lot of vital statistics which will save me many errors."[59] Brodie characterized Crawford's own research as "wonderful" adding that between the two of them they had accumulated for Joseph Smith some thirty-four wives.[60]

Also helping Brodie was a second Utah-based writer, photojournalist Claire Noall. Like Crawford, Noall was interested in the practice of Mormon polygamy in Nauvoo. Noall's interest stemmed from ongoing research on her grandfather, Willard Richards, a one-time confidant to Joseph Smith and one of the first Latter-day Saints to embrace polygamy. Noall's research would ultimately culminate in a fictionalized biography on Willard Richards entitled *Intimate Disciple*.[61] Like Crawford, Noall shared with Brodie the results of her own research. On one occasion, Brodie thanked Noall for her information on "two new wives for Joseph."[62]

Brodie, moreover, developed a particularly close friendship with Noall, which led to frank discussions concerning the operation and morality of Mormon polygamy in Joseph Smith's time. "The more I work with the polygamy material," Brodie told Noall on one occasion, "the more baffled I become." She added, "Perhaps Sarah Pratt [the wife of early Mormon Apostle Orson Pratt] was right when she told the story that Joseph once said: 'Whenever I see a pretty woman I have to pray for grace.'"[63]

Brodie also speculated to Noall concerning Joseph Smith's prime motive for entering polygamy: "I believe simply that [Smith] came to feel—as many men do . . . that monogamy was an intolerably circumscribed way of life" and that in his "peculiar position" as church leader "it was part of his job to define the nature of sin." It was therefore "ridiculously easy to transform relative promiscuity into a religious duty."[64] Brodie theorized that the promiscuous nature of plural marriage initially appealed to Mormon women as well as men. In response to Brodie's disclosure, Noall lamented: "It is hard to take, but I can swallow it, if such promiscuity did exist on the part of the women too. Certainly the truthful writer must not hesitate to deal with the question."[65] Brodie then confessed that she, too, had been "trying to fathom the secret of the magnetism of plural marriage for the women." In stark terms, Brodie asserted: "I think polygamy was disguised whoredom. But the disguise was so good that it meta-morphosed the system into something quite different. After all the difference between fornication and sacred matrimony is merely a few mumblings from any mangy justice of the peace. The word is the thing, after all. Most of the polygamous women were very certain that it was a commandment of God. Read the revelation again, and see how shockingly specific it is. 'Unless a man enters this covenant he shall be damned, etc.'"[66] Brodie then added, "I am certain that the secrecy of the system [in Nau-voo] lent to its attractiveness" plus the fact that "there was more trading around among married couples in those days too. Women as well as men, have an impulse to variety, and when that impulse is loosed under the guise of a profound religious duty, there is no telling where it will lead."[67]

Despite the mutual attraction that Brodie detected in polygamy for both Latter-day Saint men and women in the early church, she disclosed to Noall moral outrage at Joseph Smith. Brodie pointed specifically to the Mormon leader's actions in taking as plural wives women already married to other men. According to Brodie's still incomplete research " four out of five of Joseph's wives" were wives to other men. Brodie moralized, "What about these poor husbands? Some of them left the Church; some of them took several more wives; none of them could have been very happy about the arrangement, either for time or eternity."[68]

A third Utah writer who aided Brodie was Juanita Brooks, a teacher and administrator at Dixie College, located in Saint George in southern Utah. Like Claire Noall and Vesta Crawford, Brooks was interested in certain controversial aspects of early church history, in particular the Mountain Meadows Massacre. This was an 1857 incident which involved the murder of the Fancher Party—a group of non-Mormon immigrants passing through southern Utah, nearly one hundred individuals in all, including women and children. The massacre was committed by a group of Mormons, aided by local Indians. In its wake, the Mor-mons attempted to cover up their involvement. Brooks, despite the controversial nature of her research, remained an active, practicing Latter-day Saint, like Claire Noall and Vesta Crawford.[69] Brooks, nevertheless, expressed admiration for Brodie's "courage" in undertaking the controversial topic of Joseph Smith, offering to provide Brodie with whatever useful information she came across in her own research.[70] Eventually, Brooks obtained and passed on to Brodie "an autobiography of one of Joseph [Smith's] wives—Mary Rollins Lightner."[71]

A fourth Utah-based scholar providing Brodie with an even greater amount of help was M. Wilford Poulson, a professor of psychology at Brigham Young University. Like Dale L. Morgan, whom he knew well, Poulson was very interested in early Mormon church history, primarily through his activities as an avid collector of old Mormon books and diaries.[72] Apparently, Brodie's initial contact with Poulson came either through Morgan or through her uncle, Dean Brimhall, a fellow psychologist who had, at one time, taught with Poulson at Brigham Young University. Poulson provided Brodie with a copy of a manuscript written by Benjamin F. Johnson, which in the words of Brodie, "confirms a good deal of what I had suspected about Joseph's first 'wife.'" It also provided her with another wife to add to her "ever-growing list."[73]

More important, Poulson influenced Brodie's view on other crucial aspects of Joseph Smith's career, like certain parallels between Joseph Smith and the schismatic Mormon leader James J. Strang. Poulson had deciphered the coded portions of Strang's diary, which revealed Strang to be "intensely ambitious but frustrated until he deliberately became a fake prophet strictly for what was in it for Strang—the pomp and trappings of authority, the wealth from tithes, the adulation of the flock and the choice of pretty girls for plural wives." Accordingly, when Brodie learned of Strang's code from Poulson, she applied Strang's attitudes to Joseph Smith![74]

In addition, Poulson, according to Brodie's later recollections, told the author "he thought Joseph Smith wrote the Book of Mormon to make money."[75] Poulson also agreed with Brodie's view that Thomas Dick's *The Philosophy of a Future State* "was extremely important in fixing the source of many of [Joseph Smith's] metaphysical conceptions."[76]

All of the help from Wilford Poulson, Juanita Brooks, Claire Noall, and Vesta Crawford notwithstanding, Brodie relied most heavily on Dale Morgan, looking to him for aid and comfort as she pushed ahead toward final completion of her manuscript. In a November 1943 letter, Brodie confessed to Morgan, "The book is already getting much too long," chastising herself that she "simply must stop trying to write the history of the church, and start writing a biography." Then in a startling note of self-confession, she admitted, "Perhaps I am dodging the man because I am still not quite certain what I want to do with him."[77]

Brodie encountered other problems as she pushed ahead with her manuscript throughout the winter and spring of 1943–44. She had become tired of basic research. "I am rapidly getting to the point" she told Morgan "where the thought of hunting down stray pieces here and there appalls me rather than exciting me, as it used to be."[78] By mid-December, Brodie had "finished writing up the whole Missouri period, in a first draft" and was "well into the Nauvoo period." But she confessed to "quietly tearing my hair to find the right technique for introducing polygamy." She then elaborated, "It's the old problem of being smothered in [the] affidavits" taken by Utah Mormon leaders during the late nineteenth century from numerous women alleged to have been married to Joseph Smith. These affidavits had been collected to counter the claims of the rival Reorganized Church of Jesus Christ of Latter Day Saints that the martyred founder of Mormonism had never practiced polygamy. Brodie expressed her ambivalence: "If the damned Reorganites weren't in existence," Brodie lamented, "I wouldn't have to worry so much about documentation. (But then I wouldn't have so many documents either)."[79]

Brodie, moreover, was forced to balance time devoted to her research and writing against her demanding role as a wife and mother, looking after the needs of husband Bernard and her

growing and increasingly active son, Richard. Brodie was ambivalent concerning her role as a mother, confessing to Dale Morgan
that her one-year old son was "such fun to play with that I usually
succumb to his begging, [but] the book suffers as a consequence."[80] Fawn not only accepted responsibilities as a mother
but looked forward to increased commitment in that role when
she became pregnant again in late 1943. But tragically she suffered a miscarriage in early January 1944, leaving her bedridden
for a month.[81]

Despite a two-month interruption of work on the manuscript, on April 1, 1944, Brodie wrote Morgan, announcing that
she was "in a celebrating mood" because, as she put it, "I finally
succeeded in putting five bullets in the prophet." That is, she had
written her story of Joseph Smith up through his murder by an
armed mob in Carthage, Illinois, on June 27, 1844. Brodie then
told Morgan, "While I don't yet have [Smith] buried I feel that
the book is done. Now I can toss all my notes in the closet and go
to work on the revision."[82]

But Brodie's mood of celebration was short-lived as she
encountered new problems during the process of revision. In
confronting her early chapters on Mormon origins, she confessed
to Morgan, "I am quietly tearing my hair over the Book of Mormon again. Those chapters are the ones I have worked over the
most and are still the least satisfactory."[83] She continued to have
difficulty in her revision, writing to Morgan in early May that it
was going "rather badly. I am too prone to cling to what I have
written before, even though it doesn't satisfy me. What I
rewrite," she continued, "doesn't satisfy me either."[84]

In late May, Brodie was further distracted when she
received shocking news that her father had suffered "a bad heart
attack," causing him to be bedridden "for an indefinite period."
Brodie expressed extreme anxiety, sensing a relationship between
her father's condition and her own writing and research. She
confessed to being "haunted by the thought" that her father
"might die shortly after [her] book came out," adding, "the consequences for my own peace of mind would be simply unbearable."

Brodie continued, "If I didn't have such an affection for my father, who is the soul of kindness, perhaps I wouldn't be so troubled." She admitted to Morgan, "This whole business complicates an already melancholy personal problem. Sometimes I wish to God I'd never started the book."[85]

Fawn's father did not die, and in fact recovered to the point that he was soon able to resume his church duties as an assistant to the Quorum of the Twelve. Brodie meanwhile continued revising her manuscript. In early June she told Morgan of her "engrossing interest" in trying to locate definitive evidence that Joseph Smith had fathered children through one or more of his polygamous wives. Frustrated in her efforts, she lamented to Morgan that it "piqued" her to think that the Reorganized church might be right in its assertion that the only children fathered by Smith were those through Emma Hale—proof, according to the Reorganized church, of its long-standing claim that Mormonism's founder never practiced polygamy.[86] Brodie then speculated to Morgan the reason for the apparent lack of offspring from Smith's numerous plural wives. She suspected that the Mormon leader was instructed "in some kind of primitive birth control" by John C. Bennett, a medical doctor living in Nauvoo and a one-time Mormon leader who was one of Smith's closest advisors.[87]

By mid-July Brodie had the first fourteen chapters of her manuscript completely revised. She had, moreover, "pretty well completed" revision on another thirteen, which, in total, constituted the bulk of her biography. She confessed to Morgan, however, that the chapters on Joseph's wives and on Mormon metaphysics needed "a great deal of work yet. I seem able to handle the political narrative much better than the theological matter, most of which bores me."[88]

In August 1944, after completing her revisions, Brodie sent her completed manuscript on to Morgan for evaluation and comment. Morgan's own response was prompt and after a careful reading, he returned it to Brodie with a number of insightful comments. He described Brodie's work as "thoroughly engrossing" and "downright fascinating." He found "the research . . .

wide and deep without being ostentatious; the prose . . . admirably muscular" and the text "full of stimulating ideas" with a rapidly moving storyline. Most important, Morgan felt that Brodie
now had "a biography" rather than a mere "history of Joseph's
life." Brodie was "clearly the master" of her material, writing with
"insight and understanding," plus he thought she exhibited
"practical shrewdness and deftness" particularly evident in the
chapters carrying the story up through the Missouri period.[89]

Despite overall praise, Morgan did express a number of continuing concerns. He saw a "grave defect" in the way Brodie presented Nauvoo events, telling her, "More work is required of you
here." He felt she was not in control of her material as in the earlier chapters. Morgan then told Brodie that "the greatest part of
[her] trouble" was her failure to make "the necessary final analysis
of [Joseph] Smith's character." The manuscript, he continued
belied "a certain tentativeness" toward the Mormon leader. He
felt Brodie had not "exactly explained the extraordinary magnetism" that Smith "had for his followers." Smith, according to
Morgan gave his followers "something they never got from anyone else" and "left an indelible impress upon their minds." In
return these same individuals gave Smith "a love they never had
given anyone else."[90]

Morgan, also expressed "a general criticism" of Brodie's
"bold judgements on the basis of assumptions." He urged Brodie
to "give [immediate] careful attention" to this point, warning
that if such "generalizations" were carried forth into the final
book manuscript, they would expose the author to strong attack
from those Mormons already hostile toward the book and "looking for ways to discredit" it. Finally, Morgan urged Brodie to add
another chapter analyzing the character of Joseph Smith. He felt
that understanding the man's "character in all its final complexity is essential to the reader's understanding of the final events of
his life."[91]

Brodie responded positively to Morgan's varied criticisms,
characterizing them as "stimulating and instructive." Accordingly she "reorganized the Nauvoo chapters," a task that she

found less trying than she expected and added a concluding chapter analyzing Joseph Smith's character.[92]

Brigham Young University Professor Wilford Poulson also commented on Brodie's completed manuscript. Poulson's evaluation, however, was much more critical, giving Brodie a preview of the kind of criticism the biography would likely encounter from inside the Mormon establishment. "Frankly," he stated, "I had hoped your presentation would be more worthy of being characterized as DEFINITIVE. I had hoped [that] you would bring to bear the appropriate canons of historical criticism upon your sources." Then getting to the nub of his criticism, he proclaimed, "I believe the future truly great biography of the Prophet Joseph Smith will not ungenerously trim him down to the proportions of a liar, an impostor, an adulterer and anything else mostly bad." But at the same time, Poulson praised Brodie for her effort. He confessed that "many good things" would result from her book. It was "bound to stimulate wide and careful reading, pro and con" into "the early history of the church," leading ultimately to "a really objective and truly critical work in this field." He then told Brodie, "You have courage and you do get things done. You are probably much aware of imperfections and big gaps in [your] presentation. You have been big enough to even ask for and welcome straight-out-from-the-shoulder criticism. You will not be spoiled by either praise or blame that may come."[93]

Finally, in October 1944, Brodie sent her revised manuscript on to Alfred A. Knopf. In turn, Knopf moved Brodie's work through the final phases of editing in response to the suggestions made by Dale L. Morgan and two other individuals; namely, Wilson Follett, an in-house editor at Knopf, and Milo M. Quaife, an outside reader who was curator of manuscripts at the Detroit Public Library. Follett characterized Brodie's manuscript as "thoroughly viable . . . alive," noting that he as "a general non-specialist reader" found the "total effect" of the book satisfying. Brodie's work, he noted, would be "taken as [the] final" authority on Joseph Smith "by everyone except those

speaking for the official point of view by the Mormon hierarchy."
Follett did, however, "complain about . . . a rather chronic slop-
piness in the manuscript—some of it the consequence of mere
failure to proofread adequately, [and] some of it ingrained in the
author's rhetorical habits." For example, he was bothered that
the manuscript was "peppered and salted with gawky phrases like
'revelations born of crisis situations.'"[94]

Also noteworthy were the suggestions made by Milo M.
Quaife. Like Dale L. Morgan, whom he knew well, Quaife was
noted for his own extensive writings on the Mormons and the
western American experience. Also like Morgan, Quaife was
generally impressed by what Brodie had written, characterizing it
as an "excellent manuscript . . . scholarly [with] an easy, pleasant
narrative style." He then went on to characterize the entire work
as "laudably free from bias . . . as [is] reasonably possible to
achieve." But then Quaife quickly added: "Yet to tell the truth
about the career of Joseph Smith requires the statement of many
things which are painful to Mormon devotees. It necessarily follows that it will probably be criticized by church spokesmen, but
this possibility should not deter any publisher from bringing it
out who dares to discuss candidly a controversial subject.[95]

Brodie's manuscript received final in-house editorial clear-
ance in January 1945. Wilson Follett after subjecting the book to
"a slow and searching examination" found it "even better than I
thought to begin with" describing it as "an extremely impressive
piece of historical scholarship as well as a fascinating story, and I
am sure it will both win good opinions and sell gratifyingly."[96]

Meanwhile, in late 1944, Brodie became pregnant once
more. Eagerly anticipating the birth of a second child she made
every effort to limit her activities in order to prevent a repetition
of the miscarriage earlier that year. But in January 1945 she suffered a second miscarriage, and lamented at being "overwhelmed
with a sense of frustration and loss . . . I had all the pain and mis-
ery of childbirth without anything to show for it."[97]

Concurrently, Brodie was confronted with another family
tragedy. In late 1944, she received shocking news that a cousin to

whom she was very close, Lieutenant McKeen Eccles Brimhall, had been killed in combat in France. McKeen was Dean Brimhall's only son. To Dale Morgan she described her personal anguish and expressed deep concern that her uncle was "terribly depressed," adding, "I find it difficult to get the tragedy off my own mind." McKeen, she explained, "was practically like a brother . . . and clearly the favorite of all my male cousins."[98] Brodie's sense of profound personal loss prompted her to dedicate her forthcoming biography to the memory of her cousin.[99]

As Brodie put the finishing touches on her manuscript in early February 1945, she stumbled onto an unexpected surprise. While tying up some loose details in her research at the Library of Congress, she came across a photograph of Oliver Buell, the son of Presendia Huntingon Buell, one of Joseph Smith's plural wives. In examining the photograph, Brodie became convinced that Buell was the son of the Mormon leader, telling Dale Morgan that "he looks astonishingly like Joseph Smith." And with a bit of wry humor, she added, "If Oliver Buell isn't a Smith then I'm no Brimhall." She announced her intention to include this photograph in the biography together with pictures of Emma and Joseph's four sons.[100] In late March, Brodie received her copy-edited manuscript back from Knopf, noting the editor's discovery of "plenty of errors in punctuation, and occasional omissions." This combined with other oversights previously unnoticed forced Brodie to concede, "There will be errors in the book in its final form . . . I might as well reconcile myself to that fact."[101]

Brodie then waited several months for the final galleys, which arrived for her inspection in early August 1945. She was "pleased with the printing job, and elated that" Knopf had decided to include "26 out of the 27 pictures" that she had submitted. Knopf, moreover, allowed her "to place many of them in the exact spot where they would do the most to heighten the effect of the narrative." The only thing left was the actual publication of *No Man Knows My History*, which came on November 22, 1945.[102]

In conclusion, *No Man Knows My History* must be placed in proper perspective relative to Fawn Brodie's overall life and career. The Joseph Smith biography was only one of five biographies that Brodie wrote during the course of her life and the only one dealing with a Mormon subject. Brodie's second biography, *Thaddeus Stevens: Scourge of the South*, published in 1959, focused on the fiery Congressional Republican leader of the Radical Reconstruction. In her third biography, *The Devil Drives: A Life of Sir Richard F. Burton*, published in 1967, Brodie dealt with a fascinating, multifaceted nineteenth-century English explorer and author. Brodie's fourth biography, *Thomas Jefferson: An Intimate History*, published in 1974, became her best-known work, particularly outside of Utah. It was also her most controversial in that she focused on Jefferson's alleged amorous relationships, first with the already married Maria Cosway and then with Sally Hemings, his mulatto slave. Brodie's final biography, *Richard Nixon: The Shaping of His Character*, a rather harsh portrait of the resigned ex-president, was completed just before Brodie's death and published in 1981. Notwithstanding these fine works, *No Man Knows My History* is of special importance in that it brought Fawn Brodie her first recognition as a biographer of national stature—a most noteworthy accomplishment given that the young writer had just barely reached her thirtieth birthday.

Notes

1. Fawn M. Brodie to Nephi Jensen [n.d.]. Original in Fawn M. Brodie Papers, Marriott Library, University of Utah.
2. Fawn M. Brodie, "Biography of Fawn M. Brodie," oral interview conducted by Shirley E. Stephenson, October 30, 1975. Original in Oral History Collection, Fullerton State University, Fullerton, California, p. 6.
3. Ibid., 7.
4. Fawn M. Brodie to Dale L. Morgan, January 19, 1946. Original in Dale L. Morgan Papers, Bancroft Library, University of California, Berkeley.
5. Dale L. Morgan to Juanita Brooks, May 23, 1946. As reprinted in *Dale Morgan on Early Mormonism: Correspondence and a New History*, ed. John Phillip Walker (Salt Lake City: Signature Books, 1986), 121.
6. Fawn M. Brodie to Dean R. Brimhall, November 4, 1959. Original in Dean R. Brimhall Papers, Marriott Library, University of Utah. For a

closer examination of Brodie's background and the personal factors influencing the author see Newell G. Bringhurst, "Fawn Brodie and Her Quest of Independence," *Dialogue: A Journal of Mormon Thought* 22 (summer 1989): 79–95; Bringhurst, "Fawn M. Brodie—Her Biographies as Autobiography," *Pacific Historical Review* 59 (May 1990): 203–99; and Bringhurst, "Fawn McKay Brodie: Dissident Historian and Quintessential Critic of Mormondom," in *Differing Visions: Dissenters in Mormon History*, ed. Roger Launius and Linda Thatcher (Urbana: University of Illinois Press, 1994), 279–300.

7. Fawn M. Brodie, "The Libraries in My Life," *Utah Libraries: Journal of the Utah Library Association* 22, no, 1 (spring 1979): 14. Brodie was referring specifically to Elias Boudinot, *A Star in the West; or a Humble Attempt to Discover the Long Lost Tribes of Israel* (Trenton, N. J.: D. Fenton, S. Hutchinson, and J. Dunham, 1816); Ethan Smith, *View of the Hebrews; or the Ten Tribes of Israel in America* (Poultney, Vt.: Smith & Shute, 1825, 1823).

8. Brodie, "The Libraries in My Life," 14.

9. Fawn M. Brodie to Dean R. Brimhall, June 14, 1939. Original in Dean R. Brimhall Papers.

10. Ibid.

11. Thomas B. McKay, oral interview conducted by Newell G. Bringhurst, July 24, 1987.

12. Ibid.

13. Fawn M. Brodie to Dean R. Brimhall, June 14, 1939. Original in Dean R. Brimhall Papers.

14. Fawn M. Brodie to Revere Hansen, January 29, 1979. Original in Fawn M. Brodie Papers.

15. Fred Kaplan, *The Wizards of Armageddon* (New York: Simon and Schuster, 1983) gives the best overview of Bernard Brodie's early academic career and scholarly activities while at the University of Chicago and in the years immediately after. See pp. 11–19.

16. Fawn Brodie, *Our Far Eastern Record: A Reference Digest on American Policy*, vol. 2 (New York: American Council Institute of Pacific Relations, 1942); Fawn M. Brodie, *Peace Aims and Postwar Planning: A Bibliography* (Boston: World Peace Foundation, July 1942).

17. Fawn M. Brodie to Dean R. Brimhall, June 18, 1942. Original in Dean R. Brimhall Papers.

18. Ibid.

19. Fawn M. Brodie to Dean R. Brimhall, November 3, 1942. Original in Dean R. Brimhall Papers.

20. Fawn M. Brodie to Thomas E. and Fawn B. McKay, May 18, 1943. Original in Fawn M. Brodie Papers, Bx 2, Fd 1.

21. Fawn M. Brodie to Alfred A. Knopf, February 14, 1943. Original in Alfred A. Knopf Papers, Harry Ranson Humanities Research Center, University of Texas, Austin. In outlining the interim nature of the biography at this point, Brodie noted: "Of the period covering the Mormon 'wars' in Missouri during the 1830s, I have written a first draft. But the final four-year period during which Joseph Smith built Nauvoo, Illinois, making of it at the same moment a holy shrine and a political cauldron, remains to be studied as well as written. I hope to have the book finished in time for publication in 1944, since it is the centennial of [Smith's] death."

22. Fawn M. Brodie to Alfred A. Knopf, February 14, 1943.

23. Ibid.

24. M. Rugoff, "Biography Fellowship Evaluation," March 17, 1943. Original in Alfred A. Knopf Papers.

25. Ibid.

26. It should be noted that favorable opinion rendered by Alfred A. Knopf was not unanimous. In contrast to M. Rugoff, a second Knopf reader, H. Strauss, submitted a very negative evaluation stating, "I don't like her present project," expressing his belief that her "book would encounter very substantial sales obstacles." This reader was, moreover, critical of her writing, stating, "I cannot call [it] the least bit exciting. She never made me want to read on in the extensive sample section," adding, "the book remains for me a bit on the dull side." Original in Alfred A. Knopf Papers.

27. Kaplan, *The Wizards of Armageddon*, 18–19.

28. Fawn M. Brodie to Thomas E. and Fawn B. McKay, May 18, 1943. Original in Fawn M. Brodie Papers, Bx 2, Fd 1.

29. Fawn M. Brodie to Thomas E. and Fawn B. McKay, May 24, 1943. Original in Fawn M. Brodie Papers, Bx 2, Fd 1.

30. *Deseret News*, April 7, 1941.

31. Fawn M. Brodie to Thomas E. and Fawn B. McKay, May 18, 1943. Original in Fawn M. Brodie Papers, Bx 2, Fd 1.

32. "Fawn Brodie, Donald W. Mitchell Receive Alfred A. Knopf Literary Fellowships for 1943," press release, May 28, 1943. Original in Alfred A. Knopf Papers. Brodie's award was featured in various newspapers throughout the United States, including the *Washington Post*, May 22, 1943; the Salt Lake *Tribune*, May 30, 1943; and the Ogden *Standard-Examiner*, May 23, 1943.

33. Fawn M. Brodie to Thomas E. and Fawn B. McKay, May 24, 1943. Original in Fawn M. Brodie Papers, Bx 2, Fd 1.

34. Fawn M. Brodie to Thomas E. and Fawn B. McKay, May 18, 1943. Original in Fawn M. Brodie Papers, Bx 2, Fd 1.

35. Fawn M. Brodie to Thomas E. and Fawn B. McKay, May 18 and 24, 1943. Originals in Fawn M. Brodie Papers, Bx 2, Fd 1.

36. Fawn M. Brodie to Thomas E. and Fawn B. McKay, May 24, 1943. Original in Fawn M. Brodie Papers, Bx 2, Fd 1.

37. *Washington Post*, May 22, 1943.

38. Brodie, "The Libraries In My Life," p. 14-5.

39. Fawn M. Brodie, "Interview," KUTV, Salt Lake City Broadcast, March 8, 1978. Typescript in Fawn M. Brodie Papers.

40. Fawn M. Brodie to Dale L. Morgan, September 9, 1943. Original in Dale L. Morgan Papers. According to Brodie, the restrictive policy of the Mormon Church Historical Department was implemented in reaction to an essay dealing with the Mormons in a somewhat critical light by R. English, "The Mormons Move Over" *Colliers* 110 (December 12, 1942): 86–87.

41. Fawn M. Brodie to Dale L. Morgan, September 9, 1943. Original in Dale L. Morgan Papers.

42. Ibid. The existence of the Joseph Smith diary had been disclosed to Brodie by Professor M. Wilford Poulson, professor of psychology at Brigham Young University, according to Brodie in "The Libraries in My Life," 15.

43. Fawn M. Brodie to Dale L. Morgan, September 9, 1943. Original in Dale L. Morgan Papers.

44. Ibid.

45. Ibid. In a later account Brodie described her "rather difficult interview with my uncle, David O. McKay who told me at first that he would rather I would not use the library at all, and who later the next day sent me a note telling me I could use it. Seeing his anxiety, I decided then not to use it further, I wrote him a letter telling him I would not. I never returned." (Brodie, "The Libraries in My Life," 15.)

46. Fawn M. Brodie to Dale L. Morgan, September 9, 1943. Original in Dale L. Morgan Papers.

47. Ibid.

48. Brodie, in "The Libraries in My Life," 14–15.

49. Fawn M. Brodie to Dale L. Morgan, December 29, 1950. Original in Dale L. Morgan Papers.

50. Fawn M. Brodie to Dale L. Morgan, September 9, 1943. Original in Dale L. Morgan Papers.

51. The best overview of the life and activities of Dale L. Morgan is John Phillip Walker, ed., *Dale Morgan on Early Mormonism.*

52. Fawn M. Brodie, *No Man Knows My History: The Life of Joseph Smith* (New York: Alfred A. Knopf, 1945), xi.

53. "Memo from Dale Morgan" [n.d.]. Original in Dale L. Morgan Papers.

54. Ibid.

55. A term coined by Edward A. Geary in "Mormondom's Lost Generation: The Novelists of the 1940," *BYU Studies* 18 (fall 1977): 89. The varied interactions between Brodie and other members of Mormonism's so-called

lost generation are discussed in Newell G. Bringhurst, "Fawn M. Brodie, 'Mormondom's Lost Generation,' and *No Man Knows My History*," *Journal of Mormon History* 16: 11–23.

56. Vesta Crawford, although completing a significant research on this topic never actually completed her projected book-length study on Emma Smith. Material relative to this research is contained in the Vesta Crawford Papers, Special Collections, Marriott Library, University of Utah.

57. For a brief description of the activities of Vesta Crawford see Allene A. Jensen, "Utah Writers of the Twentieth Century: A Reference Tool" (M.Sc. thesis, University of Utah, 1977), 27.

58. Fawn M. Brodie to Claire Noall, April 8, 1944. Original in Claire Noall Papers, Special Collections, Marriott Library, University of Utah.

59. Fawn M. Brodie to Claire Noall, June 7, 1944. Original in Claire Noall Papers.

60. Fawn M. Brodie to Claire Noall, June 22, 1944. Original in Claire Noall Papers.

61. Two brief descriptions of the life and career of Claire Noall are contained in her obituaries as carried in the *Salt Lake Tribune*, September 3, 1971 and the *Deseret News*, September 3, 1971.

62. Fawn M. Brodie to Claire Noall, October 14, 1943. Original in Claire Noall Papers.

63. Fawn M. Brodie to Claire Noall, December 13, 1943. Original in Claire Noall Papers.

64. Fawn M. Brodie to Claire Noall, December 31, 1943. Original in Claire Noall Papers.

65. Claire Noall to Fawn M. Brodie, January 4, 1944. Original in Claire Noall Papers.

66. Fawn M. Brodie to Claire Noall, January 17, 1944. Original in Claire Noall Papers.

67. Ibid.

68. Fawn M. Brodie to Claire Noall, February 5, 1944. Original in Claire Noall Papers.

69. Levi S. Peterson, *Juanita Brooks: Mormon Woman Historian* (Salt Lake City: University of Utah Press, 1988) discusses the various aspects of this Utah writer's life and career. For a fuller discussion of the interaction between Brooks and Brodie see Newell G. Bringhurst, "Juanita Brooks and Fawn Brodie—Sisters in Mormon Dissent," *Dialogue: A Journal of Mormon Thought* 27 (summer 1994): 105–27.

70. Juanita Brooks to Dale L. Morgan, October 7, 1943, as quoted in Levi Peterson, *Juanita Brooks*, 141.

71. Fawn M. Brodie to Claire Noall, April 8, 1944. Original in Claire Noall Papers.

72. See "Martin Wilford Poulson," in *Utah's Distinguished Personalities*, 173. Levi S. Peterson in *Juanita Brooks: Mormon Woman Historian*, has suggested that Poulson was "a closet dissenter" or "disaffected Mormon" with "an inquiring mind" (65, 266–67). However one close family member, a son-in-law, has vigorously refuted Peterson's assertion, stating that Poulson "was not a dissenter or a disaffected Mormon . . . a critic yes," but at the same time Poulson strongly "believed the Church was true and that Joseph Smith was the Prophet of the restoration of the Church." Glen E. Soulier to Newell G. Bringhurst, August 29, 1994. Original in possession of the author.

73. Fawn M. Brodie to Dale L. Morgan, December 7, 1943. Original in Dale L. Morgan Papers.

74. As described by Samuel W. Taylor in *Rocky Mountain Empire: The Latter-day Saints Today* (New York: Macmillan Publishing, 1978), 232.

75. Fawn M. Brodie to Dale L. Morgan, February 7, 1946. Original in Dale L. Morgan Papers.

76. Fawn M. Brodie to Dale L. Morgan, March 22, 1944. Original in Dale L. Morgan Papers.

77. Fawn M. Brodie to Dale L. Morgan, November 19, 1943. Original in Dale L. Morgan Papers.

78. Ibid.

79. Fawn M. Brodie to Dale L. Morgan, December 18, 1943. Original in Dale L. Morgan Papers.

80. Ibid.

81. Fawn M. Brodie to Claire Noall, ca. January 1944. Copy in Dale L. Morgan Papers.

82. Fawn M. Brodie to Dale L. Morgan, April 1, 1944. Original in Madeline McQuown Papers, Special Collections, Marriott Library, University of Utah.

83. Fawn M. Brodie to Dale L. Morgan, April 26, 1944. Original in Dale L. Morgan Papers.

84. Fawn M. Brodie to Dale L. Morgan, May 6, 1944. Original in Dale L. Morgan Papers.

85. Fawn M. Brodie to Dale L. Morgan, May 31, 1944. Original in Dale L. Morgan Papers.

86. Fawn M. Brodie to Dale L. Morgan, June 7, 1944. Original in Dale L. Morgan Papers.

87. Fawn M. Brodie to Dale L. Morgan, June 30, 1944. Original in Madeline McQuown Papers. In a second letter, Fawn M. Brodie to Dale L. Morgan, August 15, 1944, the author in following up this "hunch" found a volume in the Library of Congress by a writer named Himes entitled *Medical History of Contraception*. She found this volume "extremely interesting on this

point." "Robert Dale Owen," she continued, "published a pamphlet on the subject in the 1830s which sold thousands of copies, also a fellow named Knowlton. The techniques they recommended were by no means primitive. If John C. Bennett didn't know those pamphlets intimately, he was not the man I believe him to have been."

88. Fawn M. Brodie to Dale L. Morgan, July 13, 1944. Original in Dale L. Morgan Papers.

89. Dale L. Morgan to Fawn M. Brodie, August 28, 1944. Original in Fawn M. Brodie Papers.

90. Ibid.

91. Ibid.

92. Fawn M. Brodie to Dale L. Morgan, September 2, 1944. Original in Dale L. Morgan Papers.

93. Wilford Poulson to Fawn Brodie, January 5, 1945. Original in Fawn M. Brodie Papers.

94. Wilson Follett to Alfred A. Knopf, December 6, 1944. Original in Alfred A. Knopf Papers.

95. Milo M. Quaife, "Report on Fawn M. Brodie Narrative," April 3, 1945. Original in Alfred A. Knopf Papers.

96. Wilson Follett to Alfred A. Knopf, "Memo," January 16, 1945. Original in Alfred A. Knopf Papers.

97. Fawn M. Brodie to Dale L. Morgan, January 20, 1945. Original in Dale L. Morgan Papers.

98. Fawn M. Brodie to Dale L. Morgan [ca. late 1944]. Original in Dale L. Morgan Papers.

99. Fawn M. Brodie's dedication in *No Man Knows My History* states: "To the Memory of my Cousin Lieutenant McKeen Eccles Brimhall killed in France September 20, 1944."

100. Fawn M. Brodie to Dale L. Morgan, February 17, 1945. Original in Dale L. Morgan Papers.

101. Fawn M. Brodie to Dale L. Morgan, March 24, 1945. Original in Dale L. Morgan Papers.

102. Fawn M. Brodie to Dale L. Morgan, August 9, 1945. Original in Dale L. Morgan Papers.

2

—— ❧ ——

Applause, Attack, and Ambivalence
Varied Responses to
*No Man Knows My History**

NEWELL G. BRINGHURST

In November 1945 Alfred A. Knopf published the first edition of
Fawn M. Brodie's *No Man Knows My History: The Life of Joseph
Smith*. Brodie, in terms of her background and intelligence,
seemed highly qualified to write a biography of Mormonism's
founder.[1] Born Fawn McKay in Ogden, Utah, on September 15,
1915, she was the daughter of Thomas E. McKay, an assistant to
the Council of the Twelve, the Mormon church's ruling elite,
and the niece of David O. McKay, the future church president
who in 1945 was already a member of the church's First Presidency. Brodie's mother, Fawn Brimhall (after whom she was
named), was the daughter of George H. Brimhall, a one-time
president of Brigham Young University in the early twentieth
century. Young Fawn excelled in school and by the age of nine
had already demonstrated her skills as a writer, having one of her
poems published in *Child Life*, a national periodical for children.
She sailed through school, graduating from Ogden High in 1930
at age fourteen and with highest honors from the University of
Utah in 1934 at age eighteen. She then did graduate work at the
University of Chicago, receiving her master's degree in English
in 1936 at the age of twenty.

---

*Reprinted with permission from *Utah Historical Quarterly* 57 (winter 1989).

In that same year she married a fellow student, Bernard Brodie, a non-Mormon. Bernard's family was of Latvian-Jewish immigrant stock, but Bernard himself never embraced the Jewish faith or any other religion. Meanwhile, Brodie commenced research into what would become her biography of Joseph Smith. In 1943 the fledgling author was awarded the fourth annual Alfred A. Knopf Literary Fellowship on the basis of a few preliminary chapters submitted for publication consideration. Brodie's award was noted in the *Washington Post*.[2] Her basic thesis in interpreting the life of Joseph Smith viewed the Mormon leader from a "naturalistic perspective," that is, as primarily motivated by nonreligious factors. She later noted: "I was convinced before I ever began writing that Joseph Smith was not a true Prophet."[3]

Aware of *No Man Knows My History's* potential for controversy, Herbert O. Brayer, writing in the *Mississippi Valley Historical Review*, predicted that the newly published book would "probably be one of the most highly praised as well as highly condemned historical works of 1945."[4] Brayer's prediction was certainly close to the mark on both accounts. Praise was immediately forthcoming, particularly in the eastern press. Orville Prescott of the *New York Times* characterized it as "one of the best of all Mormon books, scholarly, comprehensive, and judicial" and "scrupulously objective."[5] *Newsweek* described Brodie's book as "a definitive biography in the finest sense of the word," while *Time* magazine praised the author for her "skill and scholarship and admirable detachment" in describing Joseph Smith.[6]

No Man Knows My History was also favorably reviewed in various midwestern newspapers, particularly in Ohio and Illinois, states in which Joseph Smith and the Mormons had been influential during the 1830s and 1840s. The *Cleveland Plain Dealer* characterized the biography as "a scholarly work of accurate detail and painstaking research," prophesying it to be "the life of Joseph Smith to which all future historians and biographers must refer."[7] The *Chicago Sun* called the book "a rare combination of sound scholarship and lively, readable narrative," giving the reader "a believable picture of one of America's most interesting characters."[8]

Praise was also forthcoming from two distinguished Utah-born authors reviewing the biography for eastern publishers. The first was written for the *Saturday Review of Literature* by Dale L. Morgan, himself a noted researcher/historian of the Utah-Mormon scene. Morgan characterized Brodie's book as "the finest job of scholarship yet done in Mormon history . . . a book distinguished in the range and originality of its research, the informed and searching objectivity of its viewpoint, the richness and suppleness of its prose, and its narrative power."[9] In this same spirit, Bernard DeVoto, usually stingy with praise and generally an acerbic critic, was extremely complimentary in the pages of the *New York Herald-Tribune*. According to DeVoto, *No Man Knows My History* was "the best book about the Mormons so far published" and "in a class by itself." "Because of its general excellence," he continued, it "can be held to rigorous standards throughout" and "will stand for a long time to come."[10]

All of this favorable publicity generated local pride. In a glowing editorial entitled the "Success of Fawn McKay," the *Ogden Standard-Examiner* was "happy to congratulate Mrs. Brodie upon the success of her work," describing her as "a scholar possessing a most readable style." The *Standard-Examiner* titillated its readers: "The book commands immediate attention. Nibble at the first paragraph and you are lost, lured speedily through the work by her fascinating story."[11]

Not all Utahns shared the *Standard-Examiner's* enthusiasm—least of all spokesmen for the Church of Jesus Christ of Latter-day Saints. Initially, *No Man Knows My History*, in the words of Dale Morgan, ran up "against a wall of silence . . . in Zion" or, according to Brodie herself, "met a thunderous silence in Utah."[12] This was most evident in the reception accorded it by the church-owned *Deseret News*. At first, and in sharp contrast to the *Ogden Standard-Examiner*, the *News* completely ignored the biography. Later, the *Deseret News* did acknowledge that it had had some requests for its "appraisal" of what it termed "the so-called Brodie book." Attempting to justify its initial silence, the *News* stated that since "no copy of the book [had] ever been sent for its perusal" it had presumed that "neither the author nor the publisher wanted this book reviewed." Thus, the *News* had "no occasion to make any review."[13] However, by the spring of 1946 the Mormon church could no longer ignore *No Man Knows My History*. The book had been extensively reviewed in the eastern press and was enjoying universally brisk sales, even in Utah—sales that were reflected in its third printing by this time. Brodie's provocative biography had to be confronted head on. Leading the way was Apostle John A. Widtsoe, who attacked the book in the *Improvement Era* in March 1946. "The purported history of Joseph Smith," according to Widtsoe, "is really an attempt to portray Joseph Smith as a deceiver." The author, he continued, presents "every act in the Prophet's life . . . as the product of a dishonest man, who knew he was acting out a lie." He lashed out that "such unfairness illustrates the venomous temper of the author." Widtsoe concluded that "as a history of Joseph Smith, the book is a flat failure. . . . It will be of no interest to Latter-day Saints who have correct knowledge of the history of Joseph Smith."

The following month, other Mormon leaders responded to the book at the church's April 1946 annual general conference. These responses were less direct, not one mentioning the author or her book. In this spirit President George Albert Smith asserted, "Many have belittled Joseph Smith but those who have, will be forgotten in the remains of Mother Earth and the odor of their infamy will ever be with them."[15] Apostle Albert E. Bowen, in the words of the *Deseret News*, "made a stirring defense of the Prophet Joseph Smith against the poisonous slander of those who would make him out an imposter."[16] Throughout the conference church leaders gave "emphasis [to] the validity of the mission and accomplishments of the Prophet Joseph Smith."[17] Thus Fawn Brodie and her book cast a long shadow over this gathering, causing another Utah author, Juanita Brooks, to observe pungently to her close friend Dale L. Morgan: "We've been amused to see what Fawn's book has done to the Sunday issue of the *Deseret News*. Every number has an editorial on Joseph Smith reemphasizing all his fine qualities, but without mentioning her book at all." Brooks concluded that while none of the conference participants referred directly to Brodie or her book, "they certainly let people know what would happen to the likes of her."[18]

By May 1946, spokesmen for the church stepped up their attacks, directly confronting Fawn Brodie and her book. The "Church News" section of the *Deseret News* on May 11, 1946, presented what it termed a lengthy critique, written by "a Church Committee" of which Apostle Albert E. Bowen was apparently the principal author. This critique attacked *No Man Knows My History* as "wholly atheistic," claiming that Fawn Brodie's "intense atheism" not only colored but determined "the approach and, almost completely, the content of her book," allowing "no place in human experience for the transcendental." Also, the fact that Brodie's husband was Jewish was alluded to as influencing her lack of objectivity. This review conceded that "it is easy to grant the author the merit of a fine literary style throughout which makes the book altogether enticing reading." But it went on to note that "it is the style of the novelist and not of the historian. She has set up a pattern and cuts Joseph to fit it." The review then pointed out that "as a matter of research the author has produced nothing new," concluding that "little more can be said for the book than that it is a composite of all anti-Mormon books that have gone before pieced into a pattern comformable to the author's own particular rationale and bedded in some very bad psychology."[19] This critique apparently mirrored the official Mormon position, for it was reprinted by the church and circulated as a missionary tract under the title *Appraisal of the So-Called Brodie Book.*[20]

On the heels of the *Appraisal* came Hugh Nibley's more famous *No, Ma'am, That's Not History*. This pamphlet, subtitled *A Brief Review of Mrs. Brodie's Reluctant Vindication of a Prophet She Seeks to Expose*, attacked *No Man Knows My History* for its use of historical parallels, that is, the author's assertion that

Joseph Smith drew heavily from the social/cultural environment in which Mormonism developed. He also attacked the author for clinging "to the theory that all the prophet's thoughts and action were the result of slow and gradual evolution."[21] Nibley did concede that Brodie was "not mad at anybody" and therefore her book was "not animated by violent hatred." Brodie's book, he continued, stood in contrast to the "thumping" polemical anti-Mormon biographies of earlier times that painted Joseph Smith in "total depravity" as a "complete scamp." According to Nibley, Brodie's "Joseph Smith was a complete imposter . . . but he *meant well.*" But this "new and humane interpretation of the prophet," Nibley asserted, "far from improving things makes everything much worse" by presenting the Mormon leader as a "more plausible character."[22]

Fawn Brodie also faced strong criticism within her own family. Particularly striking was the response of Julian Cummings, an uncle married to the twin sister of Fawn's mother and to whom Fawn had been somewhat close while attending the University of Utah. In fact, she had sent Cummings a copy of *No Man Knows My History* shortly after its publication. After reading the book Cummings replied, "My dear lady, you have been laboring under a false premise and it has led you to come to false conclusions." He then called upon his niece to "humble" herself before the Lord and ask Him for a pardon for her "sins." He warned that this would be "much easier accomplished in this life," because upon death she would "have no place to hide [her] errors." He continued: "Your shame will be so mortifying that it will place you in an environment of darkness where you will see no one else and 'think' that no one else sees you. There you will wander until you become so tired with your condition and so weakened and exhausted that a feeling of repentance will begin to manifest itself." He further warned that this "is a very slow process and entails much suffering" that could "be avoided by taking advantage of repentance in this life."[23]

A cousin, Ernest McKay of Huntsville, was not content to sit back and let providence take its course relative to Brodie's alleged transgressions. He spoke out against the book as a guest lecturer at various Mormon wards in the Ogden-Huntsville area. Seeing him in action, one observer noted that McKay "knew how to choose the parts [of Brodie's book] he wanted to bring out and then tear them to pieces, and convince his audience that [Fawn Brodie] was a very naughty girl." McKay, on at least one occasion, made the rather curious statement, "One thing is certain from her book, Mrs. Jew is not convinced of the things she has written. It is plain that she has not left her CHURCH."[24] A third relative, Dr. Joseph Morrell of Ogden, an uncle through marriage, projected his hostile feelings toward Brodie and her book in a somewhat different fashion—through Madeline R. McQuown, a librarian in the Ogden Public Library, whom Brodie had known from her youth. Noted McQuown, "I have a little message for Fawn from the Church via Dr. Morrell—that she had better stay the hell out of Utah from now on." According to McQuown, "He was careful to give me the message while he drank cocoa and ate peppermint ice cream with me." She concluded, "What do they think they could do to her? Call out the Danites?"[25]

The most telling response, however, came from Fawn Brodie's most famous relative, her uncle David O. McKay. Upon the publication of *No Man Knows My History*, he expressed, within his own family, feelings of resentment, disappointment, and betrayal, declaring that his niece had gathered her information "from the garbage cans of the Church."[26] In public, however, the prominent Mormon leader expressed his anger in a more oblique fashion. On February 3, 1946, speaking to an audience at Brigham Young University, McKay related a horse story in which he made indirect, yet clear allusions to Brodie, her background, and the bringing forth of her book. He told the story of Dandy, "a well-bred colt" with a "good disposition, clean well-rounded eyes . . . well proportioned, and all in all, a choice equine possession." But Dandy resented restraint. "He was ill-contented when tied and would nibble at the tie-rope until he was free." "He hated to be confined in the pasture." His curiosity and desire to explore the neighborhood got him into trouble. One day Dandy broke through the fence getting out of his owner's field. He went into a neighbor's yard and got into an old house used for storage where he found a sack of grain. But the grain was poisoned bait for rodents. Within a few minutes Dandy was in spasmodic pain and died shortly thereafter. McKay then concluded: "My heart aches this morning because one who was pretty close to me failed—violated conventions in childhood—later broke through the fence of consideration and decency—found the poison grain of unbelief, and now languishes in spiritual apathy and decay."[27]

McKay apparently felt that the rebellious act of his niece required more drastic action. In the fall of 1945, just after the publication of *No Man Knows My History*, he apparently "initiated a resolution before the Twelve" calling for Fawn Brodie's excommunication. "But the matter was tabled on the grounds that it would make a martyr out of her."[28] However, by May 1946 such official reticence no longer remained, and Fawn McKay Brodie was formally excommunicated from the Church of Jesus Christ of Latter-day Saints. Church officials charged her with apostasy. Referring to the contents of her biography, they stated: "You assert matters as truths which deny the divine origin of the Book of Mormon, the restoration of the Priesthood and of Christ's Church through the instrumentality of the Prophet Joseph Smith, contrary to the beliefs, doctrines, and teachings of the Church."[29]

It appears that David O. McKay played a prominent role in the excommunication of his niece.[30] In assessing the motives of her uncle, Brodie suggested that he "felt keenly the need for self-protection"[31] and "of disassociating himself with me in the most dramatic possible fashion. He undoubtedly felt that he would be condemned if I were treated leniently. Moreover, he is unquestionably very angry about the book anyway, and he is not a man to take things lying down."[32]

The attacks on Fawn Brodie from David O. McKay and the Mormon church generally stood in sharp contrast to the encouragement and support that she received from within her immediate family. Her mother, whom Fawn described as a "quiet heretic," was especially supportive, particularly as the author came under increasing attack from church spokesmen. Indeed, Fawn Brimhall McKay had been "very supportive" of her daughter all along, even from the earliest stages of her research and writing.[33] This support continued unabated in the wake of Brodie's excommunication. She proclaimed, "I venture this prediction: This is one excommunication the Church will some day be ashamed of."[34] The besieged author also drew comfort from her older sister, Flora, and two younger sisters, Barbara and Louise, who in the words of Barbara "were supportive right from day one."[35]

Outside her immediate family, Fawn's uncle Dean Brimhall also encouraged his niece. From the earliest stages of her research she was inspired by Brimhall, Columbia-educated, a psychologist by training, outspoken, and known as somewhat of a maverick within the Latter-day Saint community. Brodie dedicated *No Man Knows My History* to the memory of Brimhall's son, Lt. McKeen Eccles Brimhall, who had been killed in France during World War II. After reading Brodie's book, Brimhall proclaimed that his niece "had a hero in her book and that hero was TRUTH." He went on, "She has raised our family to new levels of achievement. I know her grandfather, George H. Brimhall, would have been deeply moved with pride by the success of his granddaughter in the field of great creative writing."[36] In response to Brodie's excommunication he critically noted, "The Church has made some unhappy history for itself."[37]

Thus Brimhall's response to the book stood in sharp contrast to those of David O. McKay, her other two uncles, and cousin. In fact, a family feud developed as Brimhall lashed out against David O. McKay in response to the "Dandy" horse story that McKay had told at Brigham Young University. In writing his sister, Fawn's mother, he proclaimed: "D. O. McKay's attack on the family at the BYU meeting must be answered. . . . I must say something because by indirection he attacked [Fawn's] 'upbringing.' He insulted father and since the book was dedicated to McKeen his slander about Fawn spread over me. There is no reason for David O. McKay to be protected in such unseemly action—even dishonest words about Fawn's unconventionality as a child. McKeen died to preserve free criticism."[38] Brimhall then concluded with a question: "Should I fail [McKeen] now by letting this dishonest attack go unpunished just because D. O. McKay is supposed to be a prophet of God?"[39]

In contrast to her uncle Dean Brimhall, the male members of Fawn Brodie's immediate family were ambivalent in their reactions. Thomas E. McKay, her father, found himself in an extremely awkward situation by virtue of his high church position as an assistant to the Council of Twelve and because of his relationship to David O. McKay. Well aware of this, Fawn had initially offered to publish her biography under a pseudonym in order to protect her father. But he said, "Definitely not," wanting his daughter to be completely up front in what she was doing. He supported his daughter's "right to write the book and to do the research" when questioned by outsiders. But he was not supportive of the book's content and basic interpretation.[40] He refused to discuss the book with his daughter or even acknowledge its existence in her presence,[41] creating a barrier between them. In later years, Brodie reflected on her father's response (or lack thereof): "My father never did read the Joseph Smith biography. . . . I always felt . . . that his not reading it was an act of real hostility . . . and his refusal to discuss it, hurt me more, I think, than an angry argument about the contents would have done. At any rate, we both found it impossible to communicate on the subject, as on most others."[42] Brodie's brother, Thomas Brimhall McKay, was also ambivalent in his response. Like his father he was a devout, practicing Latter-day Saint, but unlike the elder McKay he was willing to discuss and debate with his sister the crucial issues raised in the biography. In fact, he carried out an open dialogue with Fawn as the book was in progress. Once it was completed, he defended Fawn and her right to write the book. But, like his father, he did not defend the book itself and felt that his sister's excommunication was justified. The Mormon church, he believed, had no other choice because of what Fawn had written and who she was.[43]

Outside of the McKay family ambivalence to *No Man Knows My History* was also evident in the reactions of various Mormon writers and historians. The noted Utah novelist Vardis Fisher in the book review section of the *New York Times* gave the book a mixed evaluation. He praised Brodie as "zealous and industrious and about as impartial as any biographer can be," noting that "she has ably presented her thesis in a biography that is well worth reading." But Fisher also took the author to task for quoting "copiously . . . from books by embittered apostates" which "sometimes carelessly leaves the impression that such sources are as trustworthy as . . . court records." He also asserted that "now and then she appears to state as indisputable facts what can only be regarded as conjectures supported by doubtful evidence." In one of his most telling criticisms Fisher noted that her book was "almost more a novel than a biography because she rarely hesitates to give the content of a mind or to explain motives which at best can only be surmised." He then went on to predict (inaccurately) that "it is this reviewer's notion that she will turn novelist in her next book, and that she should." Fisher noted that Brodie's book was "not the definitive biography" of Joseph Smith, adding parenthetically, "Has there ever been one of anybody?" But he concluded, "It is nevertheless a probing and very satisfying volume."[44]

Likewise, Juanita Brooks, then deep into her own research on the controversial topic of the Mountain Meadows Massacre, offered a mixed reaction to *No Man Knows My History*. In a letter to Dale Morgan (a friend of both Brooks and Brodie) Brooks praised the book as one that "needed to be done." She continued, "It is scholarly . . . it is literary . . . it sets up new points from which to judge Joseph Smith. It certainly shows careful and patient research. I like especially her work on backgrounds and social conditions and current interests."[45] But she questioned Brodie's basic thesis. "I do not believe that [Joseph Smith] was a conscious fraud and imposter. The things that were real to him may not seem so to her nor to you or to most other people, but I think they must have been to him. I have felt it was his own deep and sincere convictions that attracted and held his following. For a fraud, he inspired loyalties too deep in too many. Certainly he had something. Men, catching their spark from him, were willing to sacrifice too much to further his cause." Elaborating on this point Brooks continued: "I believe that it is possible for human beings to tap the great source of all good—to contact God direct, if you will. I believe that there were times, rare perhaps, when Joseph Smith did that. I believe that it was those times that held his people to him in spite of all his human blunderings and frailties and mistakes."[46]

Brooks also questioned Brodie's interpretations derived from contemporary, controversial statements made by Smith, noting, "Different people put entirely different interpretations even on simple statements. So with some of Fawn's material, I didn't always arrive at the same conclusions from her evidence that she did." Brooks predicted that "not many" Latter-day Saints would read Brodie's book, rejecting it out-of-hand as "just another" anti-Mormon book. She concluded, with greater accuracy, "But if Mormon laity will not read it, Mormon scholars should. Some of them will. And the book cannot but help have its effect, and in the long run, a very profound effect."[47]

Indeed, the profound effect predicted by Juanita Brooks for *No Man Knows My History* has been reflected by the varied responses expressed by scholars in the field of Mormon history since 1945. Leonard J. Arrington, the dean of Mormon historians, reflected his own ambivalence, declaring in *Dialogue* in 1966 that "despite the evidence of prodigious research, despite the charming imagery of its style and its stirring chronicle of an enigmatic career, the book has two methodological weaknesses." The first involved Brodie's limited "appreciation of religious phenomena generally" and her refusal "to accord integrity to the many men of undoubted intellect and character who associated with the Mormon prophet and believed him to be an inspired leader." Second, according to Arrington, Brodie was concerned "with painting a pen portrait rather than with writing a work of history." That is, she began her work "by studying this historical background sufficiently to formulate what she regarded as a reasonable and believable approach to Joseph Smith and then proceeded to mobilize the evidence to illustrate and support her interpretation."[48]

Also ambivalent in his reaction was Robert B. Flanders, author of *Nauvoo: Kingdom on the Mississippi* and a leading scholar within the Reorganized Church of Jesus Christ of Latter Day Saints. According to Flanders, also writing in *Dialogue* in 1966, Brodie was "so anti-Mormon in her own intellectual orientation that she succumbed to the temptation to bring nineteenth century literature of Mormon countersubversion uncritically and in large doses into her own work." He noted the author's "zeal to create the grand and ultimate exposé of Mormonism," describing the book as her "subtle yet emphatic declaration of spiritual and intellectual independence from her Mormon origins and antecedents, set in a format of wide research and a popularized journalistic writing style, with an abundance of blood, sex, and sin." But Flanders conceded that *No Man Knows My History* was "so exhaustive in its coverage and painstaking in its use of primary sources that it has become a recognized standard work on Mormon origins and early history . . . unparalleled in the field, and may remain so for some time, a guide to those who undertake less ambitious studies."[49] Writing eight years later, again in *Dialogue*, Flanders reaffirmed his earlier assessment that Brodie's book was a "transitional work." "A new era," he continued, "dawned with her book. All subsequent serious studies of early Mormonism have necessarily had Brodie as a referent point."[50]

Ambivalence among scholars of Mormon history continued in the wake of the publication of a second and enlarged edition of *No Man Knows My History* in 1971. This occasion generated two lengthy critiques by Marvin S. Hill, professor of history at Brigham Young University. The first appeared in *Dialogue* in 1972 and the second in *Church History* in 1974. Hill recognized Brodie's book as "the most influential book on early Mormonism, a status it has retained."[51] Among the contributions made by Brodie's biography, according to Hill, were the

author's convincing rejection of the Spaulding theory concerning the origins of the Book of Mormon, her consideration of
Joseph Smith within the context of the social and intellectual
currents of his time, and her depiction of Smith as "a rational
human being" (through her rejection of the earlier view of I.
Woodbridge Riley that Smith was an epileptic and the later
interpretation of Bernard DeVoto that the Mormon leader was
paranoid). Hill also credited Brodie with bringing out Smith's
"human qualities, his loves, his hates, his fears, his hopes and
ambitions." In Hill's words, "She helped many Mormons to recall
that the prophet had a human side and that not all of what he
did was done in the name of the Lord nor with transcendental
significance." Hill also credited Brodie with stimulating historical debate and further investigation on a number of crucial, controversial topics, including the first vision, authorship of both
the Book of Mormon and the Book of Abraham, and the whole
question of Mormon polygamy.[52] He pointed to entire issues of
Dialogue and *Brigham Young University Studies* that had been
devoted to various controversial issues raised in Fawn Brodie's
biography.[53] "Thus it should be evident," Hill asserted, "that
Brodie has written an immensely important book, a powerful
book, which greatly influenced the thinking of Mormon liberals
and conservatives with respect to the life of the prophet."[54]

Despite these positive responses to the book, Hill took care
to note that *No Man Knows My History* "falls short of greatness"
because of certain "fundamental weaknesses." Hill, like earlier
Mormon critics, felt that Brodie was incorrect in her basic thesis
that Smith was a "deliberate deceiver who played out his masquerade for personal advantage" and that Smith's "religious
efforts were play-acting for the benefit of an appreciative audience." Along this same line, Hill maintained that Brodie's biography "was external only" and that she "was never able to take us
inside the mind of the prophet, to understand how he thought
and why."[55] Hill seemed to attribute this deficiency in part to
Brodie's failure (and/or inability) to utilize primary source materials written by and to Smith and contained in the Mormon

church archives and, more important, to her preconceptions or assumptions that prevented her from getting "back into Joseph Smith's nineteenth century world which was so religious in its orientation." Hill continued: "She cannot handle the religious mysticism of the man or of the age because there is too much of modern science in her make-up, too much Sigmund Freud, too much rationalism. For Brodie to believe in the reality of another world, a world of the spirit seems incredible."[56]

He attributed Brodie's naturalistic portrait of Smith to her rebellion against her Mormon heritage coupled with a general "cynicism toward religion" that existed "among many intellectuals" during the 1930s and 1940s—the very time Brodie was writing her biography. According to Hill, this made the author "anxious to destroy the image of Mormonism [and that she] saw it as something to be sneered or laughed at. Such concerns may have caused Brodie to over-stress the prophet's rationality, play down his mysticism, and dismiss his religious thought which was perhaps embarrassing as a 'patchwork of ideas and rituals.'"[57] Hill also felt that Brodie's biography suffered from what he termed its "sectarian" orientation, that is, her highly moralistic either-or approach—an approach ironically rooted in her Mormon background. Brodie's "moral indignation" over Smith's limitations and indiscretions caused her to "overstate her case" by concluding that such foibles meant that Joseph Smith could not possibly have been a true prophet. Hill concluded with some irony that Brodie's thesis with its "either-or alternatives was precisely the same" as that "presented by the early Mormon and missionary Orson Pratt in the 1840s and 1850s." Whereas Pratt affirmed that in the light of Smith's accomplishments "he must have been a true prophet," Brodie, a hundred years later, "looking at [Smith's] limitations concluded he was a fraud." Brodie's original thesis, Hill noted, "opens considerable room for speculation. . . . Historians should . . . explore the broad, promising middle ground . . . neither Pratt nor Brodie fully perceived."[58]

Despite such ambivalence among Mormon writers, *No Man Knows My History* has continued to enjoy a high degree of respect among scholars in the general field of American religious history.[59] This is the case even with the appearance of four subsequent book-length studies on Joseph Smith published within the last twenty years. These include Carl Carmer's *The Farm Boy and the Angel* published in 1970; Donna Hill's *Joseph Smith: The First Mormon*, which appeared in 1977; Francis M. Gibbons's *Joseph Smith: Martyr, Prophet of God*, also published in 1977; and Richard L. Bushman's *Joseph Smith and the Beginnings of Mormonism*, 1984. Each of the four has limitations that have prevented it from supplanting *No Man Knows My History* as the most widely respected biography of the Mormon leader. Carmer in *The Farm Boy and the Angel* apparently started out to write an in-depth definitive biography but ended up, for various reasons, writing a popular narrative on the church's early years. Donna Hill's *Joseph Smith: The First Mormon*, while incorporating a great deal of the current scholarship of the "new Mormon history," suffers from chronic organizational problems that produced a cross between a biography and a narrative of early church history. Francis M. Gibbons's *Joseph Smith: Martyr, Prophet of God* is little more than a faith-promoting hagiography, virtually ignored by serious scholars both within and outside of the Latter-day Saint community. Finally, Richard L. Bushman's *Joseph Smith and the Beginnings of Mormonism*, despite being carefully researched and written, is not really a true biography of the Mormon leader in that it does not go beyond 1831 in exploring Smith's life and activities. Thus Fawn M. Brodie's *No Man Knows My History* continues to be, by default, the closest thing to a definitive biography of the Mormon leader.

Even Brodie herself seemed somewhat surprised by this fact. In 1975 she confessed, "It is astonishing to me that there has not been . . . a better biography," and in 1980 she wrote her friend and fellow iconoclast Samuel W. Taylor, declaring that her "Joseph Smith book is going to be a thorn for a long, long time."[60] Brodie, however, was a bit too limited in her latter assessment. Sterling M. McMurrin in a tribute to Fawn Brodie written for *Dialogue* shortly after her death in 1981 proclaimed that *No Man Knows My History* represented "a watershed in the treatment of Mormon history by Mormon historians" because in its wake "Mormon history produced by Mormon scholars . . . moved toward more openness, objectivity, and honesty." This involved "a more genuine commitment to the pursuit of truth, and greater courage in facing criticism or even condemnation," creating what McMurrin termed "a new climate of Liberation."[61] In this same vein, Richard S. Van Wagoner, writing for *Sunstone*, concluded, "Though we may disagree with [Brodie's] assessment of the truth respecting Mormonism, *No Man Knows My History* may be the major impetus in the quest for a less apologetic, more objective Mormon history."[62] Thus it is apparent that *No Man Knows My History* has and will continue to have a potent influence on the writing of early Mormon history, at least until someone produces a more comprehensive, thoroughly researched, and more deftly written biography of Joseph Smith—a task that remains undone some fifty years after the first appearance of Brodie's provocative biography.

Notes

1. Information relative to Brodie's early life has been drawn from a number of sources. The most useful were Fawn M. Brodie, "Biography of Fawn McKay Brodie," oral history interview conducted by Shirley E. Stephenson, November 30, 1975. Original in Oral History Collection, Fullerton State University, Fullerton, California; Flora McKay Crawford, "Flora on Fawn," unpublished recollections, n.d.; Barbara McKay Smith, "Recollections of Fawn M. Brodie," address to Alice Louise Reynolds Forum, Provo, Utah, 1982.
2. *Washington Post*, May 22, 1943.
3. Brodie, "Biography of Fawn McKay Brodie," 10.
4. *Mississippi Valley Historical Review*, March 1946, 601–3.
5. *New York Times*, January 9, 1946.
6. *Newsweek*, November 26, 1946; *Time*, January 28, 1946.
7. *Cleveland Plain Dealer*, November 25, 1945.
8. *Chicago Sun*, November 25, 1945.
9. *Saturday Review of Literature*, November 24, 1945.
10. *New York Herald-Tribune*, December 16, 1945.

11. *Ogden Standard-Examiner*, December 2, 1945.
12. Dale L. Morgan to Lydia Clawson Hoopes, January 29, 1946. Original in Dale L. Morgan Papers, Bancroft Library, University of California, Berkeley. Dale L. Morgan to Fawn M. Brodie, March 7, 1946. Original in Fawn M. Brodie Papers, Special Collections, University of Utah Library, Salt Lake City.
13. *Deseret News*, May 11, 1946.
14. *Improvement Era*, March 1946.
15. *Deseret News*, April 8, 1946.
16. Ibid.
17. Ibid.
18. Juanita Brooks to Dale L. Morgan, April 15, 1946. Copy in Juanita Brooks Papers, Utah State Historical Society, Salt Lake City.
19. *Deseret News*, May 11, 1946.
20. *Appraisal of the So-Called Brodie Book*, reprinted from the *Church News*, May 11, 1946 (Salt Lake City, 1946).
21. Hugh Nibley, *No, Ma'am, That's Not History* (Salt Lake City: Bookcraft, 1946), 21. Nibley in refuting what he considered Brodie's extreme arguments made some rather extreme statements of his own. For example, on p. 46 Nibley asserted that "of all the Churches in the world only this one has not found it necessary to readjust any part of its doctrine in the last hundred years" and on pp. 61–62 he argued, "The gospel as the Mormons know it sprang full-grown from the words of Joseph Smith. It has never been worked over or touched up in any way, and is free of revisions and alterations." Taking note of Nibley's scholarship, Brodie made the following observations concerning his pamphlet: "It is a flippant and shallow piece. He really did me a service by demonstrating the difference between his scholarship and mine. If that is the best a young Mormon historian can offer, then I am all the more certain that the death of B. H. Roberts meant the end of all that was truly scholarly and honest in orthodox Mormon historiography." Fawn M. Brodie to Thomas E. and Fawn B. McKay, May 27, 1946, original in Brodie Papers.
22. Nibley, *No, Ma'am, That's Not History*, 7–8. Also attacking Brodie with the apparent approval of Mormon church leaders were Milton R. Hunter, a member of the church's First Quorum of the Seventy, who reviewed *No Man Knows My History* in the *Pacific Historical Review* 15 (June 1946): 226–28; and Francis W. Kirkham through his *A New Witness for Christ in America* (Independence, Mo.: Zion's Publishing Co., 1947), 359–94.
23. J. M. Cummings to Fawn M. Brodie, November 5, 1945. Copy in Brodie Papers, Bx 9, Fd 14. Brodie wasted little time in publicly disclosing the contents of Cummings's letter to the press, declaring, "One of my uncles has me eternally damned and wandering forever on the outer fringes of

eternity." See Clip Boutell, "Writer Burns Bridges with Mormon Story," *Washington Post*, January 13, 1946. This same article with Brodie's quote found its way into at least one other newspaper—the *Portland (Oregon) Journal*, January 2, 1946.

24. Beatrice Johnson to Dale L. Morgan, October 7, 1946. Original in Morgan Papers. For a description of Ernest McKay's activities see "Kaysville Class to Hear Current Book Discovered" from "Kaysville Papers—September 1946." Typescript in Brodie Papers.

25. Dale L. Morgan to Fawn M. Brodie, March 2, 1947. Original in Brodie Papers. Brodie's reaction to her uncle's warning is interesting: "It makes me angry . . . I shall, of course, go back there, but what annoys me most is the realization that I am not entirely thick-skinned and those people will be able to needle me in some fashion or other—if only by cutting me dead. What I am trying to say is that until I get to the point where I am completely indifferent to what they say and do, I am not entirely free from them. And I am not quite there yet. But give me time." Fawn M. Brodie to Dean Brimhall, March 8, 1987. Dean R. Brimhall Papers, University of Utah Library.

26. Edward R. McKay, "Recollections," oral history interview conducted by Newell G. Bringhurst, July 23, 1987.

27. As printed in the *Deseret News* "Church Section," February 23, 1946. A somewhat different version of this story in typescript form, entitled "The Thoroughbred" and identified as "Taken from a Talk by David O. McKay at BYU in 1946," was brought to my attention by Barbara M. Smith.

28. Dale L. Morgan to Juanita Brooks, June 3, 1946. Original in Juanita Brooks Papers, Utah State Historical Society, Salt Lake City.

29. William H. Reeder Jr. to Fawn M. Brodie, May 23, 1946. Copy in Brodie Papers. Even though the story of Brodie's excommunication received national attention, going out on the AP wire and thus being written up in newspapers throughout the United States, it received scant notice in the two major Salt Lake City newspapers. The *Salt Lake Tribune*, June 16, 1946, carried a short news article, "Utah Author Loses L.D.S. Membership," buried on page 8B. The *Deseret News* did not accord Brodie even that much recognition, merely listing the church's official action in its usual weekly list of those "Excommunicated from the Church" as contained in its Saturday "Church Section."

30. This according to Thomas B. McKay, "Recollections," oral history interview conducted by Newell G. Bringhurst, July 28, 1986, and Flora McKay Crawford, "Recollections," oral history interview conducted by Newell G. Bringhurst, September 30, 1988.

31. Fawn M. Brodie to Thomas E. and Fawn B. McKay, May 27, 1946. Original in Brodie Papers.

32. Fawn M. Brodie to Thomas E. and Fawn B. McKay, June 2, 1946. Original in Brodie Papers.
33. As related in Brodie, "Biography of Fawn McKay Brodie." Indeed, as early as 1940 Brodie noted that her mother had become "a thorough going heretic" and that it was "almost as much fun to discuss the Church with her" as with her outspoken uncle Dean Brimhall. See Fawn M. Brodie to Dean Brimhall, March 26, 1940. Original in Brimhall Papers.
34. Fawn B. McKay to Dean Brimhall, June 18, 1946. Original in Brimhall Papers.
35. Barbara McKay Smith, "Recollections," 24, oral history interview conducted by Newell G. Bringhurst, July 21, 1986.
36. Dean Brimhall to Preston Nibley, May 26, 1946. Copy in Brimhall Papers.
37. Dean Brimhall to Fawn B. McKay, June 16, 1946. Copy in Brodie Papers.
38. Dean Brimhall to Fawn B. McKay, March 24, 1946. Copy in Brodie Papers.
39. Ibid.
40. Smith, "Recollections," 23–24.
41. Louise McKay Card, "Recollections," 14, oral history interview conducted by Newell G. Bringhurst, August 1, 1986.
42. Fawn M. Brodie to Dean Brimhall, November 4, 1959. Original in Brimhall Papers.
43. Thomas B. McKay, "Recollections."
44. New York Times, November 25, 1945.
45. Juanita Brooks to Dale L. Morgan, December 9, 1945. Copy in Brooks Papers.
46. Ibid.
47. Ibid.
48. Leonard J. Arrington, "Scholarly Studies of Mormonism in the Twentieth Century," Dialogue 1 (spring 1966): 24–25. Arrington also pointed to what he considered a third major defect in Brodie's biography in a letter to William D. Russell: "In fact . . . the chief defect of her book is that it was written from materials in the New York Public Library, Yale Library, and Chicago Historical Library, which were essentially anti-Mormon collections, plus the research she did in the RLDS Library. That she did not use material in [the LDS archives] largely explains her portrait of Joseph Smith. Certainly, if she were to see the documents which are now available, not only to me but to others, it would certainly be a different portrait." Leonard J. Arrington to William D. Russell, October 24, 1972. Copy in Brodie Papers.
49. Robert Bruce Flanders, "Writing the Mormon Past," Dialogue 1 (autumn 1966): 58–59.

50. Robert B. Flanders, "Some Reflections on the New Mormon History," *Dialogue* 9 (spring 1974): 35.
51. Marvin S. Hill, "Secular or Sectarian History? A Critique of *No Man Knows My History*," *Church History* 43 (March 1974): 78, reprinted in this volume.
52. Marvin S. Hill, "Brodie Revisited: A Reappraisal," *Dialogue* 7 (winter 1972): 73–74.
53. See *BYU Studies* 9 (spring 1969) and 10 (spring 1970), also *Dialogue* 3 (summer–autumn 1968). Although, as Hill notes, "her book is rarely cited in the footnotes" of these two journals which "have published the bulk of the anti-Brodie articles." Hill, "Secular or Sectarian History," 78.
54. Hill, "Brodie Revisited," 74.
55. Ibid., 74–75.
56. Ibid., 75.
57. Ibid.
58. Hill, "Secular or Sectarian History?" 93–96.
59. For example, Sidney E. Alhstrom, in *A Religious History of America* (New Haven: Yale University Press, 1972), 504, called Brodie's biography a "sympathetic and insightful account . . . unequaled" as a life of the Mormon prophet. More recently, however, Davis Bitton and Leonard J. Arrington in *Mormons and Their Historians* (Salt Lake City: University of Utah Press, 1988), 108–25, discuss Brodie and her biography of Joseph Smith within the context of a group of historians without history degrees who were considered part of a "lost generation" of writers of Mormon history.
60. Brodie, "Biography of Fawn McKay Brodie," 9; Fawn M. Brodie to Samuel W. Taylor, May 21, 1980. Original in Samuel W. Taylor Papers, Utah State Historical Society.
61. Sterling M. McMurrin, "A New Climate of Liberation: A Tribute to Fawn McKay Brodie, 1915–1981," *Dialogue* 15 (1982): 73–76.
62. Richard S. Van Wagoner, "Fawn Brodie: The Woman and Her History," *Sunstone* 7 (July–August 1982): 37.

3

Secular or Sectarian History?
A Critique of
*No Man Knows My History**

MARVIN S. HILL

When Herbert O. Brayer reviewed *No Man Knows My History*, Fawn Brodie's biography of the Mormon prophet, Joseph Smith, in the *Mississippi Valley Historical Review* in 1946, his words were prophetic. "This book," he said, "which purports to be a 'definitive biography' will probably be one of the most highly praised and highly condemned historical works of 1945."[1] The book has indeed been highly praised and highly condemned, with plaudits coming generally from professionals in the field of American history. It quickly became the standard life of Joseph Smith and the most influential book on early Mormonism, a status it has retained. Evidence of the respect it still commands is provided by Sidney Ahlstrom of Yale University who recently termed it a "sympathetic and insightful account" which is "unequaled" as a life of the Mormon prophet.[2]

The condemnations have come from historians who are also members of the Mormon church. In dissertations, innumerable articles and books circulated largely among the Mormon community,[3] these students have questioned Brodie's denial of Smith's first vision, her thesis that Smith was a gold digger before he turned prophet and her argument that the Book of Mormon

* Reprinted with permission from *Church History* 43 (March 1974).

and the Book of Abraham, two of Smith's works considered ancient scripture, were written by Smith himself.[4] While not all of these works are genuinely scholarly and worthy of the attention of the American historical profession, some are carefully researched and frequently based upon sources in the church archives to which Brodie did not have access. One suggestive study is by Richard Bushman of Boston University, who, after reexamining the Book of Mormon against the background of American political ideals of the 1820s, argues that contrary to Brodie the book did not consistently reflect American democratic values of that period.[5]

While these works have had small impact on non-Mormons, several studies in the field of American economic and cultural history have gained national recognition. Among these are books by Leonard Arrington, Robert Flanders, Klaus Hansen, and Thomas F. O'Dea, which have been published by university presses.[6] However, only the works of Flanders and Hansen dealt to any extent with the Mormon prophet, whom they considered in their treatment of the Mormon kingdom of God. Thus, despite great vitality in the field of Mormon studies, comparatively little significant work has been done on Joseph Smith. This perhaps explains why Alfred A. Knopf issued a second edition of *No Man Knows My History* in 1971, and it provides one reason why Brodie claimed in the preface to the new edition that the discovery of new sources has not made necessary any important revisions in her biography.[7]

That Brodie's work has gone so long without effective challenge or criticism is peculiar. During the half century since her book appeared the factual, "scientific", external sort of history that characterized the Progressive period, and her book to a considerable extent, has been discarded. In its wake has come the rise of American intellectual and religious history,[8] including the revitalization of social history through use of demographic and other methodological techniques,[9] and the reconsideration of ethnic groups and their role in shaping American religious history.[10] Most of this has taken place within the broad context of what Sidney Ahlstrom called a "moral and theological revolution" in America.[11] That Brodie's biography has maintained its status in the face of so much change and revision is remarkable, especially when so many new sources on the prophet's life have been made available, sources which Herbert Brayer said were indispensable to any definitive study of the Mormon prophet.

Brodie's considerable influence with professional historians is attributable to her skill as a narrator, to her impressive research in many areas—especially her background on the Book of Mormon and the Spaulding theory of its origin, as well as that on the Book of Abraham[12] and to her insistence on the importance of the political kingdom in alienating non-Mormons in Missouri and Illinois.[13] But Brodie's continuing influence rests too on the fact that Mormon scholars, perhaps concerned about losing status professionally or in the church, have utilized the church archives but have been reluctant to attempt a biography. Also, only a few of them have been well versed in the field of American studies and thus adequately prepared for the task.[14] As for the non-Mormons, they generally have not been aware of the opportunities now open to them in Salt Lake City.[15] Further, they have perhaps been satisfied with what Brodie had to say and seem hesitant to deal with Smith's visions, his golden plates and his witnesses, all of which are awkward to handle objectively.[16]

Despite its strengths, *No Man Knows My History* seems particularly deficient and deserving of critical reevaluation in two aspects. One of these was noticed in 1946 by Ralph Gabriel of Yale, who observed that Brodie's work was largely external in its treatment of Smith and that it "may be called appropriately secular history."[17] When it is recalled that Mormonism was a religious movement and Smith a religious leader this is no small deficiency. The other aspect is its sectarian tendencies—Brodie's inclination to dwell upon the truth or untruth of the prophet's claims and to evaluate his career from a highly moralistic perspective. This results in her bringing to her assessment of Smith some overly simple and rather inflexible standards by which to judge him. It may be that Brodie's sectarian disposition is related to her early years in the Mormon church as the daughter of a high-ranking official.[18]

To be sure, Brodie did perceive the church initiated by Smith as "a real religious creation, one intended to be to Christianity what Christianity was to Judaism: that is a reform and a consummation,"[19] and she did compare the prophet perceptively to other radical religious leaders.[20] But her book is not entirely adequate as a religious history because she did not consider Smith to be religiously motivated. Further, she made no attempt to trace the religious forces which brought the followers of Smith together in a movement but sought to account for Mormonism on the basis of his charisma alone.[21] She never explained how so many of mystical persuasion were attracted to him when he was supposedly cynical, contemptuous of sectarianism and revivalism, and an opportunist who exploited the piety of others for his own aggrandizement.[22] Brodie told a correspondent for the *New York Times* shortly after her book was published that her research was two-thirds completed before she discovered that Joseph Smith was an imposter.[23] But once she made the deduction it permeated her book and influenced what she said about Smith's visions, his gold digging, his Book of Mormon, his and his family's alleged irreligion, his history, his witnesses and his polygamy.[24] Scattered throughout her early chapters are assertions of Smith's deliberate deceptiveness and religious insincerity. Smith only gradually "acquired the language and accent of sincere faith" (84), and not until 1832 was he "now taking himself seriously as a prophet of the Lord" (123). She says in her supplement, "Here are evidences not only of unbridled fantasy but also contrivance and seeming fraud" (412). Too often Brodie fails to consider the possibility that Mormonism as a movement has its own inner dynamic which was impossible for the prophet to generate or fully control.

Despite Brodie, scholars like David Brion Davis[25] and Mario De Pillis have argued persuasively that Mormonism was a religious movement. In a paper that has not been given adequate circulation, De Pillis has shown that early Mormonism was rooted in a quest for religious authority and emerged as a reaction to the conflicting doctrines of the competing sects in the burned-over district of western New York.[26] This helps to tie together some of the miscellaneous insights of Whitney Cross, who demonstrated how important the influences of sectarian preachers were in providing the background of contention against which Mormonism arose, but failed to make clear Mormonism's relationship to this sectarian activity.[27] In a paper read at one of the recent sessions of the Western History Association at New Haven, De Pillis elaborated his thesis by maintaining that early Mormon visions and dreams brought surcease from emotional and intellectual stress among those confused and bewildered by ideological and emotional turmoil in western New York. If this be so, then it may raise the question whether Joseph Smith's visions were not prompted by the same social stress and whether they deserve the label of fraudulent which Brodie put upon them.

The matter of questioning the reality of Joseph Smith's visions stems from Brodie's skepticism about his celebrated "first vision," which he claims to receive in 1820 but which Brodie said he fabricated, since he did not publish it until 1838 and his relatives and most intimate followers either failed to mention it or confused it with the vision of the angel who revealed the golden plates of the Book of Mormon.[28] Smith's official history recounted how he was disturbed by the many contradictory claims of the several sects in his home town of Manchester and how, discovering a passage of the Epistle of St. James that those who lack wisdom should ask of God, he went into the woods to pray. Shortly after this, he

> . . . saw a pillar of light [which was] exactly over my head, above the brightness of the sun, which descended gradually until if fell upon me.
>
> It no sooner appeared . . . when . . . I saw two personages, whose brightness and glory defy all description standing above me in the air. One of them spoke unto

me, calling me by name, and said—pointing to the other—'THIS IS MY BELOVED SON, HEAR HIM.'

My object in going to inquire of the Lord was to know which of all the sects was right, that I might know which to join. No sooner, therefore, did I get possession of myself, so as to be able to speak, than I asked the personages who stood above me in the light, which of all the sects was right—and which I should join. I was answered that I must join none of them, for they were all wrong, and the personage who addressed me said that all their creeds were an abomination in His sight: that those professors were all corrupt; that 'they draw near to me with their lips, but their hearts are far from me.[29]

But Smith did not relate this vision often before the 1840s and, as Brodie noted, nothing was said about it in the local newspapers at the time,[30] although he said he told a local minister and was ridiculed.[31] Brodie surmised that the first vision story was composed by the prophet after he had gained national recognition, to account for his interest in religion in a manner different from that advanced by his enemies, that he was a money digger and prophet come-lately.[32]

Since Brodie first published her findings new evidence shows that Smith recorded his vision in the initial manuscript of his history in 1832; however, he described the visitation of one heavenly messenger, not two as in 1838.[33] We now know that he told his story in 1835,[34] and frequently in the 1840s.[35] Despite the new evidence, Brodie still maintains that the first vision account was calculated and contrived.[36] She attempts to bolster this viewpoint by noting that Wesley Walters has argued that the revival which Smith said encouraged his inquiry of the Lord could not have come in 1820 since there were no general revivals in Palmyra at that time, and must have occurred, if at all, in late 1823 or early 1824.[37] Only then were George Lane and Benjamin Stockton, the two ministers whom the prophet's brother William said were in attendance, actually in Palmyra together.[38] Brodie also notes that neither Smith nor his followers were consistent as to the year when the vision took place.[39] She indicates that according to some newly discovered records the prophet's mother and his brother Samuel remained active members of the Presbyterian church in Palmyra until mid-1828, a fact which seems strange in light of the Lord's denunciation of the churches as corrupt and his command to Joseph to join none of them. Brodie concludes that even his mother and Samuel did not give credence to Joseph's visions.[40]

But additional research suggests that Brodie dismissed the first vision prematurely. Milton Backman, a Mormon trained at the University of Pennsylvania, has demonstrated that a number of revivals occurred within a twenty-mile radius of Palmyra in 1819 or 1820. He reminds us that Smith said revivals "became general among all the sects in that *region of country*."[41] My research shows that Smith employed the term "region of country" to include the whole area occupied by the Mormons along the Mississippi, including Iowa, in the 1840s,[42] and that Charles G. Finney used it to designate the entire burned-over district.[43] Thus Walters was too restrictive in trying to limit the revival to Palymra.

That Smith and his intimate friends did not agree on the date of the revival does not prove that he did not have the visionary experience but only that the date was not important to him until later, when he worked out some of its theological implications. The point made by Walters that the revival must have come in 1823 or 1824 does not bear up under scrutiny. In an account which dates much earlier than that relied on by Walters,[44] which Brodie herself cites in her text,[45] William Smith said that "it was the suggestion of the Rev. M.——— that my brother asked of God."[46] William was obviously confused on this point, which is understandable since he was very young and indifferent toward religion at the time of the revival, and quite old when he recalled the incident.[47] Walters errs in saying that Oliver Cowdery confirms that Lane and Stockton were both there,[48] for Cowdery does not mention Stockton.[49]

Brodie's contention that Lucy and Samuel must have had doubts about Joseph's visions or they would not have joined the Presbyterian church rests on speculation, not evidence.[50] An unpublished account of Samuel Smith's conversion to Mormonism is revealing in this regard. It informs us that the prophet in 1829 "labored to persuade him [Samuel] concerning the gospel of Jesus Christ which was now to be revealed in its fulness; Samuel was not however, very easily persuaded of these things, but after much inquiry and explanation he retired in order that by secret and fervent prayer he might obtain from the Lord wisdom."[51] Nothing is said here about any doubts Samuel had as to Joseph's integrity but only that he required explanation and a personal witness. This would suggest that there was no collusion within the Smith family and that Joseph had to persuade each member individually. Those, like Samuel, who were already committed to Presbyterianism, did not give up their commitments easily. However, the prophet's father accepted his son's story at an earlier date.[52] Joseph Sr. had for some time been convinced that the existing churches were apostate and was looking for the true one.[53] He, like Lucy, was a seeker but for personal reasons would not join the Presbyterians.[54] Lucy, on the other hand, was converted at a revival in Palmyra.[55] William tells how his mother had "made use of every means which her paternal love could suffest [sic] to get us engaged in seeking our soul's salvation," which suggests her possible concern for her children at the time of her conversion.[56] This gains support from the fact that her sons Hyrum and Samuel as well as a daughter joined when she did.[57] It may also be that she weighed the social advantages to be gained in Presbyterianism, but this is more difficult to prove.[58] However, when Joseph told her of the discovery of the plates and began to translate them she believed him and separated from Presbyterianism. There would be little reason to do so if she doubted Joseph's vision.[59]

There is reason to think that disagreement in the family between Lucy and her husband over Presbyterianism may have provided one catalyst for the prophet's first vision. According to

a newly discovered source he said he was deeply moved by the
conversion of his mother and the others and "wanted to get Religion too wanted to feel & shout like the rest but could feel nothing."[60] His mother may have pressured him to join her church,[61]
but the emotionally oriented revivals left him numb with confusion and torn loyalties. His father's refusal to join would only
have added to his inner turmoil. Confused by contradictory doctrines and the disagreement in his family, he turned to the Bible
and the whispering spirit within. His vision which informed him
to join no denomination set him free from his mother's demands
and no doubt pleased his father, who had been looking for the
restored church. By 1829 he had converted all family members to
the new movement and thus sealed the fissure which divided the
otherwise closely knit family.

By concentrating upon whether or not Smith's vision actually occurred, Brodie missed its historical significance, which De
Pillis has demonstrated. I would only add to his point that much
of Smith's later career—his theocratic inclinations in economics,
social life and politics—can be interpreted as essentially anti-
pluralistic and closely related to his initial distaste for sectarian
variety and the sectarian conflict he encountered during the
revival. Since so much of what was unique to Mormonism related
to this anti-pluralism,[62] it would be hard to find a more revealing
explanation as to the essence of the movement than that which
Joseph Smith gave in his story of the first vision. By focusing
upon genuine or supposed inconsistencies in the story, Brodie
missed its real importance. It was perhaps her secular orientation
and Mormon background which caused her to misunderstand. If
she had been more concerned about the historical nature of the
Mormon movements and less about its ultimate truth or untruth
she might have treated the first vision differently.

Her secular-sectarian approach misleads her also in handling Smith's gold digging. Brodie maintained that the key to
Joseph Smith's early career was his gold digging, which was confirmed by her rediscovery of a published record of a trial at Bainbridge, New York in 1826, where Smith was tried and convicted

of being disorderly and an imposter.[63] The trial provided testimony that Smith had used a magic stone to hunt for buried treasure. As I have shown elsewhere, there is new evidence to confirm that Joseph Smith was tried in 1826, although we have contradictory accounts of the changes against him, whether or not he was convicted, who testified, and what was said.[64] It is significant that in one version Joseph Smith, Sr., says that he and his son "were mortified that the wonderful power [to see visions in a stone] which God has so miraculously given . . . should be used only in search of filthy lucre."[65] This uncovers a major flaw in Brodie's interpretation of Smith. She assumes that if Smith were a money digger he could not have been sincerely religious. Barnes Frisbie, the historian of Middleton, Vermont, knew better and noted that the rodsmen who flourished at Wells, Middletown and Poultney at the turn of the century were a religious group. They saw themselves as the children of Israel and believed in impending judgments. They were primitivists who hoped for the restoration of the true church and for healing gifts.[66] Frisbie's characterization of these rodsmen is substantiated by Ovid Miner who described a group of them in Rutland County in the May 7, 1828 issue of the *Vermont American*. He said,

> About the year 1800 one or two families in Rutland County, who had been considered respectable, and who had been Baptists, pretended to have been informed by the Almighty that they were the descendants of the ancient Jews, and were, with their connexions, to be put in possession of the land for some miles around: the way for which was to be providentially prepared by the destructions of their fellow townsmen. [They claimed] inspired power to cure all sorts of diseases—intuitive knowledge of lost or stolen goods, and ability to discover hidden treasures.

Some fifteen or more families became involved, but when their leaders prophesied an earthquake in 1802 which did not occur, many fled to Lawrence, New York. Frisbie insisted that Oliver Cowdery's father was a member in Orange County.[67] We do know that when Cowdery came to Smith in 1829 he had employed a rod and Smith sanctioned its use.[68]

What this suggests is not that there is an inevitable causal relationship between the Vermont rodsmen and Joseph Smith, but that Brodie's dichotomy between money digger and prophet rests on her twentieth-century rationalistic assumptions, not on the nineteenth-century situation. She tends to forget that it was only after Smith gave up frequent use of this stone that David Whitmer and Oliver Cowdery became dissenters.[69] Whitmer's comments on Joseph at this time are informative, because he said that while using his stone Smith remained humble and sincere, but after he came under Rigdon's and Brigham Young's influence he grew more worldly.[70] This, it should be noted, is the reverse of the evolution which Brodie saw in Smith. Brodie's interpretation of this is questionable from another standpoint, for he never did give up his seer stone entirely but continued to use it and speak of it highly at the apex of his power in Nauvoo. Brigham Young records that in late December 1841 Smith showed his seer stone to the Twelve Apostles and told them, "Every man who lived on earth was entitled to a seer stone, and should have one, but they are kept from them in consequence of their wickedness, and most of those who do find one make evil use of it."[71] Many of the earliest Mormons, including Cowdery, Martin Harris, Orrin P. Rockwell, Joseph Knight and Josiah Stowel, were rodsmen and money diggers[72] but became Mormons for religious reasons.[73] Within these converts and in their prophet, there was an element of mysticism which made the transition more natural than Brodie was willing to admit.

Brodie's explanation of the Book of Mormon also was influenced by her secular-sectarian assumptions. Smith, she said, initially conceived of writing a secular history of the mound builders, whose relics were scattered widely in western New York.[74] But, cynical towards religion, opportunistic and relying upon the religious credulity of his family and acquaintances,[75] he at some point, apparently at the time that Martin Harris lost the first 116 pages of manuscript in mid-1828, changed his narrative into a religious history.[76] He drew his material from Ethan Smith's *View of the Hebrews,* a book first published in 1823 which described the decline and fall of an ancient Hebrew civilization in America and argued that the American Indians were descendants of the twelve tribes of Israel.[77] To support her argument Brodie relied on the testimony of Obadiah Dogberry, actually Abner Cole, the embittered editor of the *Palmyra Reflector* who was initially neutral toward the Book of Mormon[78] but became hostile when he was discovered by the Smiths stealing portions of the manuscript from the printer's office in Palmyra in order to publish them in his newspaper.[79] Brodie quoted Dogberry that when the plates were discovered "no divine intervention had been dreamed of."[80] She thus misread Dogberry, who said that the miraculous aspects of the book's discovery came as an afterthought, not that the book was initially secular.[81]

Brodie's speculations as to the initial secular nature of the Book of Mormon are not substantiated by the earliest newspaper reports we have. The *Wayne Sentinel* noted on June 26, 1829 that "for some time past, much speculation has existed concerning a pretended discovery, through superhuman means, of an ancient record, of a religious and divine nature and origin." Other early newspapers characterized it similarly.[82] Further, Rev. John A. Clark wrote that Martin Harris spoke to him of the Book of Mormon as a religious work as early as the fall of 1827. Clark recalled that Harris told him the Golden Bible would "settle all religious controversies and speedily bring on the glorious millennium."[83]

To support her thesis, Brodie also relied upon the statements of some of the old neighbors of the Smiths at Palmyra and Manchester whose testimonies were collected by Philastus Hurlbut, an angry, ex-Mormon who had been excommunicated from the church in 1833 for sexual promiscuity.[84] They were published by E. D. Howe, editor of the *Painesville Telegraph.*[85] Brodie quotes one of these neighbors, Joseph Capron, that Joseph Smith, Sr. gave him "no intimation at that time that the Book was to be of a religious character."[86] Capron does not say when this statement was supposedly made. He only indicates that the translating of the Book of Mormon was under way at the time and that publication was planned. In all likelihood this was after March 1829, which means that Capron's testimony is contradicted by the earliest newspapers and John Clark.[87] Brodie also quoted Peter Ingersoll of Palmyra that Smith had confessed "he had no such book, and believed there never was any such book,"[88] and Abner Chase that Smith said he "had not got any such book, nor never had such an one."[89] The testimony of Ingersoll and Chase, so devastating if true, brings up the whole matter of the reliability of the testimonies published by E. D. Howe. There is much evidence to suggest that they are of limited value in an objective evaluation of Smith's early career.

The testimonies, collected four to six years after the events they purport to describe,[90] were solicited by Hurlbut, according to E. D. Howe, "to obtain affidavits showing the bad character of the Smith family."[91] With such intentions, it must be doubted whether Hurlbut would make any serious attempt to learn the truth about the Smiths. More likely he would collect all the unfavorable comments he could from known enemies, while ignoring those who spoke favorably of the family. To a considerable extent this can be shown to be the case.[92] Richard Anderson of Brigham Young University has made an intensive comparison of the statements and shows that certain characteristic phrases like "acquainted with the Smith family," and "addicted to vicious habits" appear throughout. Anderson also shows identical structuring in some of the affidavits, which suggests that they were written by a single hand, most likely that of Hurlbut or Howe.[93] Anderson's case against Hurlbut is given some additional support by his discovery of an interview with the Palmyrans in 1881 by a Reorganized Mormon, W. H. Kelley, who visited some of the same families as Hurlbut but found under close cross examination that they admitted they had no first-hand information, had not known the Smiths personally and knew nothing bad about the family or the prophet. Anderson claims too much, it seems, when he insists that the Kelley interviews refute Hurlbut and provide a more reliable source. Kelley's interviews came much later and were not with the identical people interviewed by Hurlbut. Further, in Kelley's interviews certain phrases are repeated, suggesting his influence upon the composition of these later testimonies.[94] But this evidence demonstrates what a difference an interviewer more friendly to the Smiths could make, and acts as a corrective to the temptation to put too much reliance on either group of witnesses. When Brodie's case for a cynical and deliberately deceptive prophet depends so heavily on the supposed confessions to Chase, Capron and Ingersoll, so out of character with the cunning prophet she depicts, when the confessions cited by Chase and Ingersoll are so similar and employ the words "any such book" and when the statement attributed to Smith by Chase was told to him by an unnamed neighbor, there is reason to question their dependability and begin to wonder whether Brodie was very objective in formulating her thesis.

Much of Brodie's case for the opportunistic origin of Mormonism grew out of her misreading of the religious attitudes of the prophet's forebears, for she argued that the whole family was casual or indifferent towards religion. It is noteworthy that Brodie does not define religion in her work but her usage suggests a conventional and rather restricted definition.[95] Thus, taking as evidence his advice to his children, "it is better to be a rich cobbler than a poor preacher," seeming to imply that Asael Smith was materialistic, she saw grandfather Smith as "avowedly Christian but basically irreligious." It is difficult to understand how Brodie could have so badly misjudged Asael unless she formulated her thesis before she examined his writings.

There is evidence which shows that Asael owned the covenant in the Congregational Church in Topsfield and was an active Universalist in Vermont.[96] Even without this, however, there was sufficient evidence in the writings Brodie examined to show that Asael's attitudes were anything but "irreligious." A quotation from his letter to his children is enough to show that Brodie misrepresented his views.

And now my dear Children, let me pour out my heart to you and speak first to you of the immortality of your souls. Trifle not in this point; the soul is immortal; you have to deal with an infinite Majesty; you go upon life and death; therefore on this point be serious. Do all to God in a serious manner; when you think of Him, speak of Him, pray to Him, or in any way make your address to His great Majesty, be in good earnest. Trifle not with His name, nor with His attributes, nor call Him to witness anything but is absolute truth . . .

And as to Religion, I would not wish to point out any particular form to you; but first I would wish you to search the Scriptures and consult sound reason, and see if they . . . are not sufficient to envince to you that religion is a necessary theme.[97]

In the unpublished manuscript of Lucy's history is evidence that Asael was influenced by Deistic writings, since on one occasion when his son Joseph was considering joining the Methodists in Trumbull, Vermont, Asael threw Tom Paine's *Age of Reason* at him and told him to read it.[98] But this is not inconsistent with his Universalism, for many of the Universalists were influenced by liberal thinking in New England.[99] That did not make them irreligious. Brodie's perspective appears peculiarly sectarian on this point.

Brodie's assertion that Lucy and Joseph Smith, Sr. "spent twenty years in New England, yet neither joined a denomination or professed more than passing interest in any sect,"[100] was intended to fit her thesis of religious indifference in the family but is contradicted by the fact that, like his father, Joseph Sr. was a Universalist in Vermont.[101] Lucy, of course, was a long time member of the Presbyterian church in Palmyra.

Brodie countered abundant evidence in the prophet's published revelations and his journal that he was a man of religious convictions by saying that what he wrote was always for public effect, that few men "have written so much and told so little about themselves."[102] Part of Brodie's frustration in trying to get to the real personality of the prophet grew out of the fact that she assumed he dictated much of his personal history, that it therefore contained his intimate thoughts. In some cases this is true, for a small part of his history is taken directly from his diary written in his own hand. But Brodie did not know that much of the history was not dictated but written by scribes and transferred into the first person and incorporated into the history as the prophet's own words.[103] Thus, a great amount of it is actually external in nature, a second party's look at what Smith was thinking and doing. The history is compiled in this way not to deceive but because the prophet was too busy to write it himself.[104] We now know that only two small diaries were written by him, one in 1832 and another in 1839.[105] The remainder is essentially the work of others, although he no doubt supervised some of its composition. Those parts which were written by him thus take on new importance. They reveal a man quite different from the one Brodie saw. At the beginning of the 1832 journal he wrote, "O may God grant that I may be directed in all my thoughts, O bless thy servant. Amen." Further on he wrote,

> In the morning at 4 o'clock i was awoke by Brother Davis knocking at my door saying: Brother Joseph come get up and see the signs in the heavens, and I arose and beheld to my great joy the stars fall from heaven; yea, they fell like hail stones, a literal fulfillment of the word of God as recorded in the holy scriptures and a sure sign that the coming of Christ is close at hand. O how marvelous are thy works O Lord and I thank thee for thy mercy unto me thy servant. O Lord save me in thy kingdom for Christ sake. Amen. [106]

Brodie might have made use of this in Smith's published version of his history, despite the fact she could not have known its full significance. There was other evidence available to her, however, which she deliberately dismissed. In the Chicago Historical

Society is a letter from Joseph to his wife, Emma, in 1832, which
was not written for publication:

> My situation is a very unpleasant one although I
> will endeavor to be contented the Lord assisting me I
> have visited a grove which is Just back of the town
> almost every day where I can be Secluded from the eyes
> of any mortal and there give vent to all the feelings of my
> heart in deadication and praise I have Called to mind all
> the past moments of my life and am left to morn and
> Shed tears of sorrow for my folly in Sufering the adver-
> sary of my Soul to have so much power over me as he has
> had in times past but God is merciful and has forgiven
> my sins.[107]

This Smith is consistent with the man who wrote in the
manuscript of his history that after his conversion experience in
1820 his "soul was filled with love and for many days I could
rejoice with great joy and the Lord was with me." It is consistent
with the same Smith who further on recounted that "after many
days I fell into transgression and sinned in many things which
brought a wound upon my Soul."[108]

By contrast Brodie depicted Smith as a fiendishly clever
person who had to put on the robes of religious piety, yet in the
face of persecution and even the risk of imminent and violent
death maintained his masquerade. Brodie's Smith supposedly
played out his role day after day in personal letters to his wife
and in the two diaries which he wrote. Actually, however, there
is no evidence in his published letters, in his diaries, in the
nearly two hundred letters written to him by his friends, some of
whom were with him in his gold digging days, in the numerous
minutes of church meetings he attended, nor in the large number of letters of Emma, Hyrum, Don Carlos or William his rebellious brother, that after his conversion he ever thought of
himself in other terms than as a man called of God to perform a
mission.[109]

But what about Smith's claim that he translated Egyptian papyri to obtain the Book of Abraham, his story of gold plates and his witnesses? Should not, as Brodie put it, "the casual reader . . . be shocked" at his pretentious claims in the field of religion?[110] Or are such claims to miracles basically any different from those that have traditionally given support to Christianity? If we assume that Smith wrote the Book of Abraham, which the Utah church denies,[111] for Smith to claim Abraham as author of his book may be no more fraudulent than for the writers of the early New Testament epistles to claim apostolic authorship. A new religion required an authoritarian base, particularly in the face of so many contending sects in nineteenth-century America. Smith said in his unpublished history that when the angel first came to him to tell him of the plates, he thought it was a dream but later changed his mind.[112] This suggests the possibility that some things which may have been looked upon as natural in the early years took on more miraculous significance as time passed. Rather than deception we may be dealing with a frame of mind in some ways more idealistic and mystical and thus less cynical than our own.

As for Smith's witnesses, Brodie continued her argument that Smith was a conniver and his religion a fraud by saying he had some mysterious power to make the men see visions.[113] She ignored other possibilities; for example, that the witnesses saw the plates as a result of their own psychological and religious needs. There is some evidence to suggest that the three witnesses saw the plates in vision only and said as much, for Stephen Burnett described in 1838 how Martin Harris, a few weeks earlier, said in a public meeting in Kirtland, "that he never saw the plates with his natural eyes only in vision or imagination, neither Oliver nor David [Whitmer]."[114] The prophet acknowledged frankly in a published revelation to the three witnesses how they were to see the plates: "it is by your faith that you shall view them . . . [and] ye shall testify that you have seen them, even as my servant Joseph Smith Jr. has seen them, for it is by my power that he has seen them."[115] There is testimony from several independent sources, all non-Mormon, that the three witnesses said they saw the plates with their "spiritual eyes" only. A. Metcalf, John Gilbert, Reuben P. Harmon and Jesse Townsend testified this was so.[116] This is contradicted, however, by a statement by David Whitmer in the *Saints Herald* in 1882: "these hands handled the plates, these eyes saw the angel."[117] But Whitmer told Zenos H. Gurley that "we did not touch nor handle the plates."[118]

If Stephen Burnett's and other reports are accurate, then the experience of the three witnesses was a visionary one. This does not prove them to be liars, but suggests that in their minds, as in Joseph's, visionary experiences were real and depicted ultimate truth. Stephen Burnett said that despite his confessions at Kirtland, Martin Harris declared that he still believed in the truth of the Book of Mormon. Burnett reports Harris fought hard at the meeting to put down its detractors, which is evidence that this experience seemed of sufficient reality and meaning that he wished strongly to preserve its integrity.[119]

With respect to the eight witnesses, Brodie accepted Thomas Ford's statement that these men also saw the plates in vision after Smith had chastised them for their lack of faith.[120] This view is given some support from Stephen Burnett who indicated that the eight never saw the plates and hesitated to sign a previously prepared statement. Their testimony in the Book of Mormon is slightly ambiguous, not making clear whether they handled the plates or the leaves of the prophet's manuscript.[121] But the evidence here again is contradictory. John Whitmer, one of the eight, said that he saw and handled the plates.[122] But William Smith claimed that his father, who was one of the eight, saw the plates under a frock.[123] Whether they actually saw the plates, saw them under a frock or in a vision, there can be no doubt of the effect upon them even years afterward. Hiram Page, who left the main body of Mormons in Ohio, described his feelings in 1847:

> As to the Book of Mormon, it would be doing injustice to myself and to the work of God in the last

days to say that I could know a thing to be true in 1830, and know the same thing to be false in 1847. To say my mind was so treacherous that I have forgotten what I saw . . . and to say that those holy Angels who came down and showed themselves to me as I was walking through the field, to confirm me in the work of the Lord of the last days—their own pure language; yes, it would be treating the God of heaven with contempt, to deny these testimonies.[124]

Whatever the Mormon witnesses experienced in 1829, there can be little doubt that it was of a deeply religious nature and altered their lives substantially, so that those, like Harris and Page, felt its influence life-long. I wonder then, in terms of human experience, if Brodie's viewpoint is very perceptive. Sidney E. Mead reminds us that at the turn of the century American religious leaders faced an intellectual crisis of major proportions, for Deists like Tom Paine challenged orthodoxy's faith in divine revelation by depicting it as a means of church aggrandizement.[125] R. Lawrence Moore of Cornell has shown us how in the face of scientific skepticism the spiritualists in western New York relied on physical evidence to bolster their transcendental faith.[126] Was there a need for witnesses to say that the plates existed materially and not merely in vision? Perhaps it seemed increasingly so to Smith and his witnesses in the face of an age of skepticism, the taunting doubts of the Palmyra residents and excessive sectarian conflict. For Smith and his witnesses to affirm their conviction of the reality of the plates may not deserve the label of fraud, any more than the apostles' testimony of the resurrection of Christ. Mormon religious roots go much deeper, which Brodie might have understood better were it not for her secular-sectarian bias.

Nowhere does that bias show its limiting effects more clearly than in Brodie's handling of polygamy. She views Smith as a sensualist and libertine who hid his excessive sexual needs behind the protective cloak of religion.[127] Not many would deny that sexual desires were involved at the outset of polygamy, but Brodie seems too smug in discovering the obvious. Behind her sophisticated facade is a considerable degree of sectarian moral indignation, reflected in her remark: "nothing was so sacred that it could not be recast into a new utility or a new beauty."[128] But such an approach minimizes the religious aspects of the institution. Brodie overlooked the fact that none of the earliest anti-Mormon writers, neither Dogberry or E. D. Howe, charge Smith with sexual immorality. Significantly, his name is not linked to any woman other than his wife before 1832,[129] well after his role as a prophet was established. Brodie failed to appreciate the degree to which the prophetic role liberated Smith from the social restraints which customarily control sexual behavior. Thus Benjamin Winchester recalled that when the prophet first began experimenting with plurality of wives and was challenged by some church members he replied that "he was authorized by God Almighty to establish His Kingdom . . . and that he could do what ever he should choose to do."[130] It is significant that the first intimations of new sexual standards in 1830 and 1831 were in a prophetic context.[131] According to W. W. Phelps, Smith received a revelation in July 1831 which promised the elders they would have wives among the Indians, and explained later that married elders would have the privilege "in the same manner that Abraham took Hagar and Kuturah and Jacob took Rachael, Bilhah and Zilpay, by revelation."[132] Rather than being evidence of cynicism and religious insincerity, polygamy may provide further proof of Smith's early and complete absorption in his prophetic role.

Allowing her moral indignation to cause her to overstate her case, Brodie depends heavily upon hearsay and circumstantial evidence to make it seem that Smith was largely driven in this matter by expansive sexual appetites. She lists 48 women who were Smith's plural wives and implies that he lived with most of them.[133] But she acknowledges that her list "includes several whose relationship to Joseph is admittedly little more than presumptive."[134] Upon the basis of the most reliable evidence it does not appear that Smith took benefit of his marital rights with all his wives. Benjamin F. Johnson, one of the few intimates of the prophet to write frankly about this, indicated in 1903 that Smith slept with Fanny Alger, Benjamin's sister, Almira Johnson and Eliza Partridge, and that another sister, Delcena Johnson, and Louisa Beaman were "both in his [the prophet's] care." Johnson stressed, "As to the number that came after this into the plural marriage order, before the prophet's death, I can think of but five, whose names I will not now attempt to recall." Johnson observed, "But the number soon after his death began to increase,"[135] thus suggesting that many marriages were of a celestial nature.[136] At another time Johnson drew up a list indicating that by April 1843 Smith was married to Louisa Beaman, Eliza R. Snow, Marie and Sarah Lawrence, sisters Lyon and Dibble, "one or two of the Partridge daughters," some daughters of C. P. Lott, plus two of Johnson's sisters. This would make 11 or 12 wives, but Johnson does not say Smith lived with all of these.[137] Since we have no better witness on this than Johnson, his limited count should not be dismissed lightly.[138] Referring to the Nauvoo temple record in 1846 Brodie says there were thirty marriages at this time and implies that Smith had sexual relations with these wives.[139] Actually, there were only seventeen marriages listed in the Nauvoo record,[140] and it made no indication which wives were Smith's previously nor whether or not he lived with them, but only recorded those marriages performed in January 1846 which were to go into effect as the Mormons left Nauvoo for the far west. Certain women were sealed to Smith for eternity and to other elders for time, either to provide these women with living husbands loyal to the church, or to give those dissatisfied with their current marital situation an opportunity to be married to Smith in the next life. In the latter category was Mary Ann Frost Pratt, who had quarreled with her husband, Parley P., and was sealed to Parley for time but to Smith for eternity, in the hope, as Pratt made clear in his unpublished family record, that she would cease to give him difficulty.[141] Smith was no doubt married to many women, but there were practical as well as theological reasons for this which Brodie overlooked.

Smith taught that an elder's status in the kingdom depended upon the number of wives and children he had.[142] He and others carried this to the point that they had other men and women "adopted" into their families.[143] Smith's many wives were a route to status, as they were at times for Brigham Young. Adoption and polygamy had a social function among the Mormons. Levi Richards quotes the prophet saying, "Our Father in Heaven organized the human family, but they are all disorganized."[144] Smith's stress on organization here, so characteristic, was related to his anti-pluralistic inclinations which in turn grew out of his fears of social disintegration.

In her supplement Brodie attempts to bolster her "imposter" thesis by appealing to the research of a psychiatrist, Dr. Phyllis Greenacre, who published "The Imposter" in the *Psychoanalytic Quarterly* in 1958.[145] But in utilizing Greenacre, Brodie makes a subtle but significant shift in her point of view. She now sees in the Mormon prophet not a bald-faced liar but a man with deep inner conflicts. Her new effort has difficulties. Despite the fact that a group of psychiatrists warned her of the dangers of trying to psychoanalyze the dead from their writings alone, she attempts it and argues that Greenacre's thesis that imposters are not ordinary liars but men with extraordinary inner conflicts fits Joseph Smith.[146] Brodie says that Smith had both inner tensions between fact and fantasy, between what he was and what he hoped to be, and hostile feelings toward his brothers who doubted his prophetic call.[147] The difficulty with this is that Greenacre found in the cases she studied that oedipal conflicts were a source of the fantasies and that in each case the imposter had succeeded in varying degrees in displacing the father of his mother's affections and thus had precipitated his own identity crisis.[148] Brodie in her supplement admits that Joseph Smith is very fond of his father.[149] Although there were inner tensions in Smith, there is no evidence of abnormal oedipal turmoil. It is doubtful that Greenacre's thesis is any more applicable to the Mormon prophet than DeVoto's paranoia. But in attempting a psychological explanation of Smith rather than that of daring deception, the mature Brodie seems to be telling us that her old interpretation was too simple. Perhaps what Brodie may have recognized at last is that her original interpretation perceived Joseph Smith in fallacious terms, as either prophet in the traditional Mormon sense or else as faker. Her original thesis opens considerable room for speculation because its either-or alternatives were precisely the same as those of the early Mormon apologist and missionary, Orson Pratt, presented to his potential converts in the 1840s and 1850s.[150] But between Pratt and Brodie a hundred years of Mormon experience have intervened. Whereas Pratt affirmed that with Smith's accomplishments he must have been a true prophet, Brodie, looking at the man's limitations, concluded he was a fraud. Possibly now historians should begin to explore the broad, promising middle ground which neither Pratt nor Brodie fully perceived.

Notes

1. From the March issue.
2. Sidney E. Ahlstrom, *A Religious History of the American People* (New Haven: Yale University Press, 1972), 504.
3. Most dissertations have been produced in the religious department at Brigham Young University, as have many of the books and articles. Two journals have published the bulk of the anti-Brodie articles, although her book is rarely cited in the footnotes. For examples see *BYU Studies* 9 (spring 1969) and 10 (spring 1970) and *Dialogue: A Journal of Mormon Thought* 3 (summer–autumn 1968).
4. Milton Backman, *Joseph Smith's First Vision* (Salt Lake City: Bookcraft, 1971) is based on some interesting research. Hugh Nibley, *The Mythmakers* (Salt Lake City: Bookcraft, 1961), 91–190 deals with contradictions in the gold digging stories. See also Edward T. Jones, "The Theology of Thomas Dick and Its Possible Relationship to That of Joseph Smith" (master's diss., Department of Religion, Brigham Young University, 1969).
5. Delivered at the meeting of the Mormon History Association in conjunction with the Western History Association at New Haven in October 1972. Bushman's paper was evaluated by Klaus Hansen and Sidney Ahlstrom. Bushman indicates he will submit it for publication.

6. Arrington's *Great Basin Kingdom* (Cambridge: Harvard University Press, 1958) was based on a Ph.D. dissertation completed at the University of North Carolina. Flanders' *Nauvoo: Kingdom on the Mississippi* (Urbana: University of Illinois Press, 1965) originated as a Ph.D. study at Wisconsin University. Hansen's *Quest for Empire* (East Lansing: Michigan State University, 1967) was initiated at Wayne State, while O'Dea's *The Mormons* (Chicago: University of Chicago Press, 1957) was begun in the Department of American Studies at Harvard.

7. Fawn M. Brodie, *No Man Knows My History* 2nd ed., rev. and enl. (1945; New York: Alfred A. Knopf, 1971), xi.

8. John Higham traces some aspects of the revolt against progressive history in *History: The Development of Historical Studies in the United States* (Englewood Cliffs: Prentice Hall, 1965), pp. 198-232. See also Henry F. May, "The Rediscovery of American Religious History," *American Historical Review* 70 (October 1964): 79-92.

9. This trend largely postdates Higham's study. See Herbert J. Bass, ed., *The State of American History* (Chicago: Quadrangle Books, 1970), 298–329 for an assessment by Morton Rothstein, Samuel T. McSevency, Phillip J. Greven, Jr., Robert Zemsky and Joel Silbey. See also Edward Pessen's application of quantitative methods in the Jacksonian period, 362–72.

10. Martin E. Marty, "Ethnicity: The Skeleton of Religion in America," *Church History* 41 (March 1972): 5–21.

11. "The Moral and Theological Revolution in the 1960s and Its Implication for American Religious History," in Bass, 98–118.

12. Brodie, 34–68, 168–80, 442–54.

13. Ibid., 285–88 and 355–56.

14. Richard Bushman and Klaus Hansen are two exceptions to this generalization. Richard Anderson of Brigham Young University, trained in ancient history at Berkeley, has recently published a commentary on Joseph Smith's ancestors which includes some careful research and important sources but makes no pretense of being a biography. See his *Joseph Smith's New England Heritage* (Salt Lake City: Deseret Book Co., 1971).

15. Only a few non-Mormons have made any use of the Historian's Archives. Donald R. Moorman of Weber State College, who is doing research on Brigham Young, is one example. The recent appointment of Leonard Arrington as church historian suggests that church leaders desire to establish the Archives and Historian's Department on a professional basis.

16. Recently a professor at Yale commented to me on how daring one must be to undertake a biography on the Mormon prophet.

17. In his review of her book in the *American Historical Review* 51 (July 1946).

18. Brodie is the daughter of Thomas McKay, assistant to the Twelve Apostles, now deceased, and the niece of David O. McKay, a past president of the church.

19. Brodie, viii.

20. Ibid., 22–23.

21. Ibid., ix, 73, 83.

22. See ibid., 16, 70.

23. *New York Times Book Review* 7 (January 20, 1946): 24.

24. Brodie acknowledged the central importance of this assumption in her 1971 supplement, p. 405.

25. "The New England Origins of Mormonism," *The New England Quarterly* 26 (June 1953): 147–68.

26. "The Quest for Religious Authority and the Rise of Mormonism," *Dialogue: A Journal of Mormon Thought* 1 (fall 1966): 68–88. Both Davis's article and part of De Pillis's have recently been published in Marvin S. Hill and James B. Allen, eds., *Mormonism in American Culture* (New York: Harper and Row, 1972), 13–34.

27. *Burned-Over District* (Ithaca: Cornell University Press, 1950).

28. Brodie, 21–25.

29. Joseph Smith, *History of the Church of Jesus Christ of Latter-day Saints* (Salt Lake City: Deseret Book Co., 1971), 1:5–7.

30. Brodie, 23.

31. Joseph Smith, 1:6.

32. Brodie, 25.

33. Since this is the earliest "history" written by Smith and one of the earliest major sources extant it bears weight despite the late date. The account is located in the Kirtland Letter Book, a manuscript of Smith's personal letters in the Historian's Archives in Salt Lake City. See pp. 1–6.

34. Joseph Smith, "Manuscript History," 120–22. Smith related his vision to a Jewish minister named Joshua.

35. For example, to the editor of the *Pittsburgh Gazette* and reproduced in the *Quincy Whig*, November 1, 1843.

36. See her supplement to the 1971 edition, p. 409.

37. Wesley Walters, *New Light on Mormon Origins from the Palmyra (N.Y.) Revival* (La Mesa, Calif.: Utah Christian Tract Society, 1967).

38. Brodie, 410.

39. Ibid., 24, 410.

40. Ibid., 24, 410–11.

41. Backman, 79. Backman made the point earlier in an article, "Awakenings in the Burned-Over District: New Light on the Historical Setting of the First Vision," *BYU Studies* 9 (spring 1969): 301–20. My italics.

42. Joseph Smith, 5, 356.

43. Charles G. Finney, *Memoirs of Charles G. Finney by Himself* (New York: Barnes & Co., 1878), 78.
44. William Smith said Stockton and Lane were at the revival, in his interview with E. O. Briggs, reported in the *Deseret News*, January 20, 1894.
45. Brodie, 25.
46. William made these remarks in a sermon delivered in Deloit, Iowa, June 8, 1884, or ten years earlier than the interview with Briggs. See *Saints Herald* 31: 643–44.
47. According to William, his father's "religious customs often became erksome [sic] or tiresome to me while in my younger days as I made no profession of Christianity." See "Notes Written on Chamber's Life of Joseph Smith" in the Historian's Archives, p. 18. William was 83 years old in 1894.
48. Walters, 7.
49. *L.D.S. Messenger and Advocate* 1 (December 1834): 42.
50. Brodie, 410.
51. From Samuel Smith's file of papers in the Historian's Archives.
52. Lucy Mack Smith, *History of Joseph Smith by His Mother*, ed. Preston Nibley (Salt Lake City: Bookcraft, 1954), 79–80. This edition deletes some things from the original but serves my purpose here. The original edition was published by Orson Pratt in 1853 under the title *Biographical Sketches of Joseph Smith the Prophet*.
53. Ibid., 46.
54. William Smith said Rev. Benjamin Stockton had alienated father Smith by intimating in Alvin's funeral service that since the deceased son was unconverted he had gone to hell. *Deseret News*, January 20, 1894.
55. "Journal of Alexander Neibaur," n.p., n.d. This manuscript is in the Historian's Archives in Salt Lake City.
56. *William Smith on Mormonism* (Lamoni, Iowa: Herald Steam Book and Job Office, 1883), 6.
57. According to William, the mother and three children joined. *Deseret News*, January 20, 1894.
58. One gets the impression from reading Lucy's history that she was very much interested in status. See her frequent comments upon the initial prosperity of the family, the material things they owned and the general social acceptance they received in Palmyra until Joseph announced his visions. See Lucy Smith, pp. 25, 32, 39–49, 48, 51, 65, 85.
59. William Smith wrote that "there was not a single member of the family of sufficient age to know right from wrong but what had implicit confidence in the statements made by my Brother Joseph concerning his vision and the knowledge he thereby obtained concerning the plates." In "Notes Written on Chamber's Life of Joseph Smith," 8. Compare also his similar

recollection in the *Deseret News*, January 20, 1894, where he says specifically that his mother and father believed Joseph's account.

60. "Alexander Neibaur Journal," n.p., n.d.

61. Suggested not only by William Smith's recollection, previously quoted, that his mother showed great concern for her children's salvation but also by Joseph's remark to her after his vision that "I have learned for myself that Presbyterianism is not true." This would make it likely that Lucy has been trying to persuade Joseph that her church was the true one. See *William Smith on Mormonism*, p. 6 and Joseph Smith, *History of the Church*, 1, 6.

62. I have argued this at some length in "Role of Christian Primitivism in the Origin and Development of the Mormon Kingdom, 1830–1844" (Ph.D. diss., University of Chicago, 1968).

63. Brodie, 16, 405–06.

64. "Joseph Smith and the 1826 Trial: New Evidence and New Difficulties," *BYU Studies* 12 (winter 1972): 232–33.

65. According to the recollections of the trial by W. D. Purple published in the *Chenango Union*, May 3, 1877.

66. Barnes Frisbie, *The History of Middletown, Vermont in Three Discourses* (Rutland, Vt.: Tuttle & Co., 1867), 44–46.

67. Ibid., 46.

68. *A Book of Commandments for the Government of the Church of Christ* (Independence, Mo.: W. W. Phelps, 1833), 15–19.

69. Brodie, 91; compare David Whitmer, *Address to All Believers in Christ* (Richmond, Mo.: the author, 1887), 30, 32.

70. *Saints Herald* 34 (February 1887): 89.

71. *Latter-day Saints Millennial Star* 26 (February 20, 1864): 118–19.

72. See Martin Harris's confessions to Ole A. Jensen that he searched for treasure in Grant Ivins, "Notes on the 1826 Trial," a manuscript in the Historian's Archives. Brigham Young's description of Rockwell's activities is in the *Journal of Discourses* 19 (1878): 37. Joseph Knight's gold digging is described by Emily Austin, *Mormonism: Or Life among the Mormons* (Madison, Wisc.: M. J. Cantwell, 1882), 30–33. Stowel's money digging is attested to by W. D. Purple in the *Chenango Union*, May 3, 1887.

73. No one can read Oliver Cowdery's private letters in the Huntington Library without recognizing his genuine piety. Martin Harris was more fanatical than Cowdery but no less anxious to find the true church. John A. Clark's testimony about Harris, previously cited, attests to his chiliasm. Rockwell's concern for religious things is described in Harold Schindler's *Orrin Porter Rockwell: Man of God, Son of Thunder* (Salt Lake City: University of Utah Press, 1966), 16. A revealing letter was written by Stowel to Joseph Smith on December 19, 1843. Stowel was ill and had Martha

Campbell write for him: "he says he has seen and believed. He seems anxious to get there [to Nauvoo] to renew his covenants with the Lord. . . . He gave me strict charge to say to you his faith is good concerning the work of the Lord." This letter is found in the Historian's Archives at Salt Lake City.

74. Brodie, 35.
75. Ibid., 36, 41.
76. Ibid., 55.
77. Ibid., 46–49.
78. As witnessed by his early "wait and see" editorial comments on the forthcoming book, in the *Palmyra Reflector*, January 2, 1830.
79. Lucy Mack Smith, 164–66, and compare the attitudes of Dogberry after January 2, 1830.
80. Brodie, 38.
81. Dogberry's comments are contradictory. While he says the prophet made no "serious presentations to religion until his late pretended revelation," in his earliest remarks on the book he warned, "Priestcraft is short-lived," suggesting his understanding that the book had religious import. See *Palmyra Reflector*, September 2, 1829, and February 1, 1831.
82. *The Rochester Advertiser and Telegraph*, August 31, 1829 depicted the book as having a doctrine "said to be far superior to the book of life." *The Rochester Gem*, September 5, 1829 described it as purporting to be "an ancient record of divine origin."
83. John A. Clark, *Gleanings by the Way* (Philadelphia: W. J. and J. K. Simon, 1842), 217, 222–23.
84. The official records of Hurlbut's excommunication are on file in the Historian's Archives. See Kirtland Stake High Council Minutes, pp. 21–22.
85. *Mormonism Unvailed* (Painesville, Ohio: the author, 1834).
86. Brodie, 38.
87. Very little of the Book of Mormon was translated until that time. See Dean Jesse, "The Original Book of Mormon Manuscript," *BYU Studies* 10 (spring 1970): 260. Compare Brodie, 61.
88. Brodie, 37.
89. Ibid., 38.
90. That is, in 1833, when they discuss things that happened in 1828 and 1829.
91. E. D. Howe confessed this to Arthur Deming in 1885, indicating that leading citizens of Kirtland and Mentor paid Hurlbut's expenses to New York and Pennsylvania. See the Arthur Deming file in the Mormon Collection at the Chicago Historical Society.
92. Among those whose testimonies Hurlbut gathered were Isaac Hale, Smith's disgruntled father-in-law, who opposed the marriage of Joseph and

Emma and ousted them from his land; Emma's brother, Alva, who constantly bickered with Joseph and nearly drove him to retaliation; Lucy
Harris, Martin Harris's ex-wife who had become estranged from her husband over the issue of Mormonism; Abigail Harris, Lucy's sister;
Nathaniel Lewis, a Methodist minister and relative of Isaac Hale; Jesse
Townsend, one time minister of the Presbyterian Church in Palmyra
which Lucy Smith ceased to attend; George Beckwith, Peletiah West and
Henry Jessup, three Presbyterian elders prominent in Lucy Smith's excommunication in 1830; David Stafford, who quarreled with Joseph over a dog
and was beaten by him in a fight; Peter Ingersoll and William Stafford,
who had been on money-digging expeditions with Smith and may have
been disillusioned by failure; Willard Chase, who admitted he quarreled
with the Smiths over the disposition of a magic stone found on Chase's
land. It is significant that none of Hurlbut's witnesses said anything good
of the Smiths although Thomas H. Taylor said there were many in
Manchester who knew the family and would have testified in their favor.
Information on Hurlbut's witnesses can be found in Joseph Smith, 1:17,
108. *Saints Herald* 26 (June 15, 1879): 190–91; some of the statements in
E. D. Howe, especially those of the Harris sisters, and Stafford, Ingersoll
and Chase; George Peck, " Mormonism and the Mormons," *The Methodist
Quarterly Review*, 3rd series, 3 (January 1843): 112–13; Pomeroy Tucker,
Origin, Rise and Progress of Mormonism (New York: 1867), 288 for a letter
by Townsend; BYU *Studies* 10 (summer 1970): 482–84 for the excommu-
nication proceedings against Emma and Samuel Smith; and Joseph
Smith's "Journal" kept by Willard Richards, January 1, 1843, for the David
Stafford incident. Thomas H. Taylor's statement was made to W. H.
Kelley and published in the *Saints Herald* 28 (June 1, 1881): 167.

93. "Joseph Smith's New York Reputation Reappraised," BYU *Studies* 10
(spring 1970): 283–314.

94. I believe that the responses Kelley received show more variety of expres-
sion, but notice that he has Ezra Pierce saying "everybody drank then," Mr.
Bryant saying "everybody drank whiskey in them times" and Orlando
Saunders, "everybody drank a little in those days." Also, Kelley reported
Bryant saying that he was "not personally acquainted with any of them,"
Ezra Pierce that he was "not very well acquainted with them" and Reed
that he was "not personally acquainted with them."

95. See Brodie, 4, 5, 16, 84. The closest she comes to explaining her meaning
is in her remark on page 5 that Joseph Smith, Sr. "reflected the irreligion
which permeated the Revolution which had made the federal government
completely secular." Her equation of irreligion with secularism suggests the
narrowness with which she conceived the term. Erwin R. Goodenough's
warning seems appropriate here. "Those who think they know most

clearly, for approval or disapproval, what religion 'is' seem to recognize least what amazingly different aspects of life the term has legitimately indicated." *The Psychology of Religious Experience* (New York: Basic Books, 1965), 2.

96. "Records of the Congregational Church in Topsfield," *Historical Collections of the Topsfield Historical Society* 14 (1909): 58. Also *Tunbridge Town Record*, December 6, 1797, p. 188 where Asael and some of his sons claimed exemption from paying taxes to support the Congregational Church.

97. The original is in the Historian's Archives, but published by Mary Audentia Anderson, *Ancestry and Posterity of Joseph Smith and Emma Hale* (Independence, Mo.: Herald Publishing House, 1929), 62–64. It also appears in Richard Anderson, *Joseph Smith's New England Heritage*, 124–29.

98. The original history of Lucy Mack, upon which her published history is based, is in the Historian's Archives but the page on which this entry appears, near the end of the manuscript, is unnumbered.

99. Sidney Ahlstrom indicates Hosea Ballou was one Universalist leader so influenced. See Ahlstrom, 482.

100. Brodie, 5.

101. *Tunbridge Town Record*, 188.

102. Brodie, vii.

103. A large portion, for example, was taken from a journal written by the prophet's cousin, George A. Smith. Another was written by Willard Richards covering December 21, 1842 through June 27, 1844.

104. He was only able to work on it himself periodically. See vol. 1:2, 298; 3:25 and 6:66. He lamented that some of his scribes and historians were not always satisfactory.

105. Located in Historian's Archives.

106. "Joseph Smith's Book for Record," partly in his own hand, covers the period November 28, 1832 through December 5, 1834.

107. The letter, dated June 6, 1832, is in the Mormon Manuscript Collection.

108. Joseph Smith Letter Book, covering November 22, 1832 through August 4, 1835.

109. All of these sources, so necessary for capturing the mood and mind of Smith and his fellow Mormons, are in the Historian's Archives. They were not available to Brodie.

110. Brodie, 84.

111. Orthodox Utah Mormons still see the Book of Abraham as an authentic historical work. As example, see Hugh Nibley, "What is the Book of Breathings?" *BYU Studies* 11 (winter 1971): 153–87.

112. Joseph Smith Letter Book, November 22, 1832 through August 4, 1835.

113. Brodie, 74.

114. Letter from Stephen Burnett to "Br. [Lyman?] Johnson," April 15, 1838, in Joseph Smith Letter Book, 2.

115. Doctrine and Covenants, sec. 17, vss. 2, 5.

116. See A. Metcalf, *Ten Years before the Mast* (Milad, Idaho: By the author, 1870), 70; John Gilbert to James T. Cobt, March 16, 1849, in Historian's Archives, Reuben T. Harmon's statement in *Naked Truths about Mormonism* (April 1888): 1, and Pomeroy Tucker, 288 for the Townsend letter to Phineas Stiles.

117. See *Saints Herald* 29 (June 15, 1882) for the piece by J. W. Catburn. Compare Whitmer's testimony as recorded by P. Wilhelm Poulsen of Ovid, Idaho in Historian's Archives and the report of J. L. Troughbee in *Saints Herald* 26 (November 15, 1879): 341.

118. Interview with Elder Z. H. Gurley, January 14, 1885, a copy of which is in the Historian's Archives.

119. Burnett to Br. Johnson, April 15, 1838. This is also partially confirmed by George A. Smith's report of the meeting in a letter of March 28, 1838. Smith wrote that "Martin Harris then bore testimony of its [the Book of Mormon's] truth and said all would be damned that rejected it."

120. Brodie, 79–80.

121. The testimony affirmed that Smith has "shown unto us the plates of which hath been spoken, which have the appearance of gold; and as many of the leaves as said Smith had translated we did handle with our hands." It seems unlikely that they would handle only the gold leaves Smith had already translated and not the whole book of plates.

122. *Messenger and Advocate* 2 (March 1836): 236–37.

123. *Deseret News*, January 20, 1894. Compare J. W. Peterson's interview of William in a manuscript in the Historian's Archives dated 1921.

124. Page's letter of May 30, 1847 appeared in the *Ensign of Liberty of the Church of Christ* 1 (January 1848): 63.

125. *The Lively Experiment* (New York: Harper & Row, 1963), 49.

126. "Spiritualism and Science: Reflections on the First Decade of Spirit Rappings," *American Quarterly* 24 (October 1972): 474–500.

127. In her chapter, "If a Man Entice a Maid," p. 297–308, Brodie quotes J. W. C. that Smith said, "whenever I see a pretty woman I have to pray for grace."

128. Ibid., 297.

129. William E. McClellin, a dissenter, maintained Emma Smith informed him of Joseph's affair with an unmarried woman in November 1832. See McClellin to Joseph Smith III, July 1872 in the McClellin Papers at the Reorganized Church Library in Independence, Missouri.

130. Benjamin Winchester, "Primitive Mormonism," in Charles L. Woodward, "The First Half Century of Mormonism" (unpublished manuscript in the New York Public Library), 195.

131. In Jacob, chap. 2, vs. 30 of the Book of Mormon, Smith said, "for if I will, saith the Lord of Hosts, raise up seed unto me, I will command my people; otherwise they shall harken unto these things."

132. W. W. Phelps to Brigham Young, August 12, 1861. He quotes parts of the revelation from memory and says Smith indicated in 1834 that wives would be given through revelation. Phelps's letter is among the Brigham Young papers at the Historian's Archives.

133. Brodie, 346, 436, 437, 440–41, 456, 459, 461. But the implication runs throughout her appendix on polygamy.

134. Ibid., 434–35.

135. Benjamin F. Johnson to George S. Gibbs.

136. But Johnson said in a letter to Anthon H. Lund, dated May 12, 1903, "I was well acquainted with the 'Lawrence girls' that I knew were living in the 'mansion' by Emma's consent as his wives as also others with homes elsewhere of which she knew." This letter is in the Benjamin F. Johnson file in the Historian's Archives.

137. Benjamin F. Johnson, My Life's Review (Independence, Mo.: Zion's Printing and Publishing Co., 1947), 96.

138. I know of no other contemporary of Smith, intimately acquainted with him, who comments on the number of wives with whom Smith had marital relations. Lucy Walker noted four, whom Emma personally approved, but does not say this was all there were. Brodie quoted her to this effect, p. 456.

139. Ibid., 434–35.

140. I have personally examined this record at the Genealogical Society in Salt Lake City.

141. "Family Record of Parley Parker Pratt" under date March 11, 1850. The original manuscript is in the possession of Katie Pratt of Salt Lake City. Pratt himself records that Mary Ann was sealed to him by Hyrum Smith in June 1843 but that afterwards she became "alienated from her husband." Pratt said he forgave his wife for some wrongs she did him and she was "by mutual consent of parties and by the Advise of President Young Sealed to Joseph Smith (the deceased President of the Church) for Eternity and to her former husband for time."

142. See Benjamin F. Johnson, My Life's Review, 10. Compare Parley P. Pratt, Millennial Star 5 (May 1845): 191.

143. J. W. Gunnison comments on the practice in Utah in The Mormons or Latter-day Saints in the Valley of the Great Salt Lake (Philadelphia: J. B. Lippincott, 1856), 73.

144. Levi W. Richards Papers, Historian's Archives.

145. Vol. 27 (autumn).

146. Brodie, 419.

147. Ibid., 413–18.

148. Greenacre, 362–63.

149. Brodie, 414.

150. See *Divine Authenticity of the Book of Mormon* (Liverpool: S. W. Richards, 1852), 1, where Pratt says, "This book must be either *true* or *false*. If true, it is one of the most important messages ever sent from God to man. . . . If false, it is one of the most cunning, wicked, bold, deep-laid impositions ever palmed upon the world." Compare a similar kind of reasoning applied to Joseph Smith in Pratt's *Divine Authority, or the Question, Was Joseph Smith Sent of God* (Liverpool: R. James, 1848), 1–16.

4

Fawn McKay Brodie
At the Intersection of Secularism and Personal Alienation

Mario S. De Pillis

Introduction

My analysis of *No Man Knows My History*, the landmark and still unreplaced biography of Joseph Smith, within the context of larger trends in American religion and society, is an exercise in history, biography, and autobiography.[1]

I argue that Fawn McKay Brodie's immediate environment was a rich and ambiguity-fraught intersection of modern secularism with Brodie's own personal alienation from the religious tradition that formed her. Her biography has been a scandal to orthodox Mormons for half a century and Brodie, herself excommunicated by LDS church leaders after its publication, has become the type of apostate who turns to question the historicity of the church that formed her. Thus, the personality of the author is mingled with the work itself even more than usual with historical works, and evaluations of one are frequently transferred to the other. This being the case, I believe it will be helpful to the reader to know how I situate myself as I contribute my own evaluation to this anniversary appraisal.

I met Fawn McKay Brodie only once in my life, during the summer of 1962. I had just finished a year as visiting assistant

94

professor for the history of the American West at Berkeley and was researching Mormon manuscripts at the Huntington Library in San Marino. Because I was not far from Brodie's home in Pacific Palisades, I called and asked if I might meet her. She graciously and warmly consented.

I arrived very late, disheveled and grease-stained, thanks to a coughing car and my own inexperience with the freeways. Despite my awkwardness and humiliation, Mrs. Brodie greeted me with a gracious generosity that remained unruffled by my embarrassed mumblings and spoke freely, as though to an equal, of her dedication to the honest and thorough handling of the primary sources of history. She was interested in my own research and encouraging of my efforts. The fact that I had experienced the same excitement at the University of Chicago that she had known formed an immediate link between us, and she spoke enthusiastically of how exposure to the heady confidence of the Hutchins era had forever changed her, just as it had changed me. Thus, although we had only a single meeting, I approached her work with the same respect and liking I felt for Mrs. Brodie personally.

Second, an important key to understanding *No Man Knows My History* lay in the Chicago environment which, in many ways, was the distilled essence of triumphant academic secularism in the United States during the 1940s and 1950s. I see Mrs. Brodie's experience at the University of Chicago from the dual personal perspectives that came from being raised in orthodox Catholicism and also from spending all of my professional life in the secularized environment of American academe. Working a generation later than Mrs. Brodie, I have perhaps been given more tools for the analysis and recognition of the force of her environment. That environment, which I argue was crucial in her approach to the personality and character of Joseph Smith, was characterized by three factors: (1) sweeping secularism, which replaced religion as a world view force during the 1940s and 1950s, (2) the influence of Freudian psychology in presenting a different paradigm of human nature from the religious view, and (3) the phenomenon, certainly influenced by the first two factors, of religious disaffiliation in Brodie's generation.

Seen in the context of these larger factors, I hope it will be clear why I believe that the common stereotype held by many conservative Mormons—that *No Man Knows My History* is the angry polemic of a disgruntled ex-believer—is simplistic and inaccurate. Unquestionably, the prophet emerges from her pages as a flawed, faintly fraudulent figure, an image which naturally infuriated church leaders and all loyal Mormons literate enough to have heard about the book. Brodie implies that Smith probably came to believe in a religion he had not really intended to found. The willing faith and loyalty of his followers energized his imposture, making him a believer in himself. She makes it clear that she finds the roots of Mormonism in superstitious rural necromancy and treasure hunting. From the small business of locating buried treasure, Joseph, the most spiritually inclined Smith, found golden plates of ancient scriptures, which became the new scripture of the Book of Mormon. Brodie calls this book a clumsily written "early example of frontier fiction," a "fantasy."[2]

Later, after organizing his religious polity in April 1830, Joseph doctored his own revelations and, as in the case of polygamy, had revelations of convenience to meet his own needs. Brodie characterizes this American prophet as, among other things, a literary exhibitionist, a lover of military display and public pageantry, a wine-bibber, and a vain and worldly man. Far from moderating these views after publication, Brodie, in her 1971 second edition, identifies "obvious evidences of pathology" that made her term Joseph Smith's life a classic case of the "great impostor." Prime evidence, to her mind, are his abandoning the short-lived United Order of Enoch (a feat which required denying his own revelations) to become the chief capitalist of Nauvoo and his "megalomaniac" notion that he could be elected president of the United States.[3]

She sees Joseph Smith, like the religion he founded, as attractive but deeply flawed. The granite obelisk at his Vermont birthplace (signs urge tourists, with unconscious irony: "Visit the

Joseph Smith Monument, World's Largest Polished Shaft") for her aptly "symbolizes the barrenness of his spiritual legacy." He created a theology and ritual that energized thousands, "but he could not create a truly spiritual content for that religion."[4]

Faced with such a portrait of their founding prophet, the church's fury was natural. That Brodie also chronicled and analyzed Smith's many admirable qualities, with the same judiciousness and level of documentation as his less admirable traits, was immaterial. By the very act of writing her biography of the prophet, Fawn McKay Brodie had become an apostate. Her formal excommunication came in June 1946, about six months after the book was published.

It is perhaps instructive to compare Brodie and her exclusion from the Mormon community with the oddly parallel case of a loyal and believing Seventh-day Adventist scholar, Ronald L. Numbers, who in 1976 published a critical biography of the "Mother" of Adventism, Ellen G. White.[5] In a revealing and stimulating introduction to the 1992 edition, Numbers's friend, Jonathan M. Butler, an Adventist and fellow historian, describes how, as a result of his naturalistic and candid treatment of Ellen G. White, Numbers had no choice but to leave his church.

Numbers began his research about 1970 as a respected member of his church and as a faculty member (1970–74) at Loma Linda University, the Adventist equivalent of Brigham Young University. Like Brodie, whose paternal uncle David O. McKay served as president of the Mormon church (1951–70), Numbers's maternal grandfather had been president of the Adventist General Conference (governing body) from 1950 to 1954. In 1973 when church leaders got copies of some prepublication chapters, they moved to delay publication. Numbers considered himself a faithful member at the time, but this action shook his trust. During the negotiations over the fate of his book in 1973/1974, the chairman of the Board of Trustees at Loma Linda University decreed that Numbers could not remain on the faculty. In a quiet compromise, Numbers signed a letter of resignation in exchange for a year's severance pay. Although he remains on the membership rolls of his former church at Loma Linda, Numbers has, since the 1970s, been neither a practicing nor a believing Adventist.[6]

Two particular points of his interpretation were at issue. First, his book asserted that White suffered from severe psychological disorders connected with her concept of her own body. White's childhood masturbation led her to be something of a voyeur in hearing the confessions of Adventist sisters. There is no way of knowing whether White led them on, pressed them into confession, or overemphasized their sexual indiscretions; however, it is clear that she overreacted. She deemed masturbation among the most grievous of sins—the cause of insanity, cancer, and a host of other ills. In 1869 and 1870, she published some of these private self-disclosures, complete with initials and other identifying characteristics. Even though Numbers had withheld some of these details from his 1976 book and provided full and detailed documentation only in his 1992 edition, White's medical and sexual views, presented drily and factually, were still not the type of inspiring information church leaders wanted to hear about their founder.

Second, Numbers also took the naturalistic position that White's claims of divine inspiration could not be proven. "For the sheer explosiveness of its historiographical challenge," writes Butler, "Numbers did for White what Fawn Brodie had done for Joseph Smith."[7]

After the book appeared in late 1976, a firestorm of controversy broke out in the Adventist community. The January 1977 issue of *Spectrum,* an independent Adventist periodical, was devoted to the Numbers biography of White. It contained an essay by Brodie on "Ellen White's Emotional Life" from a thoroughly skeptical stance on religious visions and teachings; Brodie highlighted significant clinical material on White that should, Brodie thought, be further explored. Numbers agreed, and the results are in a psychological profile, coauthored with Janet Numbers, that appears in the second edition.

Adventist officials were understandably enraged. During a special meeting of its general governing board in 1977, one member summarized the feeling of the group about Numbers's biography: "It's as if Mrs. White had been stripped naked, stripped naked!"[8]

Brodie and Numbers both benefited from (and suffered from) being creatures of their time—just as they so adeptly pointed out that Joseph Smith and Ellen White were influenced by their own times. The changing climate of opinion within Mormonism permitted young Fawn McKay to aspire to the best education possible in her day, an education that set her in tension with her religious tradition. Thirty years later, that steadily changing climate permitted Numbers to move in a more liberal direction. Brodie herself, in her later years, became even more secular in her skeptical view of religious visions and teachings than she had been in 1945. No scholar escapes the prejudices of his or her own time and group; and Mormon historians who were active in the 1960s and 1970s experienced some of the extremes of that changing climate themselves.

The assumptions of secular history and modern social science to which Brodie and Numbers subscribed can be applied to all religious groups and to all larger modern societies. These assumptions are fundamentally secular. They are independent of any church and of any changes within any particular church. They sometimes lead to a loss of faith. Secular social science exhibits a certain arrogance of power but cannot be ignored by any serious scholar. Insiders who belong to tightly knit religious communities—and the highly educated Mormons and Adventists are no exception—too often assume that the determining forces of milieu and change can be confined within their religious boundaries. That is, to put the matter bluntly, relatively few scholars within strictly bounded communities dare speak of the larger outside society and its changes. And those who do, like Brodie and Numbers, sometimes pay a high price.

Brodie viewed her abandonment of Mormonism as an escape and once compared it to escaping from a narrow green bottle and breathing free air for the first time.[9] What was she escaping from? Why, at this moment in the history of American religious life, was it possible or likely for her to leave? What intellectual currents in her day made it possible to launch herself in a different direction? Our motives are, we think, always rational and personal, but none of us remains unaffected by the air of our own times. Brodie breathed in secularism, including psychology and an anthropological approach to religion. The result was personal alienation from her own religion, followed by disaffiliation, which her excommunication only confirmed.

American Secularism and American Religion

Fawn McKay Brodie, born in 1915, "skipped" several elementary grades and entered Weber College in Ogden in 1930 at age fourteen. Then a Mormon church–owned junior college, Weber would become a state college soon after her graduation in 1932 when she matriculated at the University of Utah. She later credited the university with giving her the first taste of intellectual freedom. She graduated in 1934, taught English at Weber State in 1934–35, and entered the University of Chicago in the fall of 1935, receiving her M.A. in English in August 1936. In the process, her outlook had become thoroughly secularized.

Brodie's educational transformation thus moved with the tide that had been rising during the 1920s of purposeful intellectual secularism on a wide scale. Social historian Ann Douglas has persuasively depicted the 1920s as "the most revealing [secular] moment in the history of our national psyche," when Americans, with a "terrible honesty" that was first seen merely as post–World War I disillusionment, tried to root out what was demonstrably false in our history. It was a task in which Black and White cultural leaders joined hands, and religion was an easy target. Although many of the results can be seen as negative, it was an endeavor rooted in the hope of betterment. As Douglas explains, to believe in an America "where there is the most hope for the most people, you have to think there is a truth that can be found, and that's not a post-modernist position. You have to be closer to religious origins—the generation of the 20's was truly secular in that it still knew its theology and its varieties of religious experience." In contrast, Americans in the 1990s are "post-secular, inventing new faiths, without any sense of organizing truths. The truths we accept are so multiple that honesty becomes little more than a strategy by which you manage your tendencies toward duplicity."[10]

Brodie, despite being raised in a Mormon home that dampened most secular influences, still fit the profile of the twenties generation. It was a profile she embraced wholeheartedly during her college years, and its impact was such that she, apparently without either hesitations or regrets, jettisoned her family's religious tradition.

Mormon values dominated Brodie's world view as a child: "We were all brought up as very devout Mormons," she recalled late in life, "and I was devout until I went to the University of Utah."[11] Her father was a mission president and her uncle the president of the church. Her maternal grandfather, George H. Brimhall, had been president of Brigham Young University. Her father, Thomas E. McKay, was briefly president of the Senate in the Utah State Legislature and she called him "a politician at heart."[12] Even in what she modestly called her "parochial" hometown of Huntsville, she was exposed to literature, history, a certain sophistication in dealing with the world of ideas, and a mother who was, in her way, a "quiet heretic."[13] When Brodie went to the University of Utah, she said, "Then is when I began to learn important things." Rather than feeling frightened or threatened by this new world, she welcomed it eagerly and launched herself joyously into the University of Chicago of Robert M. Hutchins's experiments in liberal education. A host of brilliant European emigré scholars like Franz Alexander, Bruno Bettelheim, and other major figures preached Freud. In anthropology Robert Redfield taught a whole generation of cultural relativists, and both Ruth Benedict and Margaret Mead were influential academic stars visiting from Columbia.

It was a place of indescribable excitement and liberation. Brodie compared it to "taking off a hot coat in summertime" and added, "The sense of liberation I had at the University of Chicago was enormously exhilarating. I felt very quickly that I could never go back to the old life, and I never did."[14] She accepted the secular world view with its Freudian undertow, acknowledged the importance of theistic thought, admired the high moral purpose and boundless hopefulness of the abolitionists and their contemporary counterparts, and affirmed the possibility of distinguishing truth from falsehood. She tried to approach religion according to the main currents of her time. She placed Joseph Smith and his ideas squarely in the cultural, religious, and intellectual milieu of his time. But Brodie herself, like all scholars, was a product of her time as well.

Secularization, the dominant philosophy of Brodie's generation, was reinforced by modernization, which in general refers to the supplanting of traditional social habits and institutions under the impact of industrialization. Secularization is not necessarily tied to any economic development. The essential message of secularism in North America "is that this world is self-revelatory and self-complete, and that the profferings of Christianity [or other religions] are unnecessary for life."[15] An older and less tendentious definition is that of Vergilius Ferm, a prominent theologian of the 1940s: "Specifically a variety of utilitarian social ethic named and formulated by G. J. Holyoake (1817–1906), which seeks human improvement without reference to religion and exclusively by means of human reason, science, and social organization."[16] Secularism has its origins in political developments that go back to the Renaissance and the French Revolution and forward to Darwinism and modern science, but perhaps it can best be seen as a basket into which have been heaped many political, scientific, and social ideas.

The American version of rationalism and secularism had its roots in the Jeffersonian period and was then known as "infidelity." But rationalist-secular beliefs did not become a movement until after the Civil War, when they found an effective proponent and leader in Colonel Robert Green Ingersoll (1833–99). During the 1870s, partly because of the exhaustion of the Civil War, disillusionment with lackluster political life, and the hearty financial incentives for focusing on secular pursuits, an increasing number of Americans, like Ingersoll, took a dim view of all religions.

Beginning in 1869, Ingersoll, who became increasingly famous as the "Great Infidel," launched a series of lecture tours arguing that ethical and religious conflicts should be settled by individual rational analysis. With Voltaire, Ingersoll believed that Christianity and the Bible were obstacles to rational inquiry. In 1877 he became vice-president of the National Liberal League, which advocated the secularization of all public life and defended opponents of the Comstock anti-vice laws. In 1885 he was elected president of the American Secular Union. Ingersoll's dogmatic version of secularism as a rebellious movement gradually disappeared between the 1890s and 1920s. "Infidelity" became an archaism. Secular explanations of reality became common, most notably the widespread acceptance of Darwinism and the Progressives' preaching that economic and social conditions—not just religious depravity—could cause poverty and crime. In short, so many educated Americans had become secular in so many ways that Ingersoll's "movement" now seemed somewhat comic. World War I dealt a final blow to nineteenth-century religious innocence.

Intellectuals of the 1920s and 1930s generation generally found New York and Chicago poor substitutes for Paris and London, enlisting their often-facile understandings of Freud, Havelock Ellis, Karl Marx, and Max Weber to dismiss their own society and culture as dominated by materialistic "booboisie" and ludicrous religions. Many secular ideas, and certainly secularism's contempt for organized religion, found an eloquent and sardonic voice when George Jean Nathan (1882–1958) and H. L. Mencken (1880–1956) founded the *American Mercury* in 1924. (Mencken became the sole editor in 1925.) In the back pages of every issue, one could laugh at reprinted news squibs documenting the folly of American religion, together with the mental deviants or frauds who founded and led them. A Jazz Age hero was the agnostic, free-thinking lawyer Clarence Darrow (1857–1938), defender of socialists and atheists, who in 1925 humiliated William Jennings Bryan, the champion of the midwestern and southern Protestants, in the Scopes trial.

For many historians, much of American religion was a contemptible mishmash of materialism and business, not worth devoting serious effort to. Americans are a religion-obsessed people, and religion unquestionably governed the lives of most Americans between 1929 and 1959; yet, there is little evidence of that fact in American social history and historiography of that period. This black hole is not hard to explain. Historians and most other social scientists and intellectuals simply chose to ignore religion as a significant category of American (and European) life.

The most influential social historian of 1931–60, Frederick Lewis Allen, treated religion dismissively in his history of the 1920s, *Only Yesterday*.[17] According to Allen, there was no "real" religion in America. Although the number of church members grew as fast as the population and "church wealth and expenditures grew more rapidly still," he concluded that the churches were not growing in any significant direction. They just about "maintained their position in American life . . . chiefly by force of momentum." Religion had its impact on "morals," which meant mainly a negative attitude toward sex and liquor.

There was, Allen wrote, "a loss of spiritual dynamic" that substituted golf, automobiles, and the Ku Klux Klan for the old "dynamic." This view conveniently overlooked the fact that the old dynamic of 1890 to 1910 was one of even greater materialism and the largest number of lynchings of African-Americans and foreigners in American history. Allen saw the new "colossal prestige" of science as another threat to the spiritual dynamic. He praised the leading liberal Protestant preacher Harry Emerson Fosdick, who approved of scientific progress, and he saw it as a sorry symptom of the time that Fosdick was removed from his pulpit and tried as a heretic.

Thus, Allen completely overlooked the solid achievements of popular religion. His dismissal of Protestant mainline religions did not recognize Catholicism even long enough to spurn it. But these were the glory years of traditional Catholicism, with a parochial school system that fed the spirits and formed the moral conscience of millions, an achievement that did not begin to wane until the vast losses of the 1970s. Most Catholics found spiritual sustenance in conservative TV preachers like Fulton J. Sheen and, among the leftists, in Dorothy Day, the leader of the Catholic Worker movement and its houses of hospitality. Catholicism maintained scores of major hospitals and other charitable institutions, which are now mostly bankrupt or faltering as the generation of nuns who ran them without salaries is dying unreplaced. Worker priests supported unpopular unions in the face of hostile bishops, becoming popular heroes in their own circles.

Furthermore, beyond popular religion, this period could also claim an important intellectual element. Harvard Divinity School underwent a rebirth under President Nathan Pusey, who was one of the first academic leaders after 1945 to begin restoring some academic respectability to the scholarly study of religion. But the dominant religious intellectual in America at that moment was Reinhold Niebuhr (1892–1971), the famous theologian at Union Theological Seminary in New York. If Fawn Brodie had been interested in finding a way to take religion seriously, she would have been involved with his works, but she was not. By 1936 Niebuhr had turned from the social liberalism created by the amalgam of Walter Rauschenbusch's Social Gospel and John Dewey's democratic pragmatism to a more realistic view of the nature of humankind. He asserted that human beings are not perfectible on this earth and rather idealistically outlined his beliefs in social liberalism. The first was, "Injustice is caused by ignorance and will yield to education and greater intelligence." By 1942 he had changed his mind: Christianity had to deal with power and its corruptions; he now believed that justice came from painful efforts, from "the pressures and counter-pressures, the tensions, the overt and covert conflicts." Original sin tainted all human perception. Modifying his pacifism, he began to support the war against Nazi Germany, and in 1944 he voted for Roosevelt. In short, Niebuhr had become a theological conservative but remained a social liberal.[18]

Still, Niebuhr represented a minority position in the milieu in which Fawn Brodie researched and wrote. The whole American liberal establishment after 1936 generally moved away from any sympathy with Marxist utopias while still assenting to the rightness of many of Marx's insights about class structure and capitalism. (Even Niebuhr was a socialist from 1929 to 1940.) But the liberal establishment failed to recognize the relevance of religion to social policy.[19] Those same years after 1935 were also peak years for Brodie's intellectual development. She was finishing her master's thesis and beginning her research on Joseph Smith. It was a time when few intellectuals could take American religion seriously—and then only by raising questions about the social or personal value of religious faith. Brodie's research for *No Man Knows My History* suited that moment precisely. Secularism and the culture of disbelief remained in the ascendancy throughout Brodie's adult life. They have been the touchstone of historical interpretation and philosophical inquiry for most of the period since World War I. In perhaps nothing else did this historian of a great religious figure show herself so limited by her time as in her blindness to the fact that ordinary people were still practicing their religions with piety and zeal—not as historical traditions but as living faiths.

Henry Steele Commager, like Allen, confused religion with popular "moral attitudes and practices." In a single sentence in his 453-page work, Commager dismissively characterized religion in the 1950s: "No longer able to satisfy the spiritual needs of the community, [the church] had largely forfeited its moral function and assumed, instead, a secular one—that of serving as a social organization."[20] Commager thus helped to create and to perpetuate the black hole in American historiography that should have been filled with a discussion of religion. The immensely learned scholar of American Protestantism Robert T. Handy called the 1920s and 1930s "the Great American Religious Depression."[21]

Notable exceptions to this neglect of American religious life were the anthropologists and sociologists, but their books then reached a limited audience and their journals had such forbidding titles as *Journal for the Scientific Study of Religion*. Their willingness to admit religion's social power can be traced to great figures like Max Weber, Emile Durkheim, Franz Boas, and others; but a particularly telling voice among them was Ruth Benedict, professor of anthropology at Columbia University. Her *Patterns of Culture* (1934) was not only more widely read than most anthropological works but was also immensely influential in pointing out the obvious: For the "primitive" Kwakiutls of the Pacific Northwest, religion, far from being irrelevant, was the very basis and the organizing principle of their society.

Benedict's close friend and colleague at Columbia University, Margaret Mead, noted proudly in her preface to a 1959 edition that the book had been translated into fourteen languages and had sold over 800,000 copies in one paperback edition alone. Mead asserted that the concept of cultural relativism "gives human beings a greater control over their own future than they have ever known before," an empowerment unknown to the enslaved minds of "primitive cultures." She added: "When Ruth Benedict began her work in anthropology in 1921, the term 'culture,' as we use it today for the systematic body of learned behavior which is transmitted from parents to children, was part of the vocabulary of a small and technical group of professional anthropologists. That today the modern world is on such easy terms with the concept of culture, that the words 'in our culture' slip from the lips of educated men and women almost as effortlessly as to the phrases that refer to period and to place, is in very great part due to this book."[22]

Mead did not overstate the case. Cultural relativism and indifference to religion in modern industrial societies were two basic premises of the intellectual world of Fawn Brodie—and of many readers of this essay. This secular point of view, which dominated the culture criticism of Brodie's generation and resulted in the religious black hole in mid-century historiography, is still an unstated premise of many American professional historians who have traditionally slighted religious practice as an agent of historical change.[23] In the words of the social historian Glenn C. Altschuler, scientific objectivity, the basic premise of the vast process of secularization, led to the "ghettoizing" of religious studies in academia.[24] Graduate students in history never saw religion as part of the human experience or the American experience. One school of modernization/secularization theorists takes the extreme position that secularization has led to the decline of religious practice, influence, and significance in Western countries. Clearly modernization and secularization did not destroy American religious vitality; but equally clearly, American political and intellectual leaders still devote their energies to goals that are more often defined by class, race, gender, and economics than religion.

The teaching of American history has likewise reflected this strong secular bias up to the present. Most textbooks of American history provide little evidence that most Americans had any religious beliefs after 1900. Most Americanists have, if they mention religion at all, presented such outlandish figures as Billy Sunday, Marcus Garvey, Aimée Semple MacPherson, and Father Divine, most depicted as cranks and frauds ripe for satire. In this, they follow the tradition of Sinclair Lewis's *Elmer Gantry*, whose name is a virtual synonym for fraudulent piety and exploitation, or the 1970s documentary film *Marjo*. The less than amusing "radio priest," pro-fascist Father Charles B. Coughlin, gets a paragraph in almost all college textbooks to show the response to the crisis of the Great Depression and the rise of European fascism. H. L. Mencken, Sinclair Lewis, and other pundits and writers of the 1920s and 1930s ridiculed not just sects but also the middle-class religious denominations. As recently as 1994 David Halberstam's 800-page encyclopedic narrative of the 1950s described the entire religion-saturated era without even mentioning Norman Vincent Peale or Fulton J. Sheen, whereas Billy Graham appeared only because he criticized the Kinsey report.[25] Historians of the 1970s and 1980s also routinely ignored the explosive growth since 1945 of the Southern Baptists, the Church of Jesus Christ of Latter-day Saints, the richly varied African-American churches, the Jehovah's Witnesses, the various Islamic groups, and the burgeoning Pentecostals, all of which control significant wealth and political power. As recently as October 1994, when biographer David McCullough, keynoting the annual conference of the Western History Association in Albuquerque, New Mexico, asserted that religion should be put back into history, many in his audience were startled. In short, religious historiography once again provides a telling example of how omission becomes bias.

Recently, however, the trend has been reversing itself. During the 1970s, pathbreaking anthropologists and sociologists began to show that religion exerted its power in "advanced" industrial societies as well as in "primitive" ones.[26] American historians followed in their wake, taking notice of the great significance of religion in the United States only in the 1980s.[27] By the 1990s, religion became tentatively fashionable; even the conservative *William and Mary Quarterly* planned an issue on religion in early America for 1997. The most recent college textbook histories are beginning to allude to the possible significance of religious belief and practice but usually in connection with some more important aspect of American life. For example, conservative religion is mentioned for its role in assuring the election of Ronald Reagan as president.[28] No historian of religion did research in primary Mormon sources until the 1970s, and Mormonism was usually mentioned only in connection with eccentricities of the Burned-Over District and as part of the settlement of the Trans-Mississippi West. Since the 1980s, however, some intellectuals, scholars, and book review editors have begun to accord Southern Baptists, Mormons, Catholics, and sectarians the same serious attention once given to the Kwakiutls and the Puritan divines.

Fawn McKay Brodie's identification with secular intellectual thought was, as nearly as I can judge, complete. She
explained in her oral history, "I was excommunicated for heresy—
and I *was* a heretic—and specifically for writing the book."[29]
Although she speaks regretfully of the pain her excommunication
cost her father, she says, "He really never understood the nature of
my break with my past. I think he tried to but it was always very
painful for him and he was always . . . trying to pull me . . . back
into the brotherhood. But he couldn't. I told him the university
was my world and not the church."[30]

At a conference marking the fiftieth anniversary of the
publication of *No Man Knows My History*, attended by Brodie's
siblings and children, her brother Thomas stated that he had
"never heard her express any belief in God. . . . There was no
malice in her loss of faith [and] no belief in life after death." Her
daughter Pamela, who attended Brodie during her relatively
quick death from cancer in January 1981, confirmed that: "I
never saw any sign that she was afraid of death."[31] During this
final illness, Brodie asked her faithful Mormon brother for a
blessing of comfort such as their father had often given. When
she found that this private request had been exaggerated into a
myth of deathbed repentance, she forcefully rejected any interpretation of this blessing to mean that she was asking to be taken
back into the church at that moment: "I strictly repudiate and
would for all time."[32]

Psychology and Environmentalism

The second strong influence on the modern secularism which
marked Brodie's generation was the arrival of new theories of
human psychology and a new reliance on environmental explanations of historical personages.

Freudian theory, fresh in the 1920s and strong in the 1950s,
amounted to a paradigmatic structure in Brodie's world. Although

Sigmund Freud himself had come to lecture in the United States as early as 1909, it was not until his *General Introduction to Psychoanalysis* appeared in English in 1920 that his theories began to gain wide acceptance in the United States. But the flowering of American Freudianism came in the 1930s with the translation of his *New Introductory Lectures on Psycho-analysis* (1933) and his *Basic Writings*, collected, translated, and edited by A. A. Brill (1938). Almost as important for the spread of his ideas was the influence of many refugees from Nazi Germany and Austria who settled in America, including Bruno Bettelheim, Franz Alexander, Karen Horney, and Erich Fromm. They soon joined efforts with the first generation of American psychoanalysts, such as Harry Stack Sullivan. The University of Chicago during Brodie's years was becoming a major center for the study of psychoanalysis.

By the 1940s, Freudian concepts had spread to all humanistic and social science disciplines; and although modern psychology has rejected some of Freud's notions, many have become so pervasive that their Viennese origins are lost on most Americans today: frustration-aggression theory, psychological defenses, techniques of rationalization, hidden motives, the formation of personality and identity in family interactions, and, of course, the expression of sexual energy in unexpected places. Brodie was enamored of these new trends for analyzing human nature, and she applied them in her biographies—although only tentatively in *No Man Knows My History*.

The generation of the 1990s perhaps does not understand the significance of Freudian thought in supplying intellectuals first, then the general public as a whole, with tools for appraising and understanding their cultures in terms other than those received from that culture itself. It is also true that someone like Fawn Brodie can be critiqued by a post-Freudian generation for the perhaps uncritical way in which she adopted this new psychology to the exclusion of more balanced approaches; but such ongoing critiques are merely a fact of life, not a judgment.

What can be said, however, is that Brodie's conscious decision to sever her powerful ties to Mormon religion has reverberated in Mormon culture for half a century. Her decision was possible only because of the intellectual currents of her time. Freudianism was particularly important because it gave her the skills and tools with which to come to terms with Joseph Smith—not on *his* own terms but on her own.

Toward the end of her life, Brodie asserted that she had not consciously used psychoanalytic theory in her biography of Joseph Smith but wished she had.[33] I believe most current appraisals would agree that her unconscious supplied whatever she had failed to do consciously. The slant of *No Man Knows My History* is unobtrusively but clearly Freudian even though it is also true that, contrary to caricature, she used the psychoanalytic approach least in this first biography.

She insisted that Joseph Smith had dealt in self-deception and rationalization throughout his career, projecting his own sexual drives into the doctrine of polygamy, but avoiding conscious fraud by a deep conversion to his own beliefs.[34] Brodie's affinity for Freudian psychology could be seen, perhaps, as a surrogate belief system that replaced Mormonism for her. In fact, it is the most convincing explanation of why she shows no special awareness of the religious currents of her time, a surprising blind spot for an intellectual of such sensitivity. Given her devout Mormon background and her total lack of malice (compared, say, with DeVoto), it seems strange that Brodie did not rise above other American historians of her generation and that she showed so little empathy for deep religious faith. At the very least one could have expected her to approve of religious faith as a positive "functionalist" phenomenon. But even this safe sociological way of affirming the value of faith in Mormonism did not speak to her secular sensibility. She found in psychoanalysis a far more helpful and meaningful guide to the problems of sin and society.

Her more explicit use of Freudian psychology in her later biographies of Richard M. Nixon, Thaddeus Stevens, and especially Thomas Jefferson show how thoroughly she espoused the secular world view. In her oral history she commented that her books on Thomas Jefferson, Thaddeus Stevens, and Richard Nixon were pure "psychohistory . . . although not always recognized as such." She was proud of this technique and especially of her success in substituting English words for clinical terms.[35] As for Freud, she taught her students "to relax a little bit. . . . Freud and predestination are not the same. . . . . Freud was an optimist. His point of view was that you could break out of the shackles in which you are imprisoned by your parents. You do not have to stay bound in these neurotic patterns for the rest of your life; you can get out from under with reading, with therapy. There are all sorts of ways to liberation."[36] Of psychobiographer Erik Erikson, she commented in 1975, "I admire him tremendously. I think he is an authentic genius. He will never be the great genius Freud was, but nevertheless he is having a great impact."[37]

By 1972 when she brought out her second edition, she had come to believe that the most appropriate psychological explanation of Smith's actions was his adoption of the role of "impostor," not in the colloquial sense of charlatan, but in the technical psychiatric sense of Phyllis Greenacre's classic article "The Impostor"—a person with two identities.[38] Greenacre had found inspiration for her "impostor" identities in Freudian conflict theory.

Religious Disaffiliation

Given the two broad currents of secularism and new psychological understandings in American society during the 1920s and 1950s, it is now possible to examine Fawn M. Brodie's writing of *No Man Knows My History* as an act of disaffiliation. I believe that she wrote this naturalistic explanation of the founding prophet's life not only because she had disaffiliated with Mormonism but also as a way of disaffiliating.

The Mormon church in the nineteenth century maintained tight boundaries and was in high tension with its host culture.

Reluctantly and under severe compulsion, it abandoned communitarianism, political separatism, and plural marriage. These movements toward the mainstream accelerated after the turn of the century to an urgent quest for respectability and acceptability. After World War II, Mormonism in the United States found a comfortable fit in the family-centered, economically prosperous, politically conservative mainstream of American life. Today, it shares at least five basic characteristics of mainline churches: (1) a relatively high socio-economic class; (2) access to social, economic, and cultural power; (3) international growth (by 1996 there were more Mormons outside of the United States than in it); (4) the growth of bureaucracy (the twenty-six story church office building, built during the early 1970s, dominates the skyline of Salt Lake City); and (5) greater acceptance of its social environment, i.e., the larger American society.[39] Still, the boundary maintenance of Mormonism, strictly enforced by a powerful hierarchy, is so strong that many sociologists of religion still believe that Mormonism is a kind of mild sect—if one uses the recent redefinition of sect as a religious group "in high tension" with the surrounding society.[40]

Fawn McKay grew up in a church that was definitely sect-like by comparison: defensive, braced for hostility from a world that did not understand or respect Mormonism, maintaining sharp boundaries through its code against drinking and smoking (abstinence from both is now newly fashionable), and viewing as lost anyone who married out of the faith. When Fawn McKay married Bernard Brodie, a nonobservant Jew, she was committing a disloyal act. "Bernard," she said of her husband, "is marvelous. He has encouraged my writing. Without him I would never have been able to do it."[41]

Fawn Brodie belonged to the first generation of Americans that had the option of belonging to a church without really believing in all its doctrines and missions. Mormons were not part of this change. New tools of education—the scientific method and secularization—created paradigms for understanding religion as something other than total world view. Many intellectuals became completely irreligious as a result, following the Ingersoll tradition. To them, religion was a construct with little social utility and, often, downright perniciousness. Mormonism seemed immune to the new temptations. Brodie, DeVoto, and Dale Morgan exhaust the list of examples.

The 1930s and 1940s produced virtually no historical studies of religion worth reading beyond Perry Miller's heroic rescue of the Puritans, a feat as noteworthy for its solitary splendor as for its sophisticated and admirable scholarship. A small academic industry of Puritan studies followed, but its net effect was to establish Puritanism as a literary and aesthetic movement. It had virtually no influence on the status of religion as a topic in American history, especially from 1920 to 1960.[42]

In other words, Fawn Brodie was one of thousands of Americans departing from their family's religious tradition. In that context, some of the research on religious disaffiliation may prove illuminating. It is important to note that not every departure from a church-belief system is an act of anger. Hostility toward one's former faith is common enough for observers to presume hard feelings, but many leave more in sadness than in anger.[43] To be sure, apostates commonly express anger, especially against religious institutions that require intense devotion and sacrifice. Sometimes they begin by denying that they ever really believed. Less frequently they go through a period of depression followed by either a reconciliation with the original faith or the adoption of another belief system.[44]

Brodie never issued a formal statement separating herself from the church. Her lack of personal hostility is one of the remarkable facts about her decision to disaffiliate from a religion that she could no longer accept as authentic. In a 1975 interview she recalled, "The fraudulent nature of the Book of Mormon is, I think, unmistakable; that has not changed [since 1945]. The devout Mormons still believe it to be the work of God. The 'Jack Mormons' are pretty certain it is not, but still respect the organization of the church and feel that it does a great deal of good, so they stay with it."[45]

Even as a recollection in tranquility thirty years after the publication of her controversial biography and her resultant excommunication for writing it, this statement seems to be both remarkably even-handed and fair.

A second characteristic of disaffiliation—although this does not seem to have applied to Brodie—is that belief can be separated from belonging. George Gallup Jr.'s *Religion in America, 50 Years: 1935–1985* found that many "religious" Americans could answer "yes" to questions about the existence of God, the divinity of Christ, and the authority of the Bible but were not affiliated with any church or frequently, if they were, were affiliated only nominally. In contrast, nineteenth-century Christians had a close-coupled system: Belief in the divinity of Christ implied public testimonies of their conversion, active involvement in a denomination, zealous good works, and uplifting the morals of American society in a variety of ways. Believing meant commitment of hearts, hands, and purses to an organized religious group. Brodie disbelieved *and* disaffiliated.

Another illuminative parallel may be Bernard DeVoto (1897–1955), who wrote for Mencken's *American Mercury* during the 1920s and 1930s. For Mormonism's centennial in 1930, DeVoto wrote a shallow, scoffing article for the *American Mercury* terming Smith a paranoid personality.[46] Later DeVoto rose above the debunking fashions of the 1920s and 1930s, wrote for twenty years an influential column for *Harper's*, the leading serious magazine of his day, and produced solid and appreciative reappraisals of American history that won the Pulitzer Prize in history, the Bancroft Prize in history, the National Book Award, numerous honorary degrees, and the respect of thousands of readers. He also wrote the best review of Brodie's *No Man Knows My History*, praising it as "brilliant" and characterizing Brodie's style as that of "a detached, modern intelligence, grounded in naturalism, rejecting the supernatural."[47]

DeVoto was eighteen years older than Brodie, came from a family not deeply identified with the state, and was never a practicing Latter-day Saint as a youth, important differences between the two. Furthermore, despite a common past, similar interests, and transiently overlapping careers, they never became friends. DeVoto criticized *No Man Knows My History* for rejecting his own thesis—that Joseph Smith was paranoid and intermittently mentally ill; Brodie found this explanation too facile and simplistic to cover Joseph Smith's complexities.

Both, however, were similar in adopting the assumptions of intellectual secularism as young adults and, hence, in rejecting any personal religious belief system. Ogden, the birthplace of both, was the least Mormon of any major Utah city even though it was still more than 50 percent Mormon. As an intermountain center for railroading, meat-packing, canning, and milling, it had a more cosmopolitan air. Both Brodie and DeVoto attended the University of Utah and then moved on to eastern universities, DeVoto leaving for Harvard in 1915, the year Brodie was born, and Brodie leaving for the University of Chicago in the fall of 1935, when she was only twenty. Neither professed any religion after their departure from Utah.

The son of a Mormon mother and a Catholic father, DeVoto was raised as a Catholic but seems to have felt his strongest "emotional attachment towards Mormonism as an institution with a remarkable historical tradition and admirable principles of social coherence."[48] DeVoto was also indifferent to the Europe where three of his grandparents were born. He never left the United States, not even to cross the Mexican border to research his study of the Mexican War. Criticized as a provincial by cosmopolitan friends, he retorted that he had not yet seen Paris, Tennessee, or Paris, Kentucky. In 1944 DeVoto published *The Literary Fallacy*, criticizing his fellow American writers and intellectuals for their ignorance of their own history and culture. Six years later, eminent historian Henry Steele Commager acknowledged the point while sidestepping it to ask, "What is important to ask is how this situation came about. How did it happen that novelists from Lewis to Steinbeck were uniformly critical of Americans' business civilization?"[49] Commager, the son of a minister, does not, incidentally, confront even his own question—in part because the whole era of alienation was directly connected with religion, which no one took seriously.

Although neither ever denied or sneered at their Mormon roots, both Brodie and DeVoto entered relentlessly secular environments and socialized with people who still looked upon Mormonism as a ridiculous American sect. Both became successful academics later in life without Ph.D.'s in history. And both were shunned and ignored by most Utah Mormons throughout most of their working careers. It was not until 1971, sixteen years after DeVoto's death, that the historian Leland A. Fetzer, in an essay in *Dialogue*, urged a reappraisal of DeVoto's loyalty to Mormon traditions and the national status he had conferred upon the state of his birth. Brodie's first major public appearance in Utah without open vicious attacks on her as a person and as a scholar did not occur until twenty-two years after the publication of *No Man Knows My History* and just thirteen years before her death. In 1967, she was made a fellow of the Utah State Historical Society. Three years later, in September 1970, she delivered a lecture—"Can We Manipulate the Past?"—before a "standing-room only" crowd of over five hundred.[50] Her address dealt with the LDS church's attempts to manipulate and cover its own past. The mere fact of her speaking on that subject in that place amounted to a triumph of the values that had replaced Mormonism for her: secularism, objectivity, and the pursuit of truth as discovery, not as an object to be transmitted.

During Brodie's generation Mormonism was virtually impossible to leave because it was (and to some extent still is) a cultural community as well as a set of religious doctrines, an intense commonality of persons tied together emotionally. Brodie succeeded through the instrumentality of writing *No Man Knows My History.* This biography is almost literally her exiting statement. She told Dale Morgan that *No Man Knows My History* sprang out of her passionate drive "to interpret her own origins to herself" and that it "served her as the autobiographical novel serves many other writers; it has been a kind of catharsis for her."[51]

Dale L. Morgan (1914–71), a descendant of Mormon apostle and mathematician Orson Pratt, had undergone his own strenuous struggle to free himself from his Mormon past. Brodie's sympathetic confidant and helpful critic, he helped mentor her through the process. In late 1945 and early 1946 he observed: "Your intellectual detachment is only a way-station in your development—it aligns you with another culture, that of the world outside, but does not yet equip you to come to terms with the Mormons on the emotional plane." He added, "I suspect that you won't begin to have really generous feelings until you have finished disentangling yourself from the religion." A few months earlier he had written Brodie that he had expected her book to be dedicated to her husband (she had instead dedicated it to her cousin McKeen Eccles Brimhall, a casualty of World War II), "for he is the cause as well as the symbol of your personal liberation from the oppressions of Mormon orthodoxy."[52]

The distinguished literary historian and critic Paul Pickrel, who was an exact contemporary of Brodie's, concluded in a recent memoir of his life: "In the 1930s there was something I can only call a culture of aspiration that is now badly depleted. The goal of self-realization has replaced the goal of self-improvement; the notion that what is already in us would be sufficient if we could only get it out has largely replaced the notion that we should try to make more of ourselves."[53] Brodie shared that culture of aspiration and, despite considerable odds, made more of herself. It is perhaps a confession of Mormonism's narrowness before 1960 that there was no way she could do so and remain within her tradition.

Conclusion

Brodie's legacy within Mormonism has been a powerful one. Some have argued that her biography retarded Mormon intellectual life by raising so much anger and anti-intellectualism among church members. As the excommunications of 1993–95 of Mormon intellectuals demonstrate, the Mormon church still overreacts to criticism from within. On May 18, 1993, Apostle Boyd K. Packer told the All-Church Coordinating Council of middle-level managers that the church faced three major threats: "the gay-lesbian movement, the feminist movement, and the ever-present challenge from the so-called scholars or intellectuals."[54] Both before and after that date the church has used internal privileges (public speaking, the right to enter the temples, and so on) and administrative actions (disfellowshipping, ostracism, dismissal from church jobs, and even excommunication) to enforce conformity in authority and doctrine. The attention of the national press has led to the misperception that this kind of crackdown is new in Mormon history.

The emphasis on feminists and homosexuals may be new, but disciplining ranging from scoldings to excommunications over doctrinal and historical disagreements have been part of Mormonism since the nineteenth century. Orson Pratt (1811–88), a scholar, mathematician, and apostle who publicly disagreed with Brigham Young on such weighty matters as the nature of God, survived an early excommunication and a demotion in seniority. B. H. Roberts (1857–1933), the patron saint of Mormon intellectuals, was a historian, theologian, Democrat, and dissident who accused the church of infringing on his personal freedoms. When Roberts ran for the U.S. House of Representatives in 1898, Joseph Fielding Smith, a member of the First Presidency and an intensely partisan Republican, tried to thwart his election.[55] Like Pratt, Roberts retained his ecclesiastical position. Several professors were dismissed or resigned in a minipurge between 1911 and 1916 for teaching the theory of evolution at Brigham Young University, but evolution and other scientific topics were featured in church periodicals of the 1930s and 1940s.

Institutional toleration of dissent, intellectual pursuits, and internal criticism has always been grudging and cyclical. Currently Mormon scholars and intellectuals are still comparatively few and unquestionably can, if they question authority or doctrine, suffer grievous penalties inflicted on themselves and their families. Nevertheless, within the still strong communal boundaries of Mormonism, many Mormons faithful to their church have been working quietly for a new day. Although most of their output is "safe," they have been able to build, since the late 1960s, a more imposing historiography than that of any other religious group in the United States. The fact that they must also keep a cautious eye on church authorities does not negate the value of those studies. In short, there is undoubtedly some retardation of honest critical studies of Mormon history, but it was not created by Brodie; it stems from an old fear within all authoritarian churches of any approach or system with premises different from its own.

Brodie's biography of Joseph Smith, which used the premises of naturalism and secularism, had two effects. It allowed debunking critics of Mormonism to dismiss Joseph Smith as other than a prophet. But simultaneously, by those very means of secularism and naturalism, coupled with Brodie's high standard of historical research in primary documents, it required critics of Mormonism to take Joseph Smith seriously. It is the seriousness rather than the debunking that has proved to be the longer-lasting result.

This contribution must not be minimized. The hostility toward religion that suffused the scholarship of Brodie's generation consigned fervent religions like Mormonism to a particularly dreary and ludicrous role in American history. It interpreted Mormonism as both quaint and superstitious with its unlettered prophets, its powerful loyalty to unseemly institutions like polygamy, and its penchant for odd behaviors like secret temple rituals, special underwear, and dietary restrictions. Even though Mormonism was far from alone in being a target of prejudice—all religions were targets for the secular establishment—the conscious steps it took after the abandonment of polygamy to join the respectable mainstream have perhaps made it hypersensitive to remnants of bigotry from the larger community. When Mormonism matures beyond such reactions, Brodie will then be seen in her truer light—not as most orthodox Mormons still see her: as someone supplying ammunition to the "enemies" of the church. Rather, they will see that she brought Mormonism into dialogue with the national culture.

Notes

1. I wish to thank Professor Klaus Hansen, Freda De Pillis, and an anonymous reader for the Utah State University Press for helping make this three-way analysis clear and comprehensible.
2. Fawn M. Brodie, "Supplement," *No Man Knows My History: The Life of Joseph Smith, the Mormon Prophet*, 2nd ed., rev. and enl. (1945; New York: Alfred A. Knopf, 1971), 67, 421.
3. Ibid., 418–19.
4. Ibid., 403.
5. Ronald L. Numbers, *Prophetess of Health: Ellen G. White and the Origins of Seventh-day Adventist Health Reform*, 2nd ed., rev. and enl. (Knoxville: University of Tennessee Press, 1992). The second edition includes "A Psychological Profile," by Ronald Numbers and Janet S. Numbers and an insightful introduction, "The Historian as Heretic," by Jonathan M. Butler. I am indebted to Massimo Introvigne for bringing this introduction, which explicitly compares Numbers with Brodie, to my attention. The 1976 edition was titled *Prophetess of Health: A Study of Ellen G. White.*
6. I wish to thank Professor Numbers for granting me an interview on February 13, 1996, for checking the accuracy of my account, and for providing some illuminating details. He considers the parallel with Brodie's experience a fair one.
7. Butler, "Introduction: The Historian as Heretic," xxxii.
8. Quoted in Butler, "Introduction: The Historian as Heretic," li.
9. Reported to me by a scholar at Yale University in the 1950s. Although it is second-hand and anonymous, the metaphor fits well with her better-known comparison, "like taking off a hot coat in summertime." Fawn McKay Brodie, Oral History 1523, interviewed by Shirley E. Stephenson, Nov. 30, 1975, typescript (Fullerton: California State University, Fullerton, Oral History Program, 1978), 49.
10. Ann Douglas, interviewed by Tobin Harshaw, *New York Times Book Review*, Feb. 12, 1995, 17; see Douglas, *Terrible Honesty: Mongrel Manhattan in the 1920s* (New York: Farrar, Straus, & Giroux). Although Douglas was writing about Manhattan, her analysis of the temper of the times is fully applicable to Chicago as well.

11. Brodie, Oral History, 2.
12. Ibid.
13. Ibid., 4.
14. Ibid., 3.
15. "Secularism, Secularization," *Dictionary of Christianity in America*, ed. Daniel G. Reid et al. (Downer's Grove, Ill.: InterVarsity Press, 1990), 1069. Of course theories of secularization also apply to non-Christian societies, but they are not the focus of this essay. For the many other definitions of secularism, as well as a large and contentious sociological literature on its nature, sources, and effects, see Danny L. Jorgensen's summary in "Dissent and Schism in the Early Church: Explaining Mormon Fissiparousness," *Dialogue: A Journal of Mormon Thought* 28 (fall 1995): 20, n. 14. My own position in this debate lies close to that of Robert Wuthnow, *Rediscovering the Sacred: Perspectives on Religion in Contemporary Society* (Grand Rapids, Mich.: W. B. Eerdmans, 1992), which is that secular points of view do not necessarily blot out the sacred. Secularism no longer has the pretensions of a rival religion, an offensive nineteenth-century posture that has collapsed since the 1960s.
16. Vergilius Ferm, ed., *An Encyclopedia of Religion* (New York: Philosophical Library, 1945), 700.
17. Frederick Lewis Allen, *Only Yesterday: An Informal History of the Nineteen-Twenties* (New York: Harper and Brothers, 1931), 195–97.
18. See Arthur Schlesinger Jr., "Theology and Politics from the Social Gospel to the Cold War: The Impact of Reinhold Niebuhr," in *Intellectual History in America*, ed. Cushing Strout (New York: Harper and Row, 1968), 158–81.
19. This problem seems to prevail as Stephen L. Carter has recently shown in his best-selling *The Culture of Disbelief: How American Law and Politics Trivialize Religious Devotion* (New York: Basic Books, 1993).
20. Henry Steele Commager, *The American Mind: An Interpretation of American Thought and Character Since the 1880s* (New Haven, Conn.: Yale University Press, 1950; Bantam Books edition, 23rd printing, 1970), 437.
21. Handy, "The American Religious Depression, 1925–1935," *Church History* 29 (March 1960): 3–16.
22. Margaret Mead, "A New Preface," in *Patterns of Culture*, by Ruth Benedict (Boston: Houghton Mifflin Company, Sentry Edition, 1959), vii; see also viii–x.
23. See George M. Marsden and Bradley J. Longfield, eds., *The Secularization of the Academy* (New York: Oxford University Press, 1992), particularly D. G. Hart, "Faith and Learning in the Age of the University," and Marsden's "Introduction."
24. Glenn C. Altschuler, "Review Essay: Science, the State and Higher Education in America," *Journal of Social History* 28 (fall 1994): 148.

25. David Halberstam, *The Fifties* (New York: Fawcett Columbine, 1994).
26. Perhaps the most important figure in this shift was the British sociologist Bryan Wilson. See his *Religion in a Secular Society: A Sociological Comment* (London: Watts, 1966).
27. See, for example, the works of the prolific church historian Martin E. Marty, especially *The Noise of Conflict, 1919–1941*, vol. 2 of *Modern American Religion* (Chicago: University of Chicago Press, 1991).
28. This is the example Martin Gardner (1914–) cited in his brilliant assessment of American evangelicalism to show that religion is generally a source of social ills. Gardner, "Giving God a Hand," *New York Review of Books*, August 13, 1987. Gardner is a theist who belongs to no denomination.
29. Ibid., 3.
30. Brodie, Oral History, 3.
31. From my conference notes.
32. Quoted in Bringhurst, "Fawn McKay Brodie: Dissident Historian and Quintessential Critic of Mormondom," in *Differing Visions: Dissenters in Mormon History*, ed. Roger D. Launius and Linda Thatcher (Urbana: University of Illinois Press, 1994), 294.
33. Brodie, Oral History, 23.
34. See Dale Morgan's 1945 letters to historians Juanita Brooks and Bernard DeVoto for a summary and defense of Brodie's psychological theory of Joseph Smith. In John Phillip Walker, ed., *Dale Morgan on Early Mormonism: Correspondence and A New History* (Salt Lake City: Signature Books, 1986), 89, 97.
35. Brodie, Oral History, 19.
36. Ibid., 32–33.
37. Ibid., 25.
38. Greenacre's article appeared in the *Psychoanalytic Quarterly* 17 (1958). In Brodie's "Supplement" to her second edition, she discusses the tidiness of fit of Greenacre's theory.
39. See my "Mormon Power Since 1945," *Journal of Mormon History* 21 (spring 1996): 1–32 and "Viewing Mormonism as Mainline," with related essays by Marie Cornwall, Marjorie Newton, and Richard P. Howard, in *Dialogue: A Journal of Mormon Thought* 24 (winter 1991): 59–96. I do not mean to imply that Mormonism has resolved all tensions with its host society. For example, with the emergence of homosexuality as a social movement, mainline religions have conducted extensive debates and usually accepted gays as members of the religious community, sometimes ordaining homosexual ministers. The Mormon church while acknowledging that same-gender attraction is perhaps an unchosen "feeling" denies that it is an identity and insists that acting on such attraction is sinful.

Dallin H. Oaks, "Same-Gender Attraction," *Ensign* 25 (October 1995): 9–10.

40. Rodney Stark and William Sims Bainbridge, "American-Born Sects: Initial Findings," *Journal for the Scientific Study of Religion* 20 (June 1981): 131–32.

41. Brodie, Oral History, 49.

42. Miller, who preceded Brodie as a graduate student at Chicago by a few years, produced a groundbreaking collective opus. Particularly influential were his *Orthodoxy in Massachusetts, 1630–1650: A Genetic Study* (Cambridge: Harvard University Press, 1933) and *The New England Mind: The Seventeenth Century* (Cambridge: Harvard University Press, 1954).

43. In his very useful recent study of religious disaffiliation William D. Hendricks, *Exit Interviews* (Chicago: Moody Press, 1993), 258–59 studied the widespread disillusionment with Christianity during the late 1980s and 1990s by conducting detailed "exit interviews" of former denominationalists. He records that they were *not saying* that they wanted to leave their faith, that they wanted to leave their church or tradition, that their church was full of hypocrites, that all clergy were dishonest, or that they neglected the poor, social injustice, human rights, the environment, or other issues.

44. For an excellent application of the four stages of denial, anger, depression, and reconciliation to a prominent early Mormon apostate, see Craig L. Foster, "From Temple Mormon to Anti-Mormon: The Ambivalent Odyssey of Increase Van Dusen," *Dialogue: A Journal of Mormon Thought* 27 (fall 1994): 286.

45. Brodie, Oral History, 9.

46. DeVoto later repudiated his youthful essay as "ignorant, brash, malicious, and, what is worst of all, irresponsible." Quoted in Davis Bitton and Leonard J. Arrington, *Mormons and Their Historians* (Salt Lake City: University of Utah Press, 1988), 110. Bitton and Arrington, both faithful members of the church, describe the interconnections among Brodie, DeVoto, and Dale Morgan (whom they call "bridge" historians) and include Juanita Brooks in that chapter (pp. 108–24). Unlike the first three, however, Brooks never confronted the secular world view, nor do Bitton and Arrington deal with the secular influence on them. They assess Brodie as too "naturalistic."

47. *New York Herald Tribune*, Dec. 16, 1945.

48. Leland A. Fetzer, "Bernard DeVoto and the Mormon Tradition," *Dialogue: A Journal of Mormon Thought* 6 (autumn-winter, 1971): 25.

49. Commager, *The American Mind*, 278–79.

50. Newell G. Bringhurst, "Fawn McKay Brodie: Dissident Historian and Quintessential Critic of Mormondom," 293.

51. Morgan made these observations to Juanita Brooks, May 23, 1946, in *Dale Morgan*, by Walker, 121.
52. Ibid., xx, 79, 118.
53. Pickrel, "Enemies of Memory: On Recalling the 1930's," 37th Annual Katharine Asher Engel Lecture, delivered at Smith College, Northampton, Mass., Oct. 18, 1994, 20. Born the son of a farm laborer in a small village in western Illinois in 1917, not far from Spoon River, Paul Pickrel edited the *Yale Review* for seventeen years and was chief reviewer for *Harper's Magazine* in the 1950s.
54. Boyd K. Packer, "Address to the All-Church Coordinating Council, 18 May 1993," photocopy of typescript in my possession.
55. Richard S. Van Wagoner and Steven C. Walker, *A Book of Mormons* (Salt Lake City: Signature Books, 1982), 243–44; Gary James Bergera, ed., *The Autobiography of B. H. Roberts* (Salt Lake City: Signature Books, 1990), 199. Roberts won by a plurality of 7,000 votes but the House of Representatives refused to seat him in 1900 because he was a polygamist. A biographical survey of nineteen lesser figures who left for good (including Fawn Brodie) may be found in Roger D. Launius and Linda Thatcher, eds., *Differing Visions: Dissenters in Mormon History* (Urbana: University of Illinois Press, 1994).

5

———⚬⚬⚬———

Literary Style in
No Man Knows My History
An Analysis

LAVINA FIELDING ANDERSON

Perhaps the first analysis of Fawn Brodie's literary style in *No Man Knows My History* came in August 1944 when she gave a revised second draft of the manuscript to Dale Morgan for his critique, a service he had performed since their first meeting a year earlier. Among other comments he called the manuscript "downright fascinating, . . . the prose is clean and on the whole admirably muscular; . . . and at all times it moves rapidly."[1] When the publisher was looking for a cover comment for the second edition, Knopf chose an observation published in the *Saturday Review* that praised the book for "the richness and suppleness of its prose, and its narrative power."[2] The *Chicago Sun* called her work "a rare combination of sound scholarship and lively, readable narrative."[3] Juanita Brooks, despite other misgivings, conceded, "it is literary."[4]

Today, fifty years after the book's first publication, these terms of praise for the author's writing style still do not seem overstated. Among contemporary historians, Leonard Arrington noted "the charming imagery of its style and its stirring chronicle of an enigmatic career."[5] D. Michael Quinn praises her "skillful prose," and Davis Bitton acknowledges that it is "gracefully written with a compelling momentum."[6]

No Man Knows My History is, above all, an eminently read-able biography. Although Brodie's tone, naturalistic method, use of sources, and conclusions may all be properly critiqued and cer-tainly are not unrelated to her literary style, this essay does not attempt to evaluate the appropriateness of the materials she used to write her biography, which elements of Joseph Smith's life were overstressed, or which were omitted or over-generalized upon. In short, this essay does not deal with the historical accu-racy of Brodie's biography, either as a whole or in part. Rather, the focus of this essay is on the literary techniques she employed.

These two aspects—style and content—cannot, of course, be separated in the mind of the reader. Although it has become old-fashioned in recent years to ask questions about an author's intentionality and has become instead literarily correct to estab-lish ever-more sophisticated relationships between author and reader, it is not inappropriate to apply a traditional standard to a biography—and especially not to one written fifty years ago. The reader's stance in dealing with biography is, without question, that he or she expects dependability. We ask ourselves: Can we trust this author? Is this author true to the facts, drawing reason-able conclusions and marshaling the evidence in a persuasive way? As readers we resist and resent the possibility that we are being manipulated, tricked, or deceived. If we feel that we are, then the implied contract between author and reader is violated and the very skills that are the author's strengths become the most damning evidence of entrapment.

I use myself as an example. I consider myself to be a Mor-mon of orthodox beliefs although at present of unconventional status. I first heard about Fawn Brodie's biography not in positive or neutral terms, but in accents of scandal, outrage, and even contempt as a student at Brigham Young University. Although messages of any sort were few and I recall no detailed discussions, the unanimous impression I carried away was the conclusion that she did not "believe in" Joseph Smith—meaning that she did not accept the divinity of his prophetic calling as the fundamental given from which all subsequent interpretations were derived. As a result, I read Hugh Nibley's tart and spritely pamphlet "No, Ma'am, That's Not History" before I ever opened the pages of Fawn Brodie, then relaxed in the conviction that Brodie's so-called assault on the prophet had been disposed of. If anyone had asked, I would have probably replied that I did not "need" to read Fawn Brodie; there was no point in wasting my time on something that was not "good" history. I would have meant "accurate" history by that term, but the adjective carries inescapable overtones of moral well-being as well.

This undergraduate superiority stayed with me for some years after my graduation. It was while I was working at the *Ensign*, invigorated by the energetic and radiantly confident interpretations of church history emerging from Leonard Arrington's LDS Historical Department, that I faced up to the real problem. I had spent most of my life being afraid of Joseph Smith because he seemed flamboyant, extreme, and unpredictable. The church leaders I was accustomed to were staid, eminently respectable, and extremely predictable. In the wake of Leonard Arrington's influence, I developed a profound love for Joseph Smith. Tagging along behind historians I trusted, I lost my fear of Joseph Smith. Because I was no longer afraid of him, I thirsted to know more. That love was the context in which I learned details about his secret polygamy, his involvement in folk magic, his disastrous financial management, and his eschatological grandiloquence. In that context, I read Fawn Brodie for the first time with a great deal of attention and appreciation. I went on to read others of her works.

But the relationship I have as a reader with Fawn Brodie is a complicated one. Joseph Smith is *my* prophet, so I grant her her naturalistic premise but I do not accept it. The resulting tension lasts throughout the entire book and means that I relate to parts of the book differently than I do to the whole of the book. I think this complex relationship is a healthy one, although it is certainly not a relaxing nor an easy one.

I have gone into this detail because I suspect that any reading of Brodie produces a very broad range of reader-author relationships. By situating myself clearly on this spectrum, I hope to contribute to a fruitful dialogue in the three-way tensions that will inevitably be created between my perspectives, the readers' perspectives, and Brodie's perspective.

We will return to the question of the reader's contract in greater detail after a closer view of how Brodie tells her story of Mormonism's magnetic founding prophet. For convenience of discussion, I have grouped Brodie's dominant literary characteristics into four categories, beginning with the simplest and ending with the most complex: literary devices, scene structure, tone, and reader identification.

Literary Devices

Among the literary devices that Brodie employs are alliteration, allusions, foreshadowing, epigrams, periodic sentences, inversion, and parallelism. Perhaps more important than these microstyles, however, is her sheer ability to construct paragraphs that move the action forward. Her choice of verbs falls upon vigorous ones. Her descriptive details feature telling adjectives and adverbs. Her skilled use of these devices establishes a polished sequence of sentences, which the reader follows without confusion or misreadings, experiencing pleasure in the obvious craftsmanship being exhibited.

For example, after quoting Josiah Quincy's appraisal of Joseph Smith in Nauvoo, Brodie writes three paragraphs attempting to analyze the sources of Smith's charisma. Her verbs, adjectives, and adverbs are particularly well selected:

> What had overpowered Josiah Quincy, as indeed it did most of the prophet's visitors, was Joseph's magnificent self-assurance. Increased success had served to intensify his boldness and exuberance. The zest for living that he radiated never failed to inspire his own people with a sense of the richness of life. They followed him

slavishly and devotedly if only to warm themselves in the glow of his presence.

They built for him, preached for him, and made unbelievable sacrifices to carry out his orders, not only because they were convinced he was God's prophet, but also because they loved him as a man. They were as elated when he won a wrestling match as they were awed when he dictated a new revelation. They retold tales of his generosity and tenderness, marveling that he fed so many of the poor in Nauvoo at his table without stint, and that he entertained friend and enemy alike. He was a genial host, warmhearted and friendly to all comers, and fiercely loyal to his friends.

Joseph was no hair-shirt prophet. He believed in the good life, with moderate self-indulgence in food and drink, occasional sport, and good entertainment. And that he succeeded in enjoying himself to the hilt detracted not at all from the semi-deification with which his own people enshrouded him. Any protests of impropriety dissolved before his personal charm. "Man is that he might have joy" had been one of his first significant pronouncements in the Book of Mormon, and from that belief he had never deviated. He was gregarious, expansive, and genuinely fond of people. And it is no accident that his theology in the end discarded all traces of Calvinism and became an ingenuous blend of supernaturalism and materialism, which promised in heaven a continuation of all earthly pleasures—work, wealth, sex, and power. (294–95)

This passage is easy to follow and the comprehension level is high—but not for the ordinary reasons of simple style. The conventional way of computing a passage's comprehension difficulty is through the Fog Index, a development of the Reader's Digest period wherein the application of a formula to a given passage results in the approximate grade-level a reader should have to peruse the passage with 100 percent comprehension. The formula is the average number of words per sentence plus the number of words with three or more syllables. (Hyphenated words count as two words.) The resulting sum is then divided by 0.4 to yield the grade level. This particular passage consists of fifteen sentences, each averaging 20.4 words a piece. (Only three have fewer than ten words, and two of those three contain nine words). In other words, these sentences make no particular effort at brevity. The passage also contains forty-five words of three syllables or more. Applying the formula yields a grade level of 26.2—twelve years beyond graduation from college with a B.A. As a mere Ph.D., in other words, I should be struggling to follow her meaning.

However, the passage seems vivid and lucid. I argue that it has this effect because of a vigorous vocabulary and carefully structured sentences. In this passage of 240 words, the verbs are strong: *overpowered, radiated, loved, awed, marveling, enshrouded, dissolved, discarded,* and *promised.* Not a single sentence contains a passive construction. The adjectives and adverbs are far from neutral descriptors: *magnificent, radiated, slavishly, devotedly, genial, warmhearted, friendly, fiercely loyal, hair-shirt, gregarious,* and *expansive.*

Brodie further employs a variety of parallel devices in this passage: parallel verbs ("they built for him, preached for him, and made unbelievable sacrifices..."), compound objects of prepositions ("with moderate self-indulgence in food and drink, occasional sport, and good entertainment"), compound direct objects ("to intensify his boldness and exuberance"), and compound clauses containing parallel dependent clauses ("as elated when he won a wrestling match as they were awed when he dictated a new revelation").

She even constructs a sentence containing such potentially difficult-to-read structures as a noun clause for a subject and an inverted descriptor: ". . . that he succeeded in enjoying himself to the hilt" [the noun clause used as a subject] detracted not at all [the inverted descriptor] from the semi-deification. . . ." Negating structures include "was no hair-shirt prophet," "detracted not at all," and "it is no accident." All of them have the result, not of negation, but of positive intensification.

Other literary devices include alliteration, allusions, and foreshadowing. Alliteration is a device that is deep-rooted in the Anglo-Saxon heritage of English and has remained popular to the present day. Mishandled, it can become a stuttering, mechanical distraction. Used deftly, it creates a mood and a tone. For example, Brodie attributes to the name *Nauvoo* "the melancholy music of a mourning dove's call and somehow matched the magic of the site;" the reiterated "m" makes soft, prolonged, melodious sounds. A more complex triple alliteration occurs in a passage on Missouri: "They [the Saints] were weary of wearing the mantle of martyrdom and eager to unsheathe their swords" (220). The alliterated word pairs actually recall lines of Anglo-Saxon poetry with their heroic epithets and poetic conventions for descriptions of battle.

Allusions abound, their skillful interweaving into the text adding to its richness but often in a slightly ironic way. In the Nauvoo period, according to Brodie, "Joseph . . . [became] a law unto himself . . . [and] felt the Lord's thunderbolts heavy in his hand" (356). This sentence links a scriptural allusion (Romans 2:14: "When the Gentiles, which have not the law, do by nature the things contained in the law, these, having not the law, are a law unto themselves") and a second from classical mythology (the thunderbolts of Zeus). This coupling of Paul's paradox of out-of-the-law lawfulness with the Greek deity's well-known inability to refrain from wrath suggests an arbitrariness, a self-indulgence, and a dangerous temperament; but the juxtaposition also makes Joseph Smith faintly and comically grandiose.

In another allusion, also describing the Nauvoo period, Brodie observes, "It must seem that the role of prophet had finally swallowed up the man" (295), an allusion to the rod of Moses turning into a snake and swallowing the snake-rods of Pharoah's magicians. The allusion is an ambiguous one: Why is the identical feat a "miracle" when performed by Moses but "magic" when performed by Pharoah's courtiers? And is the proof of validity only who eats whom?

Foreshadowing in Brodie's hands becomes a strong summary and transitional device. For example, after discussing the "fetid" atmosphere at Kirtland after the anti-banking society disaster, Brodie describes how Joseph Smith now "realized that Kirtland must somehow be cleared of his best elders until the banking fiasco could be forgotten and the debts discharged or deferred. The best way to ensure the loyalty of his men was to send them on missions, where they could lose their petty grievances in preaching the purity of the gospel. . . . The English mission was thus born of disaster, and not even in his most extravagant day-dreams could the prophet have envisioned its success" (204). This passage thus collects the threads of Brodie's argument that Smith's mismanagement was at least partially to blame for what she terms the "banking fiasco" and that the brilliant success of the British mission was an accidental byproduct of Smith's desire to remove his loyal followers from the contamination of criticism. It then projects the image of success so strongly that the reader retains that impression over twelve intervening pages of Missouri history.

Brodie occasionally tries for an epigrammatic style and, at her best, succeeds memorably: Newell Whitney, for instance, "gave the prophet his home for a temporary residence, and his loyalty for life" (99). Less successful, because it is more complex, even turgid, is her characterization: "But Joseph had more than 'second sight,' which is commonplace among professional magicians. At an early age he had what only the most gifted revivalist preachers could boast of—the talent for making men see visions" (74).

A final literary device of which Brodie avails herself frequently is that of the periodic sentence. It heightens the structural interest by throwing the main emphasis to the end of the sentence, thereby requiring the reader to suspend the meaning in his or her mind until its end. A sentence that achieves periodicity with simple inversion is "Lovejoy's martyrdom Joseph Smith did not savor" (212). Here the direct object precedes the subject and the verb. A more complex example uses the paired correlatives "not only . . . but also": "they [the Danites] would not only defend the Saints against aggression from the old settlers, but also act as a bodyguard for the presidency and as a secret police for ferreting out dissenters" (213).

A notable paragraph, opening the chapter on Joseph Smith's escape to Kirtland, combines inversion, parallelism, and periodicity:

> Poverty Joseph had borne before; tarring and beating he had turned to advantage. [These two sentences are inverted.] But to be exiled by his own disciples and driven from the temple in which he had been intoxicated with visions and glory killed much of his tenderness and naive exuberance. [Here there is a compound infinitive acting as the subject, each infinitive being modified by its own prepositional phrase and a long clause, all of which collects and collapses upon the monosyllabic "killed" before continuing with a compound prepositional phrase.] In flight from Kirtland, Joseph reflected sorrowfully that at last he had the measure of his men's devotion, and it went no deeper than their pockets. [This is a periodic sentence.] (208)

All of these literary devices are noteworthy in their impact—but not because they are unusual or unconventional. It would easily be possible to make a collection of expressions, metaphors, and similes from *No Man Knows My History* that would plead guilty to a charge of triteness. Brodie is not exceptionally inventive. Her achievement, as categorized in this section of the essay, has been the skillful but not exceptional use of standard literary techniques of any educated writer or widely read person fifty years ago. Brodie was the widely read and very bright granddaughter of a university president. She graduated from high school at fourteen, with highest honors from the University of

Utah at eighteen, and with a master's degree in English from the University of Chicago at age twenty.[7] It is not strange that she could draw on eight hundred years of poetic devices and formal prose in English—even more if one includes the continental and Latin traditions. I argue that the result is, Fog Index notwithstanding, an absorbing, easily comprehensible narrative.

Scene Structure

Certainly, not the least of Brodie's advantages in choosing Joseph Smith for her subject is the close match between the shape of his life and that of classic tragic narrative. The hero, born in obscurity, rises to prominence through a combination of natural gifts and a confluence of environmental factors in which those gifts can flourish. His career takes the typically American form of empire-building and creating new syntheses of political, social, familial, and ecclesiastical visions. His personal gifts are precisely those factors that decree his downfall, and he dies spectacularly, assassinated in the prime of his life. The very shape of this life leads to a catharsis of pity and terror, exaltation and doom.

Within this general structure, Brodie works to create a fast-paced narrative that keeps the reader turning pages. Three of her techniques for sustaining rhythm are (1) passages of contexting which provide a significant background against which Joseph Smith's actions take on meaning, (2) dramatic vignettes at crucial scenes, and (3) vivid pen sketches of important characters.

Contexting

One of Brodie's skills is that of contexting, sketching in a national background against which the decisions and actions of Joseph Smith acquire new meaning. For example, in a remarkably concise paragraph which provides both scriptural and international background for Joseph Smith's communitarian experiment in Kirtland, she states:

> According to the Acts of the apostles, the disciples of Christ "had all things common; and sold their possessions and goods and parted them to all men as every man had need." Never in American history was this scriptural passage so influential as in the second quarter of the nineteenth century. Scores of communal societies sprang up over the country, religious, non-religious, celibate, and free-love. The Shakers were communists, as were the followers of Jemima Wilkinson. When Joseph Smith first rode into the Susquehanna Valley to find the silver mine for Josiah Stowell, he went into the province where Coleridge, Southey, and Wordsworth had planned to found Pantisocracy and where the German Harmonists, led by George Rapp, were building Economy on the banks of the Ohio. (104–5)

Brodie then draws a more extended and careful comparison between Robert Owen's New Harmony—with which, she says, Sidney Rigdon was familiar—and the beginnings of Joseph Smith's communitarian thought. This discussion then provides the foundation, and a mental counterpoint, to the history of the United Order that she offers.

Dramatic Vignettes

With a nice sense of timing and rhythm, Brodie alternates between summary passages of narrative history and dramatic vignettes. We can compare these to a film presenting footage of still photographs while a voice-over narrator dispassionately explains history, background, character, and motives. Then a still photograph comes alive, and the carefully posed actors move, speak, gesticulate, and engage each other. It is a rhythm of posed tableaux and vivid vignette. For example, Brodie employs this technique when she is describing Joseph Smith's failed bid to seize control of the Kirtland dissension once he returns from Missouri in December 1837. She telescopes much of the action of the summer, fall, and early winter, including a schism, a flood of lawsuits, a fracas in the temple, and an attempt to seize the print-ing press and copies of the Book of Mormon.

Joseph Smith, overestimating his strength, called for a "public trial in the temple," which he approached with resolu-tion and determination. It was a strategic error, in Brodie's view, that the half-crazed Sidney Rigdon was allowed to speak, denouncing the dissenters in a "savagely obscene attack." Then in two paragraphs, she moves the reader inside the temple at the very end of Rigdon's speech that "stunned the Saints."

> He let himself be helped down the long aisle to the entrance, and the congregation sat in silence while the temple doors closed behind him.
>
> There followed a bitter fight, as charges and counter-charges were hurled back and forth. Joseph com-pletely lost control. Shouting above the din, he called for an end to debate and a vote on the excommunications. "Yes," yelled a dissenter, "you would cut a man's head off and hear him afterward!" The meeting finally broke up, and Joseph left the temple conscious that he had lost, probably forever, what had been seven years in building. (207)

The literary effect of this technique is to maintain the fast pace of the narrative, with the reader pausing for summary and analy-sis, then engaging directly with the text by focusing on a vivid vignette. It is not, however, a convention of historical writing, and Robert B. Flanders disapprovingly characterized Brodie's style as "a popularized journalistic writing style, with an abun-dance of blood, sex, and sin."[8]

Quick Characterizations

A third device Brodie uses in setting scenes for the action is a quick characterization through a few vivid adjectives or a sketched-in scene. The pages are peopled with such fast-glimpsed individuals as "big sloping-shouldered Heber Kimball" (204), "half-sick" Sidney Rigdon finding "unexpected reserves of energy and vitriol" (206), Martin Harris, a "round-faced, slightly bearded man whose sad, empty eyes betrayed something of his credulous nature" (50), and "the petulant and humorless Sylvester Smith" (150).

"Young Porter Rockwell," as Brodie calls him, is never a major figure, nor does she allow him to dominate the narrative even when his actions are turning points as, for instance, they are in the attempted assassination of Lilburn Boggs. She characterizes him by his "fabulous skill with a gun and the fierceness of his love for Joseph." He had "tagged the prophet ever since his early conversion in New York State," she says, "appointed himself a guardian and hung about the jail like a shaggy and dangerous watchdog." He had "the face of a mastiff and the strength of a bear" and was "a jocose and amiable companion" (250). In other words, he was animal-like, half-human, elemental. The suggestion of danger accords with the animal imagery. His skill with a gun, which is asserted but not described, also has a magical quality to it. In such a context, the trait of "fierce loyalty" to Joseph Smith becomes a trait belonging to a subhuman species. This description evokes the powerful and loyal but inarticulate and animalistic companions of mythic heroes and demi-gods.

A valid question might be how firmly Brodie based these descriptions and characterizations on reality. Some of them seem unlikely or impossible for a twentieth-century writer to be able to defend as accurate characterization, given the lack of photographs before the mid-1840s or the level of detail provided by Brodie but not in primary sources. However, no one can challenge their vigor and vividness.

Tone

Brodie's generous use of irony makes the tone of the book a sometimes uncomfortable experience for readers who accept the spiritual heroism of the Mormon saga. And her skill in the use of irony varies greatly throughout the volume, verging on downright sarcasm sometimes, as when she comments on Moroni's 1823 night visit: "Three times that night the spirit appeared, as angels are wont to do, for, to be authentic, celestial truth must be thrice repeated" (39). This labored identification of Joseph Smith's record with fairy-tale motifs is, I suggest, Brodie's own effort to dissociate herself from belief.

Similarly, in reporting the testimony of the eight witnesses, she writes, "It will be seen that four witnesses were Whitmers and three were members of Joseph's own family. The eighth witness, Hiram Page, had married a Whitmer daughter." Brodie then finds herself unable to resist quoting the already tired jest of Mark Twain: "I could not feel more satisfied and at rest if the entire Whitmer family had testified" (79). Again, she seems to be taking pains to underscore her own skepticism about the claims of the witnesses.

In contrast, she deftly utilizes a finer irony to describe "the professionally righteous citizens of Palmyra" who persuaded the printer to abandon the Book of Mormon (80) and uses understatement to characterize Joseph Smith, during the development of polygamy: "He obviously emerged from his intensive study of Genesis with considerable detachment concerning the holiness of monogamy" (184). Similarly, restraint and understatement make witty this ironic description of Thomas Dick's influence on Joseph Smith: "Dick's whole work made a lasting impression on Joseph, whose open-mindedness, stemming no doubt from the insubstantial character of his religious credo, was unique among ministers of the gospel" (271–72).

Such passages underscore the tension of Brodie's relationship with Joseph Smith. She does not dismiss him, but she consistently diminishes him through such devices as irony and consistently maintains an authorial and ironic distance from him, even when she uses other devices to engage the reader. The result is a fast-paced and highly polished narrative.

Reader Identification

The most complicated of all the literary devices Fawn Brodie uses in her narrative of Joseph Smith's life is the identification she creates in the reader with various characters throughout the biography.

As we have already seen, Brodie has a gift for creating short but vivid portraits of characters. Some of these characters are relatively unimportant to the unfolding narrative, but some play crucial roles, not only to the action but also as foils to Joseph Smith. In such cases, they play the important function of fixing the focus of the reader's emotional attention and letting him or her live the scene through the reactions and responses of the individual portrayed. The result is an internal running commentary on the developing character of Joseph Smith. The reader continually asks, "Would I have reacted the same way? Would I have accepted this revelation, this behavior, this treatment from Joseph Smith as characteristic of a prophet? Would this have been confirmation of his divine mission or the last straw?"

For example, when John Cook Bennett becomes Joseph Smith's "most intimate friend," Brodie distances and shapes the reader's reaction by observing: Bennett was "showered with favors that older converts, who had sacrificed fortune and health to the gospel, would have given much to share" (309). Bennett's opportunism and Smith's favoritism are felt with an emotional sting as the reader identifies, not with the successful Bennett nor the generous Smith, but with the faithful, long-time, self-sacrificing, and unappreciated converts.

As another example, in a shrill and vindictive quarrel between Sylvester Smith and Joseph Smith on the Zion's Camp march, Brodie unappealingly portrays Joseph as losing his temper, then retreating to a sort of whining self-justification when he is opposed. At this point, Brodie deliberately stops narrating the action and steps into the mind of Brigham Young, whom she positions as an onlooker to the unsavory quarrel:

What passed through Brigham Young's mind as his prophet backed down, one can only guess. His years of leadership lay ahead, stretching over endless wagon trails and across dusty plains. The man who was to bring thousands of wretched outcasts to the inhospitable mountains of the West and build a homeland there would not have yielded to a mutinous upstart. This lame retreat of Joseph's was weakness, boding no good for the company's discipline in the dangerous days ahead. Nevertheless, there was something in Joseph that made Brigham content to acknowledge himself the lesser man. (151)

This passage is an important revelation of Brodie's technique. In an extended and dramatic scene, she shows Joseph Smith as less than effective and far less than admirable, contrasts him with a man whose mythic proportions she accepts without the slightest ironic qualification and holds up before the reader with the same lack of reserve, then asks the reader, rather than dismissing Joseph Smith, to accept Brigham Young's evaluation of Smith as the greater man. Although she has judged Joseph Smith negatively, she refuses the temptation to discount and discard him as unworthy of serious attention. Brigham Young becomes a foil both to reveal Smith's weakness and confirm his greatness.

In contrast is the scene in which Joseph Smith, disheartened and frightened by the *Expositor* exposé, "soft-willed" and "empty of conviction" turns in "desperation" to William Marks. Normally, the reader might expect to identify with the beleaguered and vulnerable Smith. Instead, Brodie writes an uncharacteristically heavy-handed script, forcing the reader's identification with the much-betrayed Marks. She characterizes him as having "so faithfully" rescued Joseph from "past crises" with "his wisdom and liberal purse," then describes a detailed setting and dialogue:

They walked down the street together in the bright summer sunlight, turned into a little-used lane where they could talk in private, and sat down on the grassy bank.

"We are a ruined people," Joseph began.

"How so?" Marks asked guardedly, for he had so long kept a troubled silence that he no longer knew how to talk to his leader.

"This doctrine of polygamy . . . will prove our destruction and overthrow. I have been deceived; it is a curse to mankind, and we shall have to leave the United States soon, unless it can be put down, and its practice stopped in the Church."

The older man was ready to weep with gratitude. This was what he had been hoping to hear ever since he had seen the cursed revelation on polygamy almost a year before.

"Now Brother Marks," Joseph went on, "you have not received this doctrine, and I want you to go into the high council, and I will have charges preferred against all who practice this doctrine . . . and I will . . . preach against it with all my might, and in this way we will rid the Church of this damnable heresy."

But Joseph was only striking blindly for a way out of his dilemma, and the embarrassments of this particular solution must have made him discard it by sundown. (376)

Although Brodie acknowledges in her note that Marks's "account may be colored somewhat by his profound antipathy to polygamy," there is no question that it is the hopeful Marks, not the aimlessly flailing Smith, who should engage the reader's sympathies. This being so, it is strange that Brodie abandons Marks's point of view immediately. She does not give his response even to Smith's proposal, let alone his reaction to Smith's subsequent order to wreck the *Expositor*. In fact, Marks is not mentioned again in the history. Why, then, should she have seized on Marks's point of view for this brief scene? The reader may justifiably conclude that she did it to ensure that the reader would *not* identify with Joseph Smith.

Like the example of Zion's Camp and Brigham Young, this episode shows Joseph Smith at less than his best. Unlike Brigham Young's implied acknowledgment of Joseph Smith as the greater man, there is no attempt at balance. In fact, Brodie continues with a stinging indictment of Joseph Smith that employs no authorial mask at all: "He [Smith] was betrayed by his utter incapacity for dealing skillfully with opposition, a weakness that his political and legal successes in Nauvoo had served only to intensify. He had become an autocrat who could think only in terms of suppression" (377).

Perhaps the most important foil is Emma Smith. Fawn Brodie depicts her as an essentially static character, doomed to love a charismatic and exciting but unstable man. Brodie presents their courtship without psychological subtleness: Joseph is "very much in love with" Emma and she, for her part, is "skeptical, unsure of him, and concerned over their future" but also "wildly in love with him" (31–32). Brodie's description of both characters emphasizes both physical and psychological characteristics. Emma is "a dark, serious-faced girl with great luminous hazel eyes, . . . quiet almost to taciturnity, with an unapproachable air" (29). Joseph "was big, powerful, and by ordinary standards very handsome, except for his nose, which was aquiline and prominent. His large blue eyes were fringed by fantastically long lashes which made his gaze seem veiled and slightly mysterious. Emma was probably quick to notice what many of his followers later believed had a supernatural cause, that when he was speaking with intense feeling the blood drained from his face, leaving a frightening, almost luminous pallor." (There is, in fact, no recorded evidence that Emma noticed such a trait.) Although Brodie does not speculate on Joseph's attraction to Emma, except perhaps to suggest that he was challenged by her unapproachable air, Brodie takes the time to develop a motive for Emma: "However she may have disapproved of his money-digging, she must have had faith in his insight into mysteries that common folk could not fathom; she needed no one to tell her that here was no ordinary man" (32). Thus, the connection between Emma Hale's sensing of Joseph Smith's gifts and developing blind and blinding faith in him sets up a relationship into which the reader can read himself or herself. However ill-founded such an attraction may prove to be, Brodie establishes Joseph Smith's power to create such a magnetic pull.

Another passage in which the reader is supposed to identify with an attractive and beleaguered Emma Smith comes when a revelation commands Joseph to leave the farm. This revelation, opines Brodie, was meant

> for Emma Smith. Racked anew with doubt, chagrined by their poverty and frightened by the rancor that greeted her husband's preaching, she had been the first to urge him to go back to the soil. She had seen no plates and heard no voices. She had held out six weeks after the church was organized before she was baptized, and . . . had not been 'confirmed' an official member. Her parents' contempt, her neighbors' derision, and even the death of her child she had borne with fortitude. But the prospect of living off the dubious and intermittent charity of Joseph's followers was more than this proud girl could stomach. (89)

Probably most readers could identify sympathetically with Emma's misgivings, insecurities, and hardships. When Brodie suggests that Doctrine and Covenants 25 was a convenient revelation to answer Emma's protests, it is also a comment on Joseph Smith's unappealing state of mind. The resolution, however, seems glib and undeveloped: "Emma believed in him, and nothing else mattered" (90).

Emma's faith in and love for Joseph are again suggested as motives during the Fannie Alger incident. "The scandal was insufferable to Emma," says Brodie. She then undercuts the force of this sentence by admitting in the next paragraph that "there is no record of her anger except in the dubious gossip of neighbors." Emma was "passionately fond and jealous of her husband. She had, moreover, a keen sense of the propriety and dignity of his office, and must have been humiliated for the church itself" (182). Even in nineteenth-century frontier America, there were legal and social resources for a betrayed wife. Yet Brodie sketches no alternatives for Emma Smith. As Joseph's wife, Emma appears on stage when called for, to show the depth of Joseph Smith's perfidy, but then retires conveniently until the next set piece. She thus becomes a lightning rod for the reader's (presumed) personal indignation at Joseph Smith. This function is all the more pronounced because Brodie must frequently make up Emma's reaction out of guesses, lacking any reliable documentation.

During the 1843 eruption of polygamy in Nauvoo, Brodie shows Emma as keeping a home that looked like "harmony itself," thanks largely to "her serenity and poise." Brodie quotes Charlotte Haven who reported that, during a call, Emma, although reputed for her intelligence and benevolence, virtually ignored the callers because "her whole attention [was] absorbed in what Joseph was saying." In contrast, Joseph "talked incessantly about himself, what he had done and could do more than other mortals, and remarked that he was a giant, physically and mentally" (339–40). We already know that Emma is "bitter" over Joseph's plural wives, so the serene scene of the adoring wife hanging on her husband's words is an ironic one and the adoration is a sign of pathetic insecurity and emotional doting, not of marital bliss. And Haven's wry commentary on Joseph Smith's self-serving grandiloquence provides a convenient second layer of identification for the reader who has already, in the discussion on the previous pages, followed Brodie's evidence that Joseph talked one set of rules to his wife and lived by another. The reader's sense of identification with Emma's pathetic plight is deepened by Brodie's restrained comment: "Though [Emma] may have feared that there were others, she could not have dreamed how many" (339).

Emma's characterization is static and unchanging from first love to final view of Joseph's slain body. She is doomed by her passion for a man to whom she remained a first but not an only love. Yet such an explanation is neither satisfying nor persuasive.

Brodie sells Emma Smith short by making her a mere device through which the reader can join forces with the author in deploring Joseph Smith's behavior. She turns Emma into a stock character with only the self-sacrificing character of the Patient Griselda or the jealous and dangerous character of a Medea scorned available to her. Obviously, Emma is more; otherwise she could hardly have held the interest of the Joseph Smith created in Brodie's narrative through the decades of their marriage. One of the questions that must rise in the reader's mind is why Brodie, who created a supple, complex, and even complicated psychology for Joseph Smith, saw only the simplicities of adoration or outraged betrayal for Emma. Is it possible that for Brodie herself these were the only alternatives as she contemplated the founding prophet of her rejected religion?

Conclusion

The complex historical achievement of Fawn Brodie must rest on the assessment of historians: how accurately she used the sources available to her, how limited her history was by its sources, and the extent to which she transgressed beyond their boundaries in her conclusions. But her intuition also took her to frontiers that it has taken a full fifty years to explore and where, upon exploration, that intuition has often proved astonishingly correct.

Our question here is the more limited but equally important one of the impact of style on content and on credibility. Many historians could learn a great deal from studying Brodie's writing techniques. The use of such techniques as parallelism, alliteration, stop-action contexting, allusions, foreshadowing, periodic sentences, inversion, and parallelism would provide color and sophistication to the work of anyone who learned to use them with the sophistication and skill of Fawn Brodie. All of the literary devices catalogued and demonstrated in this essay, most of them skillfully used, confirm Brodie's ability to unfold a narrative swiftly and effectively.

Nearly all of them, however, are the tools of *fictional* effect. And it is in tone, characterization, motivation, and the creation of literary foils that Brodie's work becomes simultaneously more literary and also more problematic. So noted a literary critic as Edward A. Geary has suggested that *No Man Knows My History* "perhaps should be read as a novel"; Eugene England ascribed to it "more the strengths of a novel than of biography"; and Brodie's contemporary Vardis Fisher called the book "almost more a novel than a biography," predicted that "she will turn novelist in her next book," and even wished "that she should."[9] I argue that to the extent Brodie's tools of tone, motive, and characterization are successful as literary devices, they simultaneously undercut the historical effect. The acerbic unnamed author of an extensive *Church News* review of *No Man Knows My History* made exactly this same point in 1945: "It is easy to grant the author the merit of a fine literary style throughout which makes the book altogether enticing reading. But it is the style of the novelist and not of the historian."[10]

Why should this be so? The answer is closely connected to the point with which we began: the trustworthiness of the relationship that the author establishes with the reader. These devices are not to be condemned out of hand, simply because novelists use them. Rather, we must ask: Are they persuasive? Is the relationship with the reader, as ultimately established through these stylistic devices, a trustworthy one?

Answering that question takes us into the psyche of Fawn Brodie, a journey surely as fraught with peril as her own excursion into the psyche of Joseph Smith and to conclusions that can be phrased only with the utmost tentativeness.

One of the most dramatic scenes comes at the point in the narrative in which the *Expositor* publishes its exposé of Nauvoo polygamy. Part of this scene involves the interview between Joseph Smith and William Marks already described. Brodie prefaces that conversation with a passage of analysis in which she calls the *Expositor*'s publication "the gravest crisis of [Joseph's] life," and one in which he lost his nerve. She hypothesizes that if Joseph Smith had told the truth and had gone to the platform in the unfinished temple and read the revelation on plural marriage to his church with his old magnificent assurance, he might have stripped the apostates of their chief weapon and freed his loyal followers from a burden of secrecy, evasion, and lying that was rapidly becoming intolerable. . . .

But . . . the crisis found him soft-willed. He was empty of conviction when he needed it most. (376)

This kind of hypothetical action—what Smith might have done or should have done—may simply be a kind of objective sorting through of options, a luxury for a historian with the advantage of hindsight. But in Brodie's hands, it also becomes a kind of condemnation of Smith, an analysis of his personality and morality. Is such judgment fair? And is it even accurate? Granted, historians fifty years ago may have felt perhaps less ambiguously than modern historians that judgment was a professional prerogative; but surely it is apparent even to the most cursory reader that Brodie has no objective evidence that Joseph Smith would, in fact, have been able to rally his followers if he had staged the scene she hypothesizes.

As another example, Brodie quotes Thomas Ford's explanation of suggestibility and group delusion induced by "fanatical" and protracted spiritual exercises to account for how the eight witnesses saw the gold plates. She herself is uneasy with the explanation and hypothesizes instead "some kind of makeshift deception" (80). Then in a crucial paragraph, she shifts the grounds of the argument: "Exactly how Joseph Smith persuaded so many of the reality of the golden plates is neither so important nor so baffling as the effect of this success on Joseph himself. It could have made of him a precocious and hard-boiled cynic. . . . But there is no evidence of cynicism even in Joseph's most intimate diary entries" (80). At this point, of course, Brodie could have provided an obvious (and even more cynical) reason for Smith's lack of evident cynicism. She does not. Instead, she continues: "The miracles and visions among his followers apparently served only to heighten his growing consciousness of supernatural power. He had a sublime faith in his star, plus the enthusiasm of a man constantly preoccupied with a single subject, and he was rapidly acquiring the language and even the accent of sincere faith" (80). How is it possible to create sincere faith out of psychological starshine and single-focused preoccupation? It is not—at least not if "faith" represents anything more than an internal mood. Brodie tellingly describes Joseph Smith as having "sublime faith in his star," an ironic allusion to the discredited classical notion of astrology. A deluded fanatic might have such a faith. But "the language and accent of sincere faith" cannot be acquired by a charlatan. They can only be manifestations of Joseph Smith's own developing awareness of a special relationship with God. Has Brodie here neglected to supply herself and the reader with a convenient foil by which the reader can see this sincere but misguided faith from an ironic perspective? Or has she allowed the possibility, unintentionally ironic, that the Mormon prophet was actuated by sincere faith? I suspect the latter.

Such passages are rare. For the most part, Brodie maintains an ironic disengagement through her use of literary devices, including how frequently a minor character in a scene will bear the emotional burden of the reading for and with the reader. Yet the very fact that disengagement is such an issue to Brodie raises the question of why it is so important that she maintain such a distance. There are many ways in which she seems too eager to urge her reader to regard Joseph Smith with ironic distance and a striking number of ways in which she insists perhaps too vehemently on her own superior sophistication. Take, for example, the achievement of ironic distance in the following description of what orthodox Mormons call eternal progression or the possibility of achieving godhood:

> Converts reared on a diet of harps and angels found this [Mormon] heaven exciting. To those infected with the prodigious optimism and enthusiasm of America, it seemed only reasonable that there need be no end to the

explorations of the human spirit. To men who loved their wives, it was pleasant to hear that death was no separation, and to men who did not, it was gratifying to hear that there could be no sin in taking another. To every man in love with life—with the tantalizing richness of learning, the sweaty satisfaction of hard work, the luxury of sensual pleasure—Joseph's heaven had profound meaning. (300)

In some respects, this paragraph consisting of elegantly turned phrases and exquisitely parallel constructions is consciously cynical in a way that shows its early post–World War II time of writing. Terms like "a diet of harps and angels" and the use of "infected" are both dismissive, even patronizing. Yet the qualities that she thus dismisses cannot be so lightly demeaned: the "prodigious optimism and enthusiasm of America" had unquestionably, however naively, won a major world war; and in the last sentence, there is no irony at all in the catalog of loves which shape a life. "The tantalizing richness of learning, the sweaty satisfaction of hard work, the luxury of sensual pleasure" not only give Joseph's heaven "profound meaning" but are the very qualities that give life on earth its meaning as well. The fact that this paragraph launches a discussion of Joseph Smith's polygamy is, for the moment, beside the point. Here, Brodie salutes an achievement and, I suspect, a regretted lost belief.

There may be fitting irony in applying to Brodie's monumental achievement the characterization which she made of Joseph Smith's own literary efforts. He "always dictated his journal," she observes, "with an intense consciousness of his audience" and his reconstruction of his past—like Brodie's reconstruction of that same past—"became . . . an almost impenetrable hiding-place, where he concealed himself behind a perpetual flow of words" (275).

Brodie also, in her disclosure of her view of Joseph Smith has created a flow of words through which she has simultaneously both concealed and revealed a complicated history about her complicated relationship to her childhood faith.

Notes

1. Dale Morgan, letter to F. M. Brodie, August 28, 1944. Photocopy in my possession courtesy of Newell G. Bringhurst; partially quoted in Bringhurst, "Fawn M. Brodie, 'Mormondom's Lost Generation,' and *No Man Knows My History*," *Journal of Mormon History* 16 (1990): 17.

2. Comment reproduced on the front cover of Fawn M. Brodie, *No Man Knows My History: The Life of Joseph Smith*, 2nd ed., rev. and enl. (New York: Alfred A. Knopf, 1971, printing of 1990). All other quotations from Brodie, unless otherwise noted, come from this edition and are cited parenthetically in the text.

3. As quoted in Newell G. Bringhurst, "Applause, Attack, and Ambivalence— Varied Responses to Fawn M. Brodie's *No Man Knows My History*," *Utah Historical Quarterly* 57, no. 1 (winter 1989): 48, reprinted in this volume.

4. As quoted in Bringhurst, "Applause, Attack, and Ambivalence," 57. Bernard DeVoto, who reviewed *No Man Knows My History* for the *New York Herald Tribune Book Review*, December 16, 1945, Section 7, p. 1, does not comment on Brodie's writing style except to call the book "brilliant," which may or may not refer to its literary aspects. He does, however, challenge her sharply for endowing the Book of Mormon with, as he puts it, "an integrated carefully wrought structure and subtle, eloquent and moving English style." On the contrary, he asserts pungently, "the gold Bible has neither form nor structure of any kind, its imagination is worse than commonplace, it is squalid, and the prose is lethal."

5. Leonard J. Arrington, "Scholarly Studies of Mormonism in the Twentieth Century," *Dialogue: A Journal of Mormon Thought* 1 (spring 1996): 24. He also expressed serious misgivings about her methodology.

6. D. Michael Quinn, *The Mormon Hierarchy: Origins of Power* (Salt Lake City: Signature Books, 1994), 271, n. 18, while acknowledging Brodie's "erudition . . . and insights," comments that her biography "is flawed by its inattention to crucial archival materials and by her penchant for filtering evidence and analysis through the perspective that the Mormon prophet was either a 'parapath' who believed his own lies or a fraud." Davis Bitton, "Mormon Biography," *Biography: An Interdisciplinary Quarterly* 4, no. 1 (winter 1981): 4. He then sharply critiqued Brodie's methodological weaknesses.

7. Bringhurst, "Applause, Attack, and Ambivalence," 47.

8. Robert B. Flanders, "Writing the Mormon Past," *Dialogue: A Journal of Mormon Thought* 1 (autumn 1966): 58.

9. Edward A. Geary, "Mormondom's Lost Generation: The Novelists of the 1940s," *BYU Studies* 18 (fall 1977): 90; Eugene England, "Introduction: Another View of the Garden," in *Tending the Garden: Essays on Mormon*

Literature, ed. Eugene England and Lavina Fielding Anderson (Salt Lake City: Signature Books, forthcoming); Vardis Fisher, "Mormonism and Its Yankee Prophet," *New York Times*, Book Review Section, November 25, 1945, p. 5. Photocopy in my possession courtesy of Newell Bringhurst.
Appraisal of the So-Called Brodie Book, (pamphlet) reprinted from the *Church News*, May 11, 1945 (Salt Lake City: Church of Jesus Christ of Latter-day Saints, 1945), n.p. Bringhurst, "Applause, Attack, and Ambivalence," 50, establishes the authorship of this pamphlet as a committee "of which Apostle Albert E. Bowen was apparently the principal author." The pamphlet continues by cataloging and critiquing her "fictional style" (primarily her willingness to ascribe motives to a character but also such metaphors as "Harris hung around . . . like a begging spaniel") then charging, "These and innumerable other conjectures and flippancies wholly out of character with sincere historical study, and non-existent outside her own imaginative creation, she splashes around in her narrative for the sake of atmosphere." The pamphlet then quotes an extensive passage from an unidentified reviewer who characterizes the biography as having "the pace and sweep, the bizarre incidents, and compelling suspense of the most extravagant historical novel." Interestingly enough, Dale Morgan had candidly warned Brodie in his August 1944 critique that her overgeneralizations would make her an easy mark for Mormons who would be going "over it with a fine tooth-comb [*sic*] looking for ways to discredit you." To clinch his example, he cited the "astonishing number of Mormons" who "took comfort in pointing out [Vardis] Fisher's error [in *Children of God*] in stating that the company brought to America by Lehi was a part of the lost tribes. The fact that this was an utterly irrelevant element of Fisher's larger story made no difference at all. ('Oh, it's full of errors. Why, Fisher is so uninformed about Mormon history that he even thinks the Nephites and Lamanites descended from the Lost Tribes.') . . . And this was merely a novel, mind you." Morgan, letter to Brodie, August 28, 1944, p. 2.

6

———⟨✦⟩———

Fawn Brodie on Joseph Smith's Plural Wives and Polygamy

A Critical View

TODD COMPTON

Anyone who sets out to seriously study Joseph Smith's polygamous marriages must use the appendix to Fawn Brodie's *No Man Knows My History* as a starting point.[1] This appendix is a pioneering work; before Brodie, few had studied Smith's polygamy on a scholarly level. Nevertheless, the discerning reader will use this appendix only with great caution. As is the case with many pioneers, Brodie made significant mistakes in her first survey and evaluation, both on the evidential and theoretical levels of her scholarship.

We should first emphasize Brodie's positive contributions to the study of Joseph Smith Jr.'s polygamy. She is the only scholar who has published a footnoted list of Joseph Smith's wives with small biographies of the women involved. Donna Hill, in her biography, *Joseph Smith the First Mormon*, did not provide a replacement list. Conservative scholar Danel Bachman, in his master's thesis, "A Study of the Practice of Plural Marriage before the Death of Joseph Smith," actually borrowed Brodie's list even though he was critical of it. When one considers the importance of Joseph Smith in Latter-day Saint religion and the importance of polygamy in his thought, this lacuna is surprising. So, whatever the limitations of Brodie's work, it at least looked at Joseph Smith's polygamy in a scholarly context and treated his plural wives as an important part of his story. Some scholars who might have dealt with this subject in more depth did not, for whatever reasons.

Furthermore, Brodie was a psychohistorian, interested in documenting and evaluating Joseph Smith's sexuality. Here she was pathbreaking, and was entirely justified in looking at her subject's sexual life. Sexuality is an important dimension in anyone's psyche, and to write adult, mature biography, one must feel free to treat that area, difficult as it is to document adequately and write insightfully about. The opposite extreme is ludicrously Victorian, hagiographic history; one thinks of modern devotional biographies of Brigham Young that do not find it necessary to mention that he was a polygamist.

One might also mention more general strengths in Brodie's writing—her undeniable gifts for stylistic grace and narrative power, for instance—although they are not directly relevant to the subject of this essay.

Evaluating the Brodie Method: Evidence

In 1945, Wilford Poulson, another member of Mormonism's "lost generation," wrote to Brodie, in a critique of *No Man Knows My History*, "I had hoped that you would bring to bear the appropriate canons of historical criticism upon your sources."[2] A striking aspect of Brodie's appendix on Joseph Smith's wives is her frequent use of printed anti-Mormon sources, which she often cited as if they were authoritative. However, every source in Mormon history, pro-Mormon or anti-Mormon, must be viewed skeptically and must be submitted to searching critical judgment. One must ask whether the source is first hand or second hand; whether the writer was present at important events or was close to people who were; when it was written; when it was published (the earliest source generally being most reliable, of course, although not always); whether the source is public or private (private being sometimes more reliable); whether the source blatantly contradicts another source; whether it seems extreme in tone, positively or negatively. One receives the impression, in reading Brodie's treatments of Joseph Smith's polygamy, that she did not ask these questions sufficiently of her antagonistic evidence. She almost seems to accept such evidence as unquestioningly as conservative Mormons accept hagiographic idealized Mormon history.[3]

Furthermore, in emphasizing such sources, Brodie primarily used printed materials rather than diaries and autobiographies. Diaries are especially valuable because they are usually first hand, written on the day of the event in question, and private. The contrast with Juanita Brooks is striking: Brooks edited at least three major Mormon journals and collected and studied journals throughout her life. A partial explanation for this contrast lies in the fact that early in her career, Brodie left Salt Lake City, where she might have done more research in Utah libraries, the location of most Mormon diaries. In addition, Newell Bringhurst's essay in this volume discusses in detail why she did not make more use of primary source documents in the LDS Church Historical Department.[4] It is ironic that the church's policy of limiting access to key historical documents probably influenced Brodie to rely more fully on antagonistic sources. But Brodie's residence history (living outside of Utah) was also a factor in this issue, as was the cast of her mind. Whatever the reasons, she frequently used sources biased against Mormonism, which were not first hand, and were often extreme and unreliable.

For example, Brodie quoted the following passage from William Hall's *The Abominations of Mormonism Exposed*, a source containing major factual errors: "A Mr. Henry Jacobs had his wife seduced by Joe Smith, in his time, during a mission to England. She was a very beautiful woman, but when Jacobs returned, he found her pregnant by Smith. Jacobs put up with the insult, and still lived with her."[5] This statement makes allegations that should be subjected to careful critical scrutiny. In fact, Joseph Smith did not seduce Zina Huntington Jacobs while Jacobs served a mission to England. Joseph Smith died in 1844, and Jacobs did not leave on his English mission until May 31, 1846, when he received his call;[6] he returned to Winter Quarters on November 12, 1847. Thus, the second part of the story, suggesting that Jacobs had returned home to find Zina pregnant by Smith, but continued to live with her despite that, is also completely erroneous. Henry's mission to England is documented in its entirety by Zina Huntington's brother, Oliver, who recorded it day by day in his extensive diaries, and Brodie had access to the Oliver Huntington diaries, as she cited them frequently.[7]

A similar quotation includes two factual errors that Brodie could have checked and corrected. John D. Lee, in his autobiography, wrote, "It was now June, 1842. In the summer and fall I built me a two-story brick house on Warsaw street, and made my family comfortable. . . . I then took a tour down through Illinois. H. B. Jacobs accompanied me as a fellow companion on the way. Jacobs was bragging about his wife and two children, what a true, virtuous, lovely woman she was. He almost worshiped her. Little did he think that in his absence she was sealed to the Prophet Joseph."[8]

First, Zina had been married to Joseph on October 27, 1841, so did not marry him when Lee and Jacobs were on their mission; Brodie had this date. Second, Zina only had one child, not two, at the time of Lee's mission. Brodie might have pointed this out, or dropped the quote, or she might have used other, more reliable sources to make her point. Certainly, Zina Huntington Jacobs had married Joseph Smith polyandrously; but this can be shown responsibly and clearly from affidavits and diaries (including the Oliver Huntington diary).

A third example of Brodie's use of questionable sources occurs when she treats Joseph Smith's tar and feathering in March 1832. She writes, "It is said that Eli Johnson demanded that the prophet be castrated, for he suspected Joseph of being too intimate with his sister, Nancy Marinda." The doctor brought along to perform the castration demurred, and so, writes Brodie, "Johnson had to be content with seeing the prophet beaten senseless."[9] In evaluating such a tradition, one must ask if the source is late or early, written by a witness or a person with access to a witness, if it is sympathetic or unsympathetic. In fact, it is a late, printed source, Clark Braden, published in 1884.[10] Braden is non-Mormon, unsympathetic; in fact, he introduces this story in a public debate with an RLDS antagonist. There is no mention of his source.

These are all danger signals that should have caused the historian to look at the tradition with a healthy dose of skepticism. And, in fact, in checking the story, we discover that it contains one major factual error: Marinda Johnson had no brother named Eli. An Eli Johnson was present, but he was not Marinda's brother. Another late source suggests that brothers of Marinda were in the mob but gives an entirely different motivation for the mobbing, an economic reason. Marinda's brother, Luke, tells us that a doctor was brought along to castrate Joseph, but he says nothing about any Johnson brother being present. Other sources give us different mob leaders, the apostate Mormons Ezra Booth and Simonds Ryder, and no other sources give the motivation that Braden gives.[11] This is not the place to sort out all of these traditions; but this passage shows that Brodie placed a great deal of reliance on a flawed source with a major factual error.

The Theological Development of Plural Marriage

In writing her biography of Joseph Smith, it was necessary for a historian like Brodie with an interest in psychology to consider Smith's marriages and sexuality, and she opened the discussion, on a scholarly level, in Mormon historiography. Nevertheless, she has been justly criticized as overemphasizing sexuality and arguing beyond solid evidence, both in *No Man Knows My History* and in her Jefferson biography.[12] Brodie interprets Smith's polygamy as derived entirely or chiefly from his pronounced sexual appetites; while sexual/romantic attraction must certainly be accepted as part of his motivations, to view Smith's sexuality as his only motivation is reductionist.

Brodie begins her discussion of Joseph Smith's Nauvoo polygamy by writing that monogamy seemed to Smith "an intolerably circumscribed way of life," then supports this by a second-hand quotation alleging his weakness for pretty women.[13] Then, she writes, Joseph Smith, because of his Puritan nature, "erected a stupendous theological edifice to support his new theories on marriage." (Notice the ironic hyperbole of "stupendous.") She proceeds to explain the "edifice" of Smith's Nauvoo theology. So although she does not deny the theology, she sees it as an afterthought that Smith developed to support his sensual leanings. This could be linked to Brodie's interpretation of Joseph Smith as charlatan, using religion opportunistically for unscrupulous purposes.[14]

Marvin Hill, in two important articles, Danel Bachman, in his previously mentioned thesis, and Lawrence Foster, in his *Religion and Sexuality*, have criticized Brodie for this interpretation of the origin of polygamy. Hill argues that Joseph Smith's writings reflect a sincerely religious man.[15] He writes, "With regard to plural marriage, where Brodie is so confident that the real Joseph Smith, the pleasure lover and sensualist, shows through, there is no evidence in his writings to suggest that he thought of it in other than religious terms."[16] Bachman has shown convincingly how Smith's polygamy revelations began early in the New York period of Mormon history and so precede his actual practice of polygamy. In his view, "the tenets of [plural] marriage emerged from a primarily religious context" including "Smith's work on the revision of the Bible, [and] his intense Old Testament biblicism." Bachman dates Joseph Smith's earliest significant revelations on polygamy to February 1831, years before he took his first well-documented plural wife, Fanny Alger, probably in 1833.[17] The first reference to polygamy in Mormon writing, however, is Jacob 2:30 in the *Book of Mormon*, published in 1830, dictated from 1827 to 1829, which suggests that polygamy may be practiced under certain conditions, when God commands, although unauthorized polygamy is forbidden. Thus, Bachman argues, Brodie's view of Joseph Smith's polygamy theology as a late rationalization for his sensual leanings is inadequate; Smith developed his plural marriage theology very early in the history of the Mormon church. Polygamy was, in fact, a viable restorationist doctrine, fitting neatly into the milieu of the Christian/Biblical primitivism that cradled Mormonism. And there is a Protestant tradition of "restoring" polygamy long before Joseph Smith.[18] If it was in the Bible, restorationists would logically want to restore it. A purely sexual explanation for Joseph Smith's interest in polygamy does not do justice to the complexity of Joseph Smith's personality or milieu.[19]

Good evidence supports the view that important theological impulses—Joseph Smith's biblicism and his Christian primitivism—drove his development of polygamy, not merely his sexual libido. One may argue chicken and egg here—either that the sexuality caused the theological explorations toward polygamy or that the interest in Old Testament, restorationist polygamy caused the polygamous sexuality—but it was not a matter of sexuality alone. With Brodie, the emphasis was almost entirely on sexuality.

Fanny Alger as the First Plural Wife

In keeping with this perspective, Brodie, followed by other scholars, characterized Smith's pre-Nauvoo relationships with women as non-marriages, carried on in an atmosphere of "extreme informality." She treated his first well-documented relationship with a woman outside of his first marriage—Fanny Alger, in Kirtland—as an affair, not as a marriage. This harmonized with her theory of Joseph Smith as sensualist for whom the formal marriage ceremony was unnecessary and perhaps nonexistent at this early time.[20] Certainly, some quotations from unsympathetic sources can be used to support her interpretation, including the estranged Oliver Cowdery, who in 1838 referred to "a dirty, nasty, filthy affair of his [Joseph Smith's] and Fanny Alger's."[21] But any student of rhetoric will agree that Cowdery's accusation is couched in extremist language. Other evidence suggests that Smith's early marriages were poorly documented but were nevertheless marriages. Smith had had his polygamy theology since at least the 1830–31 period, as we have seen; it seems doubtful that he would have dangerous affairs when he could have marriages. Polygamous marriages, illegal and esoteric though they were, would be much safer than affairs.[22] Even the theory of Joseph Smith as charlatan could logically include him solemnizing his relationships with women at a very early time. Furthermore, the 1835 statement on marriage published in the first *Doctrine and Covenants* proves conclusively that the Mormons were being accused of "polygamy" at that time. Richard Van Wagoner makes the attractive suggestion that this document was produced to defuse problems caused by the Smith-Alger relationship.[23] Early polygamy insider Benjamin Johnson explicitly referred to Fanny Alger as Joseph's first plural wife.[24] Brodie brushes this sympathetic witness aside; and she ignores two unsympathetic writers, Ann Eliza Webb Young, in her 1876 book *Wife Number 19*, and Chauncey Webb, quoted in Wilhelm Wyl's 1886 exposé *Mormon Portraits*, who both referred to the Alger relationship as a "sealing."[25]

An undeservedly neglected autobiography by Mosiah Hancock, a son of Fanny's uncle, Levi Hancock, explicitly documents a marriage ceremony between Joseph and Fanny, performed by Levi. Mosiah wrote, "Father goes to Fanny and said 'Fanny Brother Joseph the Prophet loves you and wishes you for a wife will you be his wife?' 'I will Levi' Said She—Father takes Fanny to Joseph and said 'Brother Joseph I have been successful in my mission'—Father gave her to Joseph repeating the Ceremony as Joseph repeated [it] to him."[26] If this document preserves a reliable tradition from Levi Hancock, it shows that Brodie's interpretation of the Fanny Alger-Joseph Smith relationship as a casual, informal sexual liaison, rather than as a polygamous marriage, must be discarded. Here we have a formal marriage ceremony, performed by a third party. Joseph Smith's proposal through an uncle of the intended is also an interesting

formal element and entirely in keeping with Smith's polygamous practice during the Nauvoo period.[27]

Dynasticism

D. Michael Quinn, in his 1976 dissertation, "The Mormon Hierarchy, 1832–1932: An American Elite," and Danel Bachman, in
his previously mentioned thesis, have demonstrated another
major, non-sexual motivation for Joseph Smith's polygamy:
dynasticism.[28] Using polygamy, Smith could link important
church leaders to himself, which would bring earthly and eschatological benefits both to him and to the church leaders. On an
earthly level, marrying a man's daughter has throughout history
created a political bond between two men. Virtually all of
Roman history will illustrate this: political alliances, *amicitiae*,
were often sealed by marriages.[29] On an eschatological level,
those who "married into" Smith's eternal family believed that
they had been given a promise of fuller exaltation and salvation.
Smith, on the other hand, by his theology of salvation through
familial quantity,[30] furthered his own exaltation. The classic
example is Joseph marrying Heber C. Kimball's daughter, Helen
Mar. She wrote about her father: "Having a great desire to be
connected with the Prophet Joseph . . . [he] offered me to him."[31]
Here we see polygamy being used to link the president of the
church to an important apostle. Helen Mar's son also wrote of
the marriage in dynastic terms: "Soon after . . . a golden link was
forged whereby the houses of Heber and Joseph were indissolubly
and forever joined. Helen Mar, the eldest Daughter of Heber
Chase and Vilate Murray Kimball, was given to the Prophet in
the holy bonds of celestial marriage."[32] It is significant that
Helen Mar was Joseph's youngest known wife, marrying him
when she was fourteen. Brodie emphasizes that he married young
women for sensual reasons, but here we find explicit evidence in
a source that Brodie knew showing that there were other motives
involved in a marriage to a young teenager. In fact, it is possible

that Joseph Smith never had sexual relations with Helen Mar; there is no unambiguous documentation, positive or negative, on the issue.[33]

Other marriages that show dynastic elements are the marriages of Joseph to Sarah Ann Whitney (linking Joseph to Bishop Newell Whitney); to Zina and Presendia Huntington (linking him to his close friend Dimick Huntington, as well as to High Councillor William Huntington, their father); to Fanny Young (linking him with Brigham Young, her brother, an apostle); to Rhoda Richards (linking him with Willard Richards, her brother, an apostle); and to Melissa Lott (linking him with loyalist Cornelius Lott).

It is possible that even Smith's polyandry, his marriage to women already married (of which there are eleven instances among the "certain" wives), had dynastic overtones. The fact that some men, after Joseph Smith's death, knowingly gave their wives to him for eternity in the Nauvoo temple suggests this, as does a passage from the anti-Mormon poem published during Joseph's life, "Buckeye's Lamentation for Want of More Wives," which hints that some men would receive greater salvation by giving their wives to the prophet.[34] The writings of Henry Jacobs, the "first husband" in the best-documented polyandrous triangle, show that he felt a great reverence for Joseph Smith even though he knew that his wife would be married to Joseph in eternity;[35] this would fit comfortably within the dynastic model for explaining some polygamous marriages.

It should also be noted, however, that polygamous marriages could serve to endanger important hierarchical relationships, as the cases of Nancy Rigdon and Elvira Cowles show. Joseph's proposal to Nancy, and her emphatic refusal, caused dramatic tensions between Joseph and his long-time counselor Sidney Rigdon. And Elvira Cowles Holmes's polyandrous marriage to Joseph was perhaps instrumental in turning her father, Austin Cowles, a counselor in the Nauvoo stake presidency, against Joseph and later into William Law's dissenting church. Cowles's affidavit in the *Nauvoo Expositor* was one of the most explicit anti-polygamy documents in that important publication. On the other hand, Jonathan Holmes, "first husband" in the polyandrous triangle with Smith and Elvira, was one of the pallbearers at Joseph's funeral.[36]

Sexuality was undoubtedly an element in Joseph Smith's plural marriages, and Brodie was correct in seeing it as an important motivating factor in his polygamy. However, to view it as the only, or by far the most important, motivating force in his theory and practice of polygamy, as she does, resulted in an unbalanced picture of Joseph Smith and his religiosity. Joseph Smith's burnt-over district biblical primitivism and his desire to arrange earthly and heavenly dynastic linkings with other Latter-day Saint leaders must also be considered.

Joseph Smith's Children by Polygamous Marriages

Brodie produced a list of six children she felt may have qualified as children of Joseph Smith by his polygamous wives. A careful evaluation of this list, however, leads to the conclusion that none of these children is a strong candidate for being a child of the Mormon prophet.[37] Brodie proposes:

1. Oliver Buell, son of Presendia Buell (see below).

2. A child Zina Huntington Jacobs had "while her husband, Henry Jacobs, was on a mission to England." This story from William Hall is discussed and rejected earlier in this essay. Brodie may mean Zebulon Jacobs, but Zina was already pregnant with Zebulon when she married Joseph on October 27, 1841.

3. John Reed Hancock, son of Clarissa Reed Hancock. There is no known documentary evidence for Clarissa Reed Hancock ever marrying Joseph Smith. Brodie can only cite family "legend," which is undocumentary, twentieth-century, unverifiable evidence.[38] In addition, the author has found that there are many descendants of Levi and Clarissa Hancock who deny this tradition. Furthermore, the autobiography of Mosiah Hancock explicitly states that Clarissa was not Joseph's wife when she

lived in his home as a maid in 1832. All these data suggest that Clarissa was not one of Joseph Smith's wives. Therefore, John Reed Hancock must also be rejected as his child.

4. Mary Elizabeth Rollins Lightner, one of Smith's polyandrous wives, Brodie writes, "bore a son in 1843 who may as easily have been the prophet's son as that of Adam Lightner." Although evidence is often ambiguous, it seems probable that Joseph Smith had sexual relations with his polyandrous wives. However, all of the polyandrous wives, with no exceptions, continued to live with their "first husbands" after Smith married them. In such a situation, it seems very likely that the "first husbands" had regular relations with their wives while Smith (married to twenty to thirty other women in 1842 and 1843, including a watchful and demanding first wife) had infrequent relations with them. Thus, unless strong evidence suggests otherwise, it is safest to attribute the children from the polyandrous marriages to the "first husbands," not to Joseph Smith. One might conjecture that a "first husband" very devoted to Smith would, at his command, refrain from sexual relations with his wife. But Adam Lightner was a non-Mormon.

5. Marinda Hyde, another polyandrous wife, had two sons born in Nauvoo. See the analysis of polyandrous situations in number 4. It is striking that Marinda had no children while Orson was on his mission to Jerusalem, then became pregnant soon after Orson returned home. (He arrived in Nauvoo on December 7, 1842, and Marinda bore Orson Washington Hyde on November 9, 1843.)

6. Moroni Pratt, a child by Mary Ann Frost Stearns Pratt, Parley Pratt's wife. There is no documentary evidence for Mary Ann marrying Joseph Smith during his lifetime, only a posthumous marriage to him in the Nauvoo temple. See the discussion of posthumous marriages below. If Mary Ann is not a strong case for being a wife of Joseph Smith, Moroni becomes a moot point. But even if Mary Ann was sealed to Smith during his lifetime, see the analysis of polyandrous situations found in number 4.

The rest of this section will concentrate on Oliver Buell, the son of Presendia Huntington Buell, the child Brodie felt was most certainly a child of Joseph Smith.[39] She was so convinced that she wrote to Dale Morgan, "If Oliver Buell isn't a Smith then I'm no Brimhall."[40] One gentle criticism by Dale Morgan to Brodie is relevant to the Oliver Buell question. He wrote to her, "Your chain of reasoning looks logical, but it is attended by a string of ifs all along the line (precisely as with the orthodox Mormon reasoning), and the probability of error increases as the chain of reasoning lengthens."[41] In other words, one uncertain link in a chain of evidence weakens it significantly; but if all the links are uncertain, the proposition is extremely unlikely.

Ettie V. Smith's 1859 exposé *Fifteen Years Among the Mormons* quotes Presendia as saying that she had a child and she did not know whether the father was Norman Buell or Joseph Smith.[42] Thus Brodie, as was entirely typical of her, takes a printed antagonistic source as her beginning point. But as was suggested above, every statement, pro-Mormon or anti-Mormon, must be looked at skeptically, and one wonders if Presendia would have said such a thing. Talk of sexuality was avoided by the Victorian, puritanical Mormons; in diaries, the word "pregnant" or "expecting" is never or rarely used. Women are merely "sick" until they have a child. Polyandry was rarely discussed openly by Mormon women. In addition, Fanny Stenhouse, another anti-Mormon writer, described Ettie Smith as "a lady who . . . in her writings, so mixed up fiction with what was true, that it was difficult to determine where the one ended and the other began."[43] This is remarkable testimony, coming from another, more reliable, unsympathetic writer. So Brodie opens with a weak link.

But even if Presendia did say what Ettie Smith attributes to her, we still must ask which child Presendia was talking about. It is certain that Presendia was a polyandrous wife of Joseph Smith. She married Norman Buell in 1827 and had seven children with him from 1829 to 1843, before separating from him in 1846. She gave her date of marriage to Joseph Smith as December 11, 1841,

which Brodie knew, and her last child by Buell, John Hiram, was
born in November 1843. Oliver Buell, however, was probably
born in 1840, two years before Presendia's marriage to Joseph. So
Brodie, in insisting on Joseph as Oliver Buell's parent, is positing
an affair, a sexual liaison, not a marriage. But which is the sim-
pler, more natural hypothesis, granting Ettie Smith's statement—
that Presendia was referring to John Hiram, who was born after
she married Joseph, or to Oliver, who was born two years before?
Clearly John Hiram (whom Brodie never mentions), given that
there is no evidence—only Brodie's assumption—that Presendia
had a liaison with Joseph before her marriage to him. And
although Ettie Smith does not name the child, she makes it clear
in a different passage of her book that she was referring to the
later child, John Hiram, not Oliver.[44]

Some might suggest that this argument makes a good case
for John Hiram Buell as a son of Joseph Smith, and John Hiram
certainly is a more likely candidate than Oliver Buell. However,
Presendia was not even living in Nauvoo while married to Joseph
Smith, and her "first husband" was a disaffected Mormon. As
noted above, it is probable that none of the polyandrous children
were Joseph's (unless there is strong evidence to the contrary); in
Presendia's case, her special conditions make it even more
improbable.

Brodie's next piece of evidence is a picture of Oliver Buell
in which she saw a striking resemblance to Joseph Smith's sons.
Of course, this kind of subjective identification is very much
open to interpretation. For one thing, it would help to have pictures of Norman Buell and George Buell to see if there were family resemblances there. So this is another weak link in the
evidence.

Next, Brodie endeavors to show that Joseph and Presendia
could have cohabited to engender Oliver, that they were in the
same vicinity at the right time. First she notes that there are two
birth dates for Oliver, January 31, 1840 (which Brodie found in
Presendia's genealogical records) and spring 1839 (found, Brodie
notes, in Augusta Joyce Crocheron's *Representative Women of*

Deseret, an article on Presendia based on an interview; it is some-what vague, "About this time was born her son Oliver."). Brodie preferred the earlier date as Joseph Smith and Presendia were both in Missouri in the summer of 1838, and Brodie could thus show the possibility of cohabitation. The fact that Joseph was living in Far West while Presendia was living in Fishing River, Ray County, and that Presendia was presumably having regular sexual relations with Norman Buell, further complicates Brodie's theory, even if Oliver was born in 1839.

But the best evidence suggests that Oliver was born in 1840. The 1839 date is found only in Crocheron. And the Janu-ary 31, 1840, date used in Presendia's genealogical records is also found in Esshom's *Pioneers and Prominent Men of Utah,* which Brodie used. A source available to Brodie, but not used by her, was the biography of Presendia found in *Women's Exponent,* "A Venerable Woman," which also gives January 31, 1840, for Oliver's birth date. Finally, a source that may not have been available to Brodie, at least in libraries, was a small holographic autobiography by Presendia. It also gives the 1840 date for Oliver's birth. So the 1840 date for Oliver's birth is the standard date and Brodie's preference for 1839 is not the strongest schol-arly judgment.[45]

However, Brodie works with the 1840 date also. She counts back nine months from January 31, 1840, and finds that Oliver's conception would have been in approximately late April 1839. In mid-April 1839, Presendia was living with Buell, who had apostatized from Mormonism, at Fishing River, Ray County, Mis-souri, southeast of Far West. The Huntington family was at Far West preparing to move to Illinois, some of the last Mormons to leave Missouri. Joseph Smith was in captivity.

On April 16, Joseph Smith escaped from his captors, some-where southeast of Gallatin, Davies County, after traveling two or three days toward Boone County; on April 22, he arrived in Illinois.

On April 18, the Huntingtons left Far West. It is possible that Presendia had gone to Far West to see them before they left.

Or it is possible that they visited Fishing River on their way east. In any event, she says she saw them at this time.

Brodie's reconstruction has Presendia go to Far West to see her family off, which is not unlikely. Then Brodie has Joseph Smith, after escaping from captivity, travel west to Far West, where he and Presendia have sexual relations that result in a child, Oliver Buell.

It is useful here to follow Smith's movements on a map to evaluate Brodie's reconstruction. According to an 1843 affidavit by Hyrum Smith, printed in *History of the Church*, Joseph and he were in Gallatin when they received a change of venue to Boone County, southeast, in the center of the state. They visited Diahman, where they spent the evening. The next day, they bought two horses and traveled "four or five" miles toward Boone. They stayed that night at Judge Morin's. On the 16th, they traveled twenty more miles toward Boone. (So now they were at least twenty-five miles southeast of Diahman.) That night, they got their captors drunk and were allowed to escape.[46]

Another source in *History of the Church*, the Lyman Wight affidavit, tells us that the group traveled three days after leaving Gallatin, then received their freedom "near Yellow Creek."[47] This is in Chariton County, about forty miles southeast of Gallatin. So, according to Hyrum Smith's and Wight's testimony, Joseph Smith was between twenty and forty miles southeast of Gallatin when he was freed.

The *History of the Church*, which may or may not reflect a first person document by Joseph Smith, clearly states that Joseph and his party immediately began traveling east to Quincy, Illinois, after being released. It records that Joseph knew that many Missourians wanted to kill him (even under armed guard, according to Wight, the party had traveled secretly miles from the main roads); it mentions the Haun's Mill Massacre. Hyrum writes, "Two of us mounted the horses, and the other three started on foot, and we took our change of venue for the State of Illinois."[48] Wight also wrote, "Here [Yellow Creek] we took a change of venue, and went to Quincy without difficulty."[49] They were delayed in their journey because they continued to stay away from the roads when traveling.

Even if these explicit testimonies were not enough, it also seems very unlikely that Smith would travel west to Far West before traveling to Quincy, as Brodie demands. In traveling to Far West, he would have had to pass Haun's Mill, where the massacre of Mormon men, women, and children had taken place just months before. And the Missourians were still in a murderous mood. When the sheriff who had freed Joseph and Hyrum returned to Gallatin, in fact, he was ridden on a rail by an angry mob.[50]

Thus, literally all the evidence suggests that Joseph Smith and his companions, fearing for their lives, hastened eastward to Illinois after they were freed. Brodie writes, however: "Since Joseph's journal entries make it clear that after his escape he was mingling with the last Mormon group to leave Far West . . . it is quite possible that he spent some time with Prescinda."[51] How did Brodie reach the conclusion that Joseph Smith was mingling with Mormons in Far West after his escape? She apparently read *History of the Church* incorrectly. From April 17 to April 21, the *History* divides its focus between the Mormons at Far West and Joseph Smith's party in eastern Missouri, hastening toward Quincy. Sometimes it switches without warning, but the Far West portions are in third person while the Joseph Smith portions, always recording hasty travel eastward, are in first person. In the same way, the *History of the Church* had covered events in Far West while Joseph Smith had been in jail in Liberty. For instance, on April 17, according to the *History*, Joseph writes, "We prosecuted our journey towards Illinois, keeping off from the main road as much as possible." April 18 begins, "This morning Elder Kimball went into the committee room and told the committee [on removal] to wind up their affairs and be off." Here we switch from the Joseph and Hyrum party, traveling to Illinois, recorded in the first person, and turn our focus to Far West, recorded in third person. But Brodie apparently misinterpreted the *History of the Church* here, confusing the geographical shifts.

Brodie's final piece of evidence is a statement in the Oliver Huntington diary purportedly saying that Oliver Buell was "sealed or adopted" to Joseph Smith in the Salt Lake temple.[52] But the Huntington journal reference does not mention Oliver Buell's name. It reads, "Friday 14 I went through for Elias Huntington, after which I stood Proxy for Louis Wight a Nephew of Lyman Wight, to have his children adopted Then I stood Proxy for the Prophet Joseph Smith in having. sealed or adopted to him a child of my Sister Presenda, had while living with Norman Buell. Wednesday Nov. 19–1884. I was endowed for Benjamin Huntington." The child in question might be any one of the seven children Presendia bore to Norman Buell.

Thus every link in Brodie's position that Oliver Buell was Joseph Smith's son is implausible, improbable, or impossible. There is no good evidence that Oliver Buell was the son of Joseph Smith, and thus there is no good evidence that Joseph had an affair with Presendia Buell before he married her in 1841. But Oliver Buell was crucial to Brodie's argument. He was her best candidate for a son of Smith; and he was her best evidence for Joseph Smith having extramarital affairs. She even published a large picture of Oliver next to a picture of Joseph's sons in *No Man Knows My History*.[53]

Morgan told Brodie once, "You are positive beyond what the facts will support, when all the obscure lights and shadows of those facts are closely examined."[54] He also advised her to express her opinion but not to "claim that [she had] Absolute Truth by the tail." This is a subtle critique—from one of her closest and most scholarly friends and a fellow non-believer in supernatural religion—of her tendency to interpret evidence inexactly and of a pronounced dogmatic streak in her nature and scholarship. The two limitations are of course related—when Brodie had an *idée fixe*, she sometimes interpreted facts imprecisely in order to arrive at her desired perspective.

One may ask why Brodie felt that she had arrived at "Absolute Truth" in portraying Oliver Buell as a son of Joseph Smith; the interpretation was clearly of great significance to her.

It portrayed Joseph as sexual, and sexual outside of the bounds of marriage, even outside of a polygamous marriage. Newell Bringhurst's forthcoming biography of Fawn Brodie will perhaps tell us why it was so important for her to pursue such a perspective. But it is strikingly like something arrived at and clung to like a religious dogma. And Dale Morgan perceptively chided Brodie, telling her she was reasoning as weakly as conservative Mormons when arranging an argument from a chain of mere possibilities—"precisely as with the orthodox Mormon reasoning" are his words.[55] Often a rigidly conservative Mormon will arrive at a crisis of faith—sometimes because of reading Brodie, ironically enough—and will then turn into a rigidly fundamentalist non-believer. Instead of making the next step of thinking about religion with less rigidity and thus being able to gain some kind of sympathetic understanding of it (like Dale Morgan, who, despite his non-belief, was sincerely sympathetic toward Mormons and Mormonism), one rejects it all in totality. Perhaps Brodie, despite her brilliance, could not escape the absolutist, doctrinaire mentality she inherited from her father and uncle, both general authorities in the Mormon church. *No Man Knows My History* may be viewed as a conservative Mormon book in this paradoxical way.[56]

On the other hand, there is some reliable evidence that Joseph Smith's polygamous marriages did produce children. There is an affidavit by Josephine Lyon Fisher, a child of Sylvia Sessions Lyon Smith Kimball Clark, one of Joseph's polyandrous wives, which asserts that Sylvia, on her deathbed, told her that she, Josephine, was the biological child of Joseph Smith.[57] Although it is safest to assume that the children of Joseph Smith's polyandrous wives were not his, barring strong evidence to the contrary, such an affidavit as this qualifies as strong evidence to the contrary.

It is possible that Eliza Snow had a miscarriage;[58] and it is possible that Fanny Alger had a child, for she became pregnant while married to Joseph, according to one source.[59] So Brodie was certainly right in asserting that sexuality was part of Joseph

Smith's marriages and probably right in asserting that there were children as a result. But she probably pointed to the wrong children.

Brodie's List of Wives

Brodie's list of Joseph Smith's wives is an important element in her book, and many authors cite Brodie as an authority for the number of Smith's wives: she lists forty-eight wives of Joseph Smith married to him during his lifetime. In her second edition, she intimates that there might have been many more.[60] However, this list, so important as a pioneering first scholarly effort, is frequently unreliable and is somewhat inflated. Some women on the list were certainly not Joseph Smith's wives during his lifetime; some women were very probably not his wives at all; and some are mere possibilities that should be not be accepted as probabilities, let alone certainties.

First of all, Brodie has some double listings. Elizabeth Davis Goldsmith Brackenbury Durfee Smith Lott, to use her full name, is listed twice, once as Mrs. Durfee, number 11, and once as Elizabeth Davis, number 38. Here Brodie's mistake is understandable: Elizabeth Davis married so many times that it is easy to confuse her names. Another woman whom Brodie doubled is Nancy Maria Winchester, number 47, who is also listed as number 44. Here Brodie repeats an error made by Orson Whitney, so again the mistake is understandable. She argues that Orson Whitney, a grandson of Heber C. Kimball, would make no mistakes in listing Kimball's wives; but Stanley Kimball points out other mistakes made by Whitney, two double listings based on confusing wives' married names.[61]

Sometimes Brodie made mistakes in her list because she did not have all of our resources, but in some cases the mistakes resulted from her use of antagonistic published sources. Brodie's number 37 is "Mrs. Edward Blossom." Her source, Richard Rushton in the anti-Mormon book *Mormon Portraits*, says that she was the wife of a Mr. Blossom, a high councilor in Nauvoo and an apostle under Brigham Young. Brodie admits the fact that there has never been a Mormon apostle named Blossom, but she nevertheless leaves Mrs. Blossom on her list, allowing the list to be padded by a source which even she admits is unreliable.[62]

Another problem in this list is Brodie's use of posthumous marriages to Joseph Smith, marriages in which the woman was sealed to Joseph after his death. For example, Cordelia Calista Morley, number 41, had an early posthumous marriage to Joseph, which admittedly is sometimes a sign that the woman married Joseph in his lifetime. But Cordelia's autobiography tells us that Joseph Smith had proposed to her; however, she had refused his marriage proposal and had never married him while he lived.[63] This is an example of how Brodie's research would have been strengthened by using more primary writings by Mormons in addition to the printed secondary sources by non-Mormon writers. This example supplies us with an important methodological principle: Posthumous marriages to Joseph Smith do not automatically give us women who were married to him during his lifetime. Such early posthumous marriages only allow us to say that the women *might* have been married to Smith while he lived. Careful scholarship requires us to put them in a different category than the certain or very probable wives. Numbers 35 (Mary Ann Frost Stearns Pratt), 36 (Olive Andrews Young), 39 (Mary H[o]uston Kimball), 42 (Sarah Scott Mulholland Kimball), 45 (Jane Tibbetts Luddington), 46 (Phebe Watrous Woodworth), and 48 ("Sophia Woodman," whose actual name was Aphia Woodman Sanburn and who married Gad Yale and perhaps David Dow) on Brodie's list are all posthumous marriages to Joseph Smith, not documented marriages to him during his lifetime.

Although Brodie's list fails to give us a definitive accounting of Joseph Smith's wives, it was a valuable first attempt at showing the extent of Joseph Smith's polygamous family, and many of the women included on it—approximately thirty-three of them—were certainly or very probably plural wives of

Joseph. The plural wives of Joseph Smith who can be reliably documented, according to my research, are now listed. The reader may compare this list with Brodie's to note additions and subtractions.[64]

1. *Fanny Alger* (Smith) (Custer), 1816–? (died after 1885), was married to Joseph Smith in approximately early 1833, at age sixteen. She then lived in Joseph's house as a maid but was expelled from the house by Emma when she became pregnant, according to one source. If this source is correct, it is not known what became of the child; possibly it died or was raised under another name. In 1836, Fanny married a non-Mormon, Solomon Custer, in Dublin, Indiana, where she lived the rest of her life. She and Solomon had nine children.

2. *Lucinda Pendleton* (Morgan) (Harris) (Smith), 1801–? (died after the Civil War), probably married Joseph polyandrously in 1838, at age thirty-seven. She was the widow of the anti-Masonic martyr William Morgan, to whom she had been married from 1819 to 1826; she bore him two children. She then married George Washington Harris in 1830, who became a prominent high councilor in Missouri, Nauvoo, and Council Bluffs. She left Harris in approximately 1853, apparently converted to Catholicism, and served as a nursing nun in Tennessee during the Civil War.

3. *Louisa Beaman* (Smith) (Young), 1815–50, married Joseph Smith on April 5, 1841, at age twenty-six. Although she became something of a folk heroine as Smith's first well-known polygamous wife, she lived a life of stark tragedy after his death. She married Brigham Young on September 19, 1844, to whom she bore five sons, including two sets of twins, all of whom died as infants, in Winter Quarters, on the plains, and in Salt Lake City. She herself died of breast cancer in Utah at age thirty-five. When Parowan was settled in 1851, Apostle George A. Smith first named it "Louisa" in her honor.

4. *Zina Diantha Huntington* (Jacobs) (Smith) (Young), 1821–1901, married Joseph Smith polyandrously on October 27,

1841, at age twenty. She had married Henry Jacobs on March 7, 1841, and bore him two children. On February 2, 1846, she married Brigham Young polyandrously, for time. (In Mormon theology and ritual, spouses were generally married for time and eternity, but under special circumstances, as when a widow had already married her first husband for time and eternity, the partners were "sealed" for time only. Most of Joseph Smith's plural marriages were re-solemnized in the Nauvoo temple, with living men standing proxy for Smith; generally, the proxy husbands were then married to the women for time.) Her marriage with Jacobs finally came to an end in May 1846, soon after the birth of their second child, when Brigham Young sent Henry on a mission to England. She and Young then began cohabiting as man and wife. In Utah, Zina bore Young a daughter, was a close friend and counselor of Eliza Snow Smith Young, and became the third General Relief Society president of the Latter-day Saint church.

5. *Presendia Lathrop Huntington* (Buell) (Smith) (Kimball), 1810–92. The older sister of Zina Huntington, she married Joseph Smith polyandrously on December 11, 1841, at age thirty-one. She had married Norman Buell in 1827, with whom she lived for nineteen years even though he became disaffected from Mormonism in 1838. She bore him seven children, five of whom died young. After Smith's death, she married Heber C. Kimball polyandrously on February 4, 1846. She finally left Buell in May 1846 and traveled to Utah, where she bore Kimball two children.

6. *Agnes Moulton Coolbrith* (Smith) (Smith) (Smith) (Pickett), 1808–76, married Joseph Smith on January 6, 1842, at age thirty-three, as the widow of Don Carlos Smith, Joseph's youngest brother, who had died on August 7, 1841. She had married Don Carlos in 1835 and bore him three daughters. After Joseph's death she married his cousin, Apostle George A. Smith for time on January 28, 1846, but when he left for Utah, she stayed in Nauvoo. She then married a lukewarm Mormon, William Pickett, in spring 1847, bore him twins and traveled to California with him, where she lived the rest of her life. Pickett, an alcoholic, left her in 1870. Her daughter by Don Carlos,

Josephine Smith (Carsley), became famous as a bohemian poetess and librarian in Oakland, using the pen name Ina Coolbrith.

7. *Sylvia Porter Sessions* (Lyon) (Smith) (Kimball) (Clark), 1818–82, married Joseph Smith polyandrously on February 8, 1842, at age twenty-three, and bore him one child, Josephine Lyon (Fisher), on February 8, 1844. Sylvia had married Windsor Lyon in 1838 and stayed with him for eleven years, bearing him four children, all of whom died as infants. He was excommunicated in Nauvoo in November 1842, due to a financial/legal conflict with Nauvoo Stake President William Marks, but was rebaptized in January 1846. Sylvia married Heber C. Kimball for time, polyandrously, on January 26, 1846, but did not go west with him, staying with Lyon. After Lyon's death in January 1849, she married a non-Mormon, Ezekiel Clark, in Iowa on January 1, 1850. She bore him three children (all of whom survived) but left him and came to Bountiful, Utah, in 1854.

8. *Mary Elizabeth Rollins* (Lightner) (Smith) (Young), 1818–1913, married Joseph Smith polyandrously approximately at the end of February 1842, at age twenty-three. She had married Adam Lightner, a non-Mormon, in 1835, with whom she had ten children. Mary and Adam lived together until his death in 1885. She also married Brigham Young for time, polyandrously, on May 22, 1845, but never lived with him as his wife. The Lightner family resided in Wisconsin for a number of years but came to Utah in 1863. Mary lived most of her later life in Minerville in southern Utah.

9. *Patty Bartlett* (Sessions) (Smith) (Parry), 1795–1892, married Joseph Smith polyandrously on March 9, 1842, at age forty-seven. The mother of Sylvia Sessions, Patty was famous as a frontier midwife and diarist. She married David Sessions in 1812, lived with him in Missouri, Nauvoo, and Utah, and bore him eight children; he died on August 11, 1850, in Salt Lake City. She then married John Parry for time in 1851; he died in 1868. She moved from Salt Lake City to Bountiful in 1872.

10. *Marinda Nancy Johnson* (Hyde) (Smith), 1815–86, married Joseph Smith polyandrously in April 1842, at age

twenty-seven, when her husband Orson Hyde was on his mission to Palestine. She had married Hyde, one of the prominent nineteenth century apostles, on September 4, 1834. She bore Hyde ten children and lived with him until their divorce in 1870. She died in Salt Lake City.

11. *Elizabeth Davis* (Goldsmith) (Brackenbury) (Durfee) (Smith) (Lott), 1791–1876, married Joseph polyandrously before June 1842, approximately at age fifty or fifty-one. She had married her first husband, Gilbert Goldsmith, on April 13, 1811; he died on December 24, 1811, leaving her with one son. She then married Joseph Brackenbury between 1815 and 1819. They converted to Mormonism and had five sons, but he died in December 1831 while serving a mission. She married Jabez Durfee in Missouri in 1834 and stayed with him until 1844 or 1845. After Joseph Smith's death, she married Cornelius Lott for time on January 22, 1845, but the marriage was short-lived. The rest of her life she spent with her Brackenbury sons in Utah, Missouri, Colorado, California, and Kansas. Ironically, she and two of her sons joined the Reorganized Latter Day Saint church in San Bernardino, California, and she died as a practicing Reorganized Latter Day Saint in Kansas.

12. *Sarah Maryetta Kingsley* (Howe) (Cleveland) (Smith) (Smith), 1788–1856, married Joseph Smith polyandrously before June 29, 1842, approximately at age fifty-three or fifty-four. She had married John Howe in 1807, with whom she had one son, but John died between 1823 and 1826. She then married John Cleveland in 1826, with whom she lived for the rest of her life and to whom she bore two children. Sarah became Mormon between 1832 and 1836, but Cleveland never converted to Mormonism, although they eventually moved to Nauvoo. She served as first counselor to Emma Smith in the first Relief Society organization. After Smith's death, Sarah married John Smith, later church patriarch, her daughter's father-in-law, in a polyandrous proxy marriage but never lived with him. The Clevelands stayed in Illinois when the Mormons went west.

13. *Delcena Didamia Johnson* (Sherman) (Smith) (Babbitt), 1806–54, married Joseph Smith before July 1842, approximately at age thirty-seven or thirty-eight. She was the widow of Lyman Sherman, a prominent early Mormon. She had lived with Sherman from 1829 to 1839 and bore him six children. After Smith's death, she married Almon Babbitt, her brother-in-law, for time, on January 24, 1846. Crippled by acute rheumatoid arthritis, she achieved her last wish, to see Utah, just before she died.

14. *Eliza Roxcy Snow* (Smith) (Young), 1804–87, married Joseph Smith on June 29, 1842, at age thirty-eight. After his death, she married Brigham Young for time in October 1844 and lived in the Lion House as his plural wife but always signed her name Eliza R. Snow Smith. A prominent poetess and intellectual, she was the dominant woman leader in nineteenth century Mormonism and became the second General Relief Society president of the Latter-day Saint church.

15. *Sarah Ann Whitney* (Smith) (Kingsbury) (Kimball), 1825–73. The daughter of Newell Whitney, a prominent early bishop, she married Joseph on July 27, 1842, at age seventeen. After the marriage to Joseph, the prophet himself solemnized her marriage to Joseph Kingsbury on April 29, 1843, in a "pretend" marriage (albeit a legal, civil marriage) to camouflage the polygamous marriage. The marriage to Kingsbury was technically polyandrous although none of the participants considered it a real marriage. After Joseph's death, she married Heber C. Kimball on March 17, 1845, and lived in his household in Utah, bearing him seven children.

16. *Martha McBride* (Knight) (Smith) (Kimball), 1805–1901, married Joseph Smith in August 1842, at age thirty-seven. Joseph married her as the widow of Vinson Knight, another important early bishop, with whom she had lived from 1826 to July 31, 1842, when he died, and with whom she had seven children. After Smith's death, she married Heber C. Kimball for time on October 12, 1844, to whom she bore one child that died at birth. Nevertheless she lived most of her

later life with relatives in Utah, especially in Ogden and Hooper.

17. *Ruth Daggett Vose* (Sayers) (Smith), 1808–84, married Joseph Smith polyandrously in February 1843, at age thirty-three. She had married Edward Sayers in 1841 and stayed with him until his death in 1861. Sayers was never baptized but lived with Ruth in Nauvoo and Salt Lake City, where they both died. She bore no children.

18. *Flora Ann Woodworth* (Smith) (Gove), 1826–? (died at Winter Quarters after 1850). The daughter of Lucian Woodworth, architect of the Nauvoo House, she married Joseph in the spring of 1843, at age sixteen. After Joseph's death, she married Gove, a non-Mormon, in 1845, with whom she had two or three children.

19. *Emily Dow Partridge* (Smith) (Young), 1824–99, married Joseph on March 4, 1843, at age nineteen. Emily and her sister Eliza were the daughters of Edward Partridge, another important early Mormon bishop. After Joseph's death, she married Brigham Young for time in September or November 1844 and bore him seven children. She was the mother of Don Carlos Young, an architect for the Salt Lake temple.

20. *Eliza Maria Partridge* (Smith) (Lyman), 1820–86, married Joseph Smith on March 8, 1843, at age twenty-two. After his death, she married Apostle Amasa Lyman on September 28, 1844, and bore him five children. Two of her sisters also married Lyman, but the three sisters left him when he was excommunicated for "spiritualist" Godbeite heresy in 1870. Eliza and her grown children joined in one of the great pioneering feats in Utah history, the mission to the nearly inaccessible San Juan County, in 1879 and 1880, which was led by Platte Lyman, her son. She lived most of her later life in Fillmore and Oak City, Utah.

21. *Almera Woodward Johnson* (Smith) (Barton), 1812–96, married Joseph Smith between April 2 and April 22, 1843, at age thirty. She was the sister of Delcena Johnson and a number of prominent Mormon Johnsons, including Benjamin, Joseph Ellis, and Joel. After Smith's death, she married Reuben Barton on November 16, 1845, with whom she had five daughters, but he

became disaffected and she left him in 1861 and came to Utah. She buried all of her five daughters, most of whom died as children; none married. The one daughter who lived the longest was retarded and lived with Almera for some thirty years in Parowan in southern Utah.

22. *Lucy Walker* (Smith) (Kimball), 1826–1910, married Joseph Smith on May 1, 1843, at age seventeen. After his death, she married Heber C. Kimball for time on February 8, 1845, and bore him nine children in Utah.

23. *Sarah Lawrence* (Smith) (Kimball) (Mount), 1826–72, married Joseph soon after May 11, 1843, at age seventeen. After Joseph's death, she married Heber C. Kimball for time on October 12, 1844, but divorced him on June 18, 1851, in Utah. She then married Joseph Mount in 1853 and with him moved to Napa, California, where she became disaffected from Mormonism. She bore no children to either husband.

24. *Maria Lawrence* (Smith) (Young?) (Babbitt), 1823–1847. The sister of Sarah Lawrence, she married Joseph Smith soon after May 11, 1843, at age nineteen. After his death, she married Brigham Young (according to some sources, denied by others), then married Almon Babbitt on January 24, 1846. She bore no children.

25. *Helen Mar Kimball* (Smith) (Whitney), 1828–95. The daughter of Heber C. and Vilate Kimball, she married Joseph Smith in May 1843, at age fourteen. After his death, she married Horace Whitney, the brother of Sarah Ann Whitney, on February 3, 1846, for time. She bore Whitney eleven children, among whom was Orson F. Whitney, a noted writer, poet, and apostle. After loathing polygamy as a young teenager in Nauvoo, she wrote two fervent pamphlets in defense of it as an older woman in Utah.

26. *Elvira Annie Cowles* (Holmes) (Smith), 1813–71, married Joseph Smith polyandrously on June 1, 1843, at age twenty-nine. She was the daughter of Austin Cowles, a counselor in the Nauvoo stake presidency, who joined William Law's dissenting church in Nauvoo, perhaps because he disapproved of Joseph's marriage to his daughter. Elvira had married Jonathan Holmes on

December 1, 1842, and stayed with him until her death, living most of her later life in Farmington, Utah. She bore Holmes five daughters from 1845 to 1856.

27. *Rhoda Richards* (Smith) (Young), 1784–1879. The sister of Apostle Willard Richards, Joseph Smith's close friend, she married Joseph on June 12, 1843, at age fifty-eight. After Joseph's death, she married Brigham Young for time on January 31, 1846, but apparently never lived in his household, living instead with relatives the rest of her life. She died in Salt Lake City.

28. *Desdemona Catlin Wadsworth Fullmer* (Smith) (Benson) (McLane), 1809–86, married Joseph Smith in July 1843, at age thirty-two or thirty-three. After his death, she married Ezra Taft Benson for time on January 26, 1846. However, the marriage did not last, and she married Harrison Parker McLane in 1852, with whom she had a son. This marriage also ended in a separation sometime between 1860 and 1863. She died in Salt Lake City.

29. *Hannah S. Ells* (Smith), 1813-1845?, married Joseph Smith between January 1 and summer 1843, approximately at age twenty-nine or thirty. She was a seamstress and Relief Society secretary and the sister of Josiah Ells, who eventually became a Reorganized Latter Day Saint apostle.

30. *Olive Grey Frost* (Smith) (Young), 1816–45, married Joseph Smith in the summer of 1843, approximately at age twenty-seven or twenty-eight. The sister of Mary Ann Frost Stearns Pratt, Parley P. Pratt's wife, she served with her in England as one of the early female missionaries in Mormon history. She married Brigham Young for time on November 7, 1844, but died of malaria less than a year later.

31. *Melissa Lott* (Smith) (Bernhisel) (Willis), 1824–98. The daughter of Cornelius Lott, a close friend of Joseph Smith, she married Joseph on September 20, 1843, at age nineteen. After his death, she married John Bernhisel, the prominent Mormon politician, on February 8, 1846, but the marriage did not last. She then married Ira Willis on May 13, 1849, with whom she settled in Lehi; she bore him seven children. Ira and a son died in a farming accident in 1863.

32. *Nancy Maria Winchester* (Smith) (Kimball) (Arnold), 1828–76. The time of marriage to Joseph Smith is unknown, but she probably married him in 1842 or 1843, approximately at age fourteen. After his death, she married Heber C. Kimball for time on October 10, 1844, at age sixteen. However, the marriage did not produce children and so Heber C. Kimball helped arrange her marriage to Amos George Arnold on October 12, 1865. She bore Arnold one child.

33. *Fanny Young* (Carr) (Murray) (Smith), 1787–1859. The older sister of Brigham Young, whom she helped raise, she married Joseph Smith on November 2, 1843, at age fifty-six, his last known plural wife. She had married Robert Carr in 1803 and either was widowed or had divorced him by 1827, then married Roswell Murray, Vilate Kimball's father in 1832. After his death in 1839 or 1840, she married Smith. She came to Utah and lived in the Lion House until her death.

In the possible wives category (due to conflicting or ambiguous evidence or very limited evidence):

1. *Vienna Jacques* (Smith?) (Shearer), 1787–1884. An early Mormon convert from Boston, Vienna lived in Joseph Smith's home in Kirtland, where, according to a late, unsympathetic witness, he married her. There is also a first person affidavit stating that Vienna married Joseph, but she evidently refused to sign it—possibly because she had not married Joseph, possibly because she was embarrassed by the marriage. She married Daniel Shearer, a Mormon, in 1838, which one would not expect of Joseph's wife, had no children, then separated from Shearer by January 1846. She was known as a midwife in Salt Lake City, where she died.

2. *Hannah Ann Dubois* (Smith) (Smith?) (Dibble), 1808–93. A sympathetic and an unsympathetic source both refer to a Sister Dibble or Mrs. Dibble as Joseph's wife. Hannah first married a John Smith in Philadelphia. After his death, she married Philo Dibble in 1841 in Nauvoo (a marriage solemnized by Joseph Smith), and she stayed with Dibble for the rest of her life,

living many years in Springville, Utah. She married Dibble, not Joseph Smith, for eternity in the Nauvoo temple, which one would not expect if she had been Joseph's wife.

3. *Sarah Bapson* (Smith?), 1793–?. Almost nothing is known of this woman. A late Salt Lake temple marriage record, dated in 1899, states that she married Joseph while he was alive. She may be a Miss B***** on John C. Bennett's list of Joseph's wives.

4. "*Mrs. G*****" (Smith?) possibly married Smith before June 1842 as she is on John C. Bennett's list of Joseph's wives. However, she is not yet identified.

5. *Sarah Scott* (Mulholland) (Smith?) (Kimball), 1817–78, was married to James Mulholland, who died in 1839. Orson Whitney referred to her as a wife of Joseph Smith, but she was sealed to Mulholland, not Joseph Smith, for eternity, and to Heber C. Kimball for time in a proxy wedding on February 3, 1846. She bore Kimball no children.

6. *Mary H[o]uston* (Smith?) (Kimball), 1818–96, was referred to by Orson Whitney as a wife of Joseph Smith. She was sealed to Joseph for eternity and to Heber C. Kimball for time in a proxy wedding on February 3, 1846. She bore Kimball no children.

7. *Mrs. Tailor* (Smith?) is linked with Patty Sessions and Elizabeth Durfee as a wife of Joseph on a seemingly reliable non-Mormon list. Nothing else is known of her.

For most of these women, there is just a hint of late evidence that they married Joseph Smith. Three of them are unidentified or barely identifiable. The two strongest cases, Vienna Jacques and Hannah Dubois, have major contradictory evidence.

Early "posthumous" marriages (married to Joseph Smith after his death):

1. *Mary Ann Frost* (Stearns) (Pratt), 1809–91, was sealed to Joseph for eternity and to Parley P. Pratt for time in a proxy marriage on February 6, 1846. The sister of Olive Frost, Mary Ann had first married Nathan Stearns, who died in 1833 after three

years of marriage and one child. Then she married Parley P. Pratt in 1837 and bore him four children. Mary Ann separated from Parley in March 1846 and later formally divorced him in 1853. There is complex, contradictory evidence for her marriage history, but the posthumous marriage to Joseph Smith is certain.

2. *Olive Andrews* (Young), 1818–? (She died after January 1846.) Olive was sealed to Joseph Smith for eternity and to Brigham Young for time in a proxy marriage on January 15, 1846. Almost nothing is known of her beyond this.

3. *Jane Tibbetts* (Luddington), 1804–? (She died after 1851.) She was sealed to Joseph Smith for eternity, to Elam Luddington for time on January 17, 1846; she separated from Luddington soon after. Almost nothing is known of her beyond this.

4. *Phebe Watrous* (Woodworth) 1805–?. (She died after 1874, perhaps in Lehi, Utah.) She was sealed to Joseph Smith for eternity, to Lucien Woodworth for time in a proxy marriage on January 19, 1846. Phebe had married Woodworth in approximately 1825 and was the mother of Flora Woodworth, who married Joseph Smith in 1843. Lucien Woodworth died in 1867, perhaps in California.

5. *Aphia Woodman Sanburn* (Dow?) (Yale), 1795–? (She died in 1846 or later.) She was sealed to Joseph for eternity, to Gad Yale for time on January 27, 1846. She had possibly married a David Dow at some point and was married to Gad Yale by 1842. She may have died soon after the proxy marriage or she left Yale, for he crossed the plains without her, and she appears no more in Mormon history.

6. *Sally Ann Fuller* (Gulley) (Fuller) (McArthur), 1815–97. Her obituary refers to her as the wife of Joseph Smith, but this may refer to a posthumous marriage. She was married to Joseph for eternity and to Samuel Gulley for time on January 29, 1849. Gulley died soon after, on July 4, 1849. She married Elijah Knapp Fuller on September 8, 1850, to whom she bore a child, Joseph Smith Fuller, but she left Elijah between 1851 and 1856. She married Daniel D. McArthur on July 5, 1857, in St. George, Utah, where she died.

7. *Lydia Kenyon* (Carter) (Kimball) (Goff), 1800–66. A Utah marriage record refers to her as a wife of Joseph Smith; again, this may refer to a posthumous marriage. She married Simeon Carter in 1818 and bore him a number of children. She married Heber C. Kimball polyandrously in 1844 but apparently never lived with him. She separated from Carter in 1849 and married James Goff on June 8, 1851. She had separated from him, evidently, by 1860. She died in Salt Lake City.

Although it is tempting to regard this last group of women as Joseph Smith's wives, the fact is that there is no documentary evidence showing that they married him during his lifetime. And it is certain that "posthumous only" marriages to Joseph Smith were being practiced in the Nauvoo temple. Thus we should look at them as promising subjects for further study but not as Joseph's wives.

Conclusion

Hopefully, this essay has demonstrated that Brodie's treatment of Joseph Smith's polygamy was not definitive. But this does not mean that she was always wrong, and it does not deny that she had great strengths as a stylist and biographer. She was an important pioneer and I owe her a great deal. But pioneers always lack balance in some ways, and all historians have failings and biases and make factual errors at times due to the fragmentary, contradictory nature of the historical record. In addition, Brodie did not have the benefit of sources and theoretical developments we have at our disposal now. Although she made errors in her treatment of Joseph Smith's polygamy, at least she made the first, valuable attempt at a footnoted list of his wives.

And even if we disallow Brodie's questionable interpretations, Joseph Smith's polygamy still has many problematic aspects—notably the details of his polyandry, as nine of his first twelve certain plural marriages were polyandrous and twelve of his total of thirty-three marriages. The details of his marriages to young teenage women are also extremely discomforting, as well as his use of theological pressure and revelation-supported authoritarianism when proposing (or rather, commanding) marriage. Those with feminist sympathies will also look askance at male church leaders using women to cement alliances between themselves, often at great cost to the women serving as links, especially the teenagers. Clearly, the woman is object, not subject, in such a social construct. Gerda Lerner speaks of the "commodification" of women,[65] and the dynastic marriages of Joseph Smith might be cited as examples of this.

Finally, although Oliver Buell was not a son of Joseph Smith, it has been adequately documented that Josephine Lyon Fisher was a daughter of Joseph and Sylvia Sessions Lyon Smith Kimball Clark, and this will remain a problem for conservative scholars who would prefer to interpret Joseph Smith's polyandrous marriages as non-sexual.

Notes

1. I would like to thank Newell Bringhurst and Linda King Newell for their invaluable editorial help with this article. It was written at the suggestion of Newell Bringhurst.
2. Wilford Poulson to Fawn M. Brodie, January 5, 1945, in Fawn McKay Brodie papers, Marriott Library, University of Utah; quoted in Newell Bringhurst, "Fawn M. Brodie, 'Mormondom's Lost Generation' and No Man Knows My History," Journal of Mormon History 16 (1990): 19.
3. Cf. C. Laurence Moore, Religious Outsiders and the Making of Americans (N.Y.: Oxford University Press, 1986), 27.
4. See also "Fawn McKay Brodie: An Oral History Interview," ed. Shirley Stephenson, Dialogue 14, no. 2 (summer 1981): 99–106; technically, Brodie could have used the archives more, but she did not want to embarrass her father or uncle, both general authorities in the Mormon church.
5. William Hall, The Abominations of Mormonism Exposed (Cincinnati: I. Hart, 1852), 43–44; Fawn M. Brodie, No Man Knows My History, The Life of Joseph Smith, 2nd ed., rev and enl. (New York: Alfred A. Knopf, 1971), 466.
6. Elden Watson, ed., Manuscript History of Brigham Young, 1801–44 (Salt Lake City: Smith Secretarial Services, 1968), and 1846-47 (1971); 175, cf.

Oliver Huntington journal, Harold B. Lee Library, Brigham Young University, Provo, Utah, June 11, 1846, which documents Henry's arrival in New York.

7. *No Man Knows My History*, 289, 462 (the Presendia Huntington section), 231, 239.

8. *Mormonism Unveiled* (St. Louis: M. E. Mason, 1877), 132; *No Man Knows My History*, 465. The quote shows that Lee and Jacobs left Nauvoo after fall 1842. The date of Jacobs's and Lee's departure, December 26, is documented by Lee's missionary journal in Utah State Historical Society; cf. a letter by Lee published in *Times and Seasons* 4, no. 20 (September 1, 1843): 311–12.

9. *No Man Knows My History*, 119.

10. Clark Braden and E. L. [Edmund Levi] Kelley, *Public Discussion of the Issues between the Reorganized Church of Jesus Christ of Latter Day Saints and the Church of Christ, Disciples* (St. Louis: C. Braden, 1884), 202. Clark Braden was a member of the Church of Christ, the "Disciples."

11. Luke Johnson, "History of Luke Johnson," *Deseret News* 8 (19 and 26 May 1858): 53–54; Joseph Smith Jr., *History of the Church of Jesus Christ of Latter-day Saints*, ed. B. H. Roberts, 2nd. ed., 7 vols. (Salt Lake City: Deseret News, 1932–51), 1:261–65 (hereafter cited as HC); cf. Linda King Newell and Valeen Tippetts Avery, *Mormon Enigma: Emma Hale Smith* (Garden City, N.Y.: Doubleday, 1985), 42; Donna Hill, *Joseph Smith, the First Mormon* (Garden City, N.Y.: Doubleday, 1977), 144–46. Hill echoes the Eli Johnson story, citing Brodie as her authority. So misinformation perpetuates itself. For the brothers of Marinda Johnson Hyde, see the family group sheet in the LDS Genealogical Society, information derived from the Johnson family bible.

12. Newell Bringhurst, "Fawn Brodie's Thomas Jefferson: The Making of a Popular and Controversial Biography," *Pacific Historical Review* (1993): 433–54, esp. 453–54; Louis Midgley, "The Brodie Connection: Thomas Jefferson and Joseph Smith," *BYU Studies* 20 (1979): 59–67. Dale Morgan, after reading a draft of *No Man Knows My History*, complained that the manuscript "was too much in the vein of 'I expose'." Morgan, "Memo from Dale Morgan," n.d., in Fawn M. Brodie papers, quoted in Bringhurst, "Fawn M. Brodie, 'Mormondom's Lost Generation,'" 16. One might object that these comments (and other comments by Morgan quoted in this essay) were directed at an early draft of *No Man Knows My History* and that Morgan had unreserved praise for the finished biography. However, in my judgment, many of Morgan's early criticisms of *No Man Knows My History* are strikingly appropriate to the finished product. It is possible that Morgan's critiques tempered a first draft that apparently was quite extreme in tone; but this does not mean that the exposé bent was completely

expunged from the book. Cf. Morgan to Brodie, January 7, 1946, Brodie collection, Marriott Library: "You have an intellectual but not yet an emotional objectivity about Mormonism. You are still in certain of a mood of rebellion and you sometimes give vent to a sharp intellectual scorn for the Mormon way of life which practically speaking is an intolerance for it. . . . I am inclined to believe that this reflects a sense of emotional insecurity which may require several more years to overcome." This was written after the publication of *No Man Knows My History* and presents an interesting contrast to Morgan's public response to the book.

13. *No Man Knows My History*, 297. For her dependence on such second-hand, unsympathetic sources, see above. It is striking that polygamy is first introduced into the book on page 184 although Joseph Smith's relationship with Fanny Alger is introduced on page 181. In other words, Brodie viewed this early relationship as "an illicit affair," 181, pre-polygamy. (See further on Fanny Alger below.) She also presents Joseph as having an affair with Marinda Johnson in 1832, on page 119 (see above for the reliability of her documentation on this point). In Brodie's view, Smith started with affairs, then developed the theology of polygamy to mask them; for her, theology was never an important motivating force in his plural marriages.

14. Cf. "An Oral History Interview," p. 106. Morgan disagreed and tried to convince Brodie that Joseph Smith, "came to believe absolutely in what he was doing; his sincerity can hardly be challenged." Dale Morgan, "Memo," quoted in Bringhurst, "Fawn M. Brodie, 'Mormondom's Lost Generation,'" 16.

15. Cf. Morgan, previous note. Brodie's thesis of Joseph as conscious charlatan should not be rejected out of hand, but it would at least need to be tempered and fine tuned. Cf. Jan Shipps, "The Prophet Puzzle: Suggestions Leading Toward a More Comprehensive Interpretation of Joseph Smith," *Journal of Mormon History* 1 (1974): 3–20; Harold Bloom, *The American Religion, the Emergence of the Post-Christian Nation* (N.Y.: Simon & Shuster, 1992), 96–112.

16. Marvin Hill, "Brodie Revisited: A Reappraisal," *Dialogue* 7, no. 4 (winter 1972): 73–85, 76. Cf. Hill's "Secular or Sectarian History? A Critique of *No Man Knows My History*," *Church History* 43 (1974): 78–96, 93–95, reprinted in this volume; Lawrence Foster, *Religion and Sexuality* (Urbana: University of Illinois Press, 1984), 126–27.

17. Danel Bachman, "A Study of the Mormon Practice of Plural Marriage before the Death of Joseph Smith," (M.A. thesis, Purdue University, 1975), 56–68, 61–73; and "New Light on an Old Hypothesis: The Ohio Origins of the Revelation on Eternal Marriage," *Journal of Mormon History* 5 (1978): 19–32, 32. Fanny Alger's marriage date can be estimated from

the Mosiah Hancock autobiography, Archives, Historical Department, Church of Jesus Christ of Latter-day Saints (hereafter, LDS Archives), MS 570, 61–63.

18. John Cairncross, *After Polygamy Was Made a Sin: The Social History of Christian Polygamy* (London: Routledge & Kegan Paul, 1974).

19. For Mormonism and Christian primitivism, see Marvin Hill, "The Shaping of the Mormon Mind in New England and New York," *BYU Studies* 9 (1969): 351–72; Richard Hughes, ed., *The American Quest for the Primitive Church* (Champaign: University of Illinois Press, 1988); Richard Hughes and C. Leonard Allen, *Illusions of Innocence; Protestant Primitivism in America, 1630-1875* (Chicago: University of Chicago Press, 1988). Foster, in *Religion and Sexuality*, puts Mormon polygamy in a wider context of social, religious, marital, and sexual experimentation in the unsettled environment of nineteenth century America.

20. *No Man Knows My History*, 301; cf. Foster, *Religion and Sexuality*, 301–2; B. Carmon Hardy, *Solemn Covenant* (Urbana: University of Illinois Press, 1992), 24, n. 29; Richard Van Wagoner, *Mormon Polygamy* (Salt Lake City: Signature, 1986), 12—all fine scholars but all overly dependent on Brodie here, perhaps.

21. Oliver Cowdery letterbook, January 21, 1838, Huntington Library, San Marino, California.

22. For instance, Fanny Alger's parents considered her relationship with Joseph to be an honor for them, according to Ann Eliza Webb Young, *Wife Number 19* (Hartford: Dustin, Gilman, 1876), 66–67; if Fanny had merely had a backstairs affair with Joseph, with a pregnancy, the parents might have been furious with Smith. Benjamin Johnson threatened to kill Joseph Smith if his sisters were debauched; but he actively helped Joseph marry his sister polygamously, Benjamin Johnson to George Gibbs, edited in Dean R. Zimmerman, *I Knew the Prophets, An Analysis of the Letter of Benjamin F. Johnson to George F. Gibbs, Reporting Doctrinal Views of Joseph Smith and Brigham Young* (Bountiful, Utah: Horizon, 1976), 41.

23. *Doctrine and Covenants* (Kirtland, Ohio: F.G. Williams, 1835), sec. 101, p. 251; cf. HC, 2:247–49. Van Wagoner to Linda King Newell, September 20, 1983, in Van Wagoner Collection, Marriott Library.

24. Zimmerman, *I Knew the Prophets*, 38–39, 44–45. Johnson also says that Heber C. Kimball stated publicly that Fanny was Joseph's wife but places him in the St. George temple when he said it, a chronological impossibility.

25. Ann Eliza Young, *Wife Number 19*, 66–67; Chauncey Webb, in Wilhelm Wyl, *Mormon Portraits* (Salt Lake City: Tribune Press, 1886), 57.

26. Mosiah Hancock, Autobiography, LDS Archives MS 570, 61–63. As of the date of writing and to the author's knowledge, the Fanny Alger passages in this document had never been published or discussed in print. As

an important new historical text, it will thus need to undergo serious scrutiny; some will accept it as reliable, others may regard it as a fabrication. It
is late, written in 1896, but it is a nineteenth-century holograph by Fanny's
full cousin; Levi Hancock, Mosiah's father and the brother of Fanny's
mother (Clarissa Hancock Alger), was a close friend of Joseph Smith in
Kirtland, so the story has the credibility of access. Parallels with Nauvoo
polygamy also incline one toward accepting it (see next note). For a fuller
discussion of this text, see my "Fanny Alger Smith Custer: Mormonism's
First Plural Wife?" *Journal of Mormon History* 22.1 (spring 1996): 174-207.

27. For instance, Joseph's final proposal to Zina Huntington Jacobs came
through a male family member, her brother Dimick; Zina Young, in "Joseph
the Prophet," *The Salt Lake Herald, Church and Farm Supplement* (January
12, 1895): 212; cf. Martha Sonntag Bradley and Mary Brown Firmage
Woodward, "Plurality, Patriarchy, and the Priestess: Zina D. H. Young's Nau-
voo Marriages," *Journal of Mormon History* 20 (spring 1994): 84–118.
Exactly the same thing happened with Benjamin and Almera Johnson, see
Zimmerman, *I Knew the Prophets*, 41. And Louisa Beaman was married to
Joseph Smith by her sister's husband, Joseph Bates Noble. Speech by Joseph
Noble, December 19, 1880, as reported in Charles Walker diaries, Andrew
Larson and Katherine Miles Larson, eds., *Diary of Charles Lowell Walker*, 2
vols. (Logan: Utah State University Press, 1980), 2:515: "Br Nobles made a
few remarks on the celestial order of marriage, He being the man who sealed
Louisa Beeman to the Prophet Joseph Smith in 1840 under his instructions."

28. D. Michael Quinn, "The Mormon Hierarchy, 1832–1932: An American
Elite," (Ph.D. diss., Yale University, 1976), 74–75; Bachman, "A Study,"
112; see also M. Guy Bishop, "The Celestial Family: Early Mormon
Thought on Life and Death, 1830–46," (Ph.D. diss., Southern Illinois Uni-
versity, 1981), 23, 30; Rex Cooper, *Promises Made to the Fathers* (Salt Lake
City: University of Utah Press, 1990), 140–41, 146–47.

29. See Gerda Lerner, *The Creation of Patriarchy* (N.Y.: Oxford University
Press, 1986), 67, on dynastic marriage. Princesses "in one sense . . . were
merely pawns of their families' diplomatic designs and imperialistic ambitions; not unlike their brothers who were sometimes forced to enter such
diplomatic marriages and had no more personal choice than did the
women." Yet it would be a mistake to view these princesses as entirely pow-
erless; they were frequently "influential, politically active, and powerful.
Their role as future wives in diplomatic marriages demanded that they be
given the best available education."

30. Zimmerman, *I Knew the Prophets*, 47.

31. "Helen Mar Kimball Smith Whitney to her children, March 30, 1881,"
MS 744, Fd. 2, LDS Archives, also in Linda King Newell Collection, Marriott Library.

32. Orson F. Whitney, *Life of Heber C. Kimball* (Salt Lake City: Kimball family, 1888), 339.
33. Stanley Kimball, *Heber C. Kimball* (Champaign: University of Illinois Press, 1981), 98, argues that Helen Mar certainly had no sexual relations with Joseph; but to me the evidence is entirely ambiguous. Helen Mar certainly found the marriage to Joseph more confining than she had expected (see the poem in her reminiscence, quoted above), but it is not known if or how sexuality entered into that feeling of confinement. One might argue from later Mormon practice that there was no sexuality; see Juanita Brooks, *John Doyle Lee* (Logan: Utah State University Press, 1992), 233, 239–40. Joseph certainly had sexual relations with some of his older teenage wives, however.
34. "Buckeye's Lamentation for Want of More Wives," Stanza 8, *Warsaw Message* (February 4, 1844), reprinted in Bachman, "A Study," App. E, 338–40, see also 264–65. Cf. HC 6:210 for Wilson Law as a possible author.
35. "All is right according to the Law of the Celestial kingdom of our God Joseph," Henry Jacobs to Zina Young, before Valentine's day 1847, Zina Brown Collection, LDS Archives; "Joseph is our Prophet stil the grate High Preist Ordained of God and sent forth to give us light," Henry Jacobs to Zina Young, September 2, 1852, Zina Brown Collection, LDS Archives.
36. For Nancy Rigdon, see Richard Van Wagoner, *Sidney Rigdon: A Portrait of Religious Excess* (Salt Lake City: Signature, 1994), 307; for Austin Cowles and Jonathan Holmes, *Nauvoo Expositor* 1 (June 7,1844). Holmes helped destroy the publication to which his father-in-law was a prominent contributor, Joseph Smith journal, June 13 and 17, 1844, see Scott Faulring, *An American Prophet's Record: the Diaries and Journals of Joseph Smith* (Salt Lake City: Signature Books, 1989), 491, 493. Holmes as pallbearer: "History of Joseph Smith," *Deseret News* (Weekly) 7.38 (November 25, 1857), 298; Brigham H. Roberts, *Comprehensive History of the Church of Jesus Christ of Latter-day Saints*, 6 vol. (Provo, Utah: Brigham Young University Press, 1965) 5:528.
37. See *No Man Knows My History*, 345.
38. Brodie admits in *No Man Knows My History*, 464 (the appendix entry for Clarissa) that this evidence is thin but still makes Clarissa wife # 5. And in the body of her biography, 345, she does not mention that the evidence for Clarissa's marriage to Joseph Smith is weak.
39. For Brodie's treatment of Oliver Buell, see especially *No Man Knows My History*, 460–62.
40. Fawn Brodie to Dale Morgan, March 24, 1945, Dale Morgan papers, Marriott Library. She was sympathizing with her mother's family here, the Brimhalls; her father was, of course, a McKay.

41. Morgan, cited in Bringhurst, "Fawn M. Brodie, 'Mormondom's Lost Generation,'" 16; cf. Gary Wills, "Uncle Tom's Cabin," *New York Review of Books* 21 (April 18,1978): 26.

42. Ettie V. Smith, *Fifteen Years Among the Mormons*, ed. Nelson Winch Green (N.Y.: Scribners, 1858), 34–35.

43. Fanny Stenhouse, *Tell It All* (Hartford, Conn.: A. D. Worthington, 1874), 618.

44. Ettie Smith, *Fifteen Years*, 45.

45. *Representative Women of Deseret* (Salt Lake City: J.C. Graham, 1884), 30. Frank Esshom, *Pioneers and Prominent Men of Utah* (Salt Lake City: Utah Pioneers Book Publishing, 1913), at the picture of Oliver Buell, which Brodie reproduced, enlarged, in her own book, *No Man Knows My History*, 299; Presendia's autobiographical sketch, in the letter dated April 16, 1881, LDS Archives; and Emmeline Wells, "A Venerable Woman," *Woman's Exponent* 11 (March 15, 1883): 155. The spacing of Presendia's children also argues for the 1840 date. In early nineteenth century America, there was usually a year and a half between children, and she had had a daughter on April 24, 1838.

46. HC 3:321. Hyrum Smith's journal, LDS Archives, supports this.

47. HC 3:449.

48. HC 3:321.

49. HC 3:449.

50. HC 3:321.

51. *No Man Knows My History*, 461–62, 301–2.

52. Lee Library, see book 16, p. 31, November 14, 1884. A film of the holograph is available at the Huntington Library.

53. And of course a major mistake like the Oliver Buell interpretation leaves one with serious questions about Brodie's critical judgment in the rest of her book.

54. Cited in Bringhurst, "Fawn M. Brodie, 'Mormondom's Lost Generation,'" 16. As noted before, these are criticisms of drafts of *No Man Knows My History*. See his letter to Brodie, August 28, 1944, Marriott Library, Bx 7, Fd 4: "I have also a general criticism of your book, to which I think you would do well to give careful attention before publishing it. It is one of the strengths as well as one of the weaknesses of your book that you have not hesitated to come to bold judgments on the basis of assumptions" (2). "On reviewing your MS, you should know where it would be wise of you to make a final check on your sources and see whether your statements are too flat and positive in the light of the facts that are available to you. Many of your judgments you can set forward tentatively . . . But it is highly important that you should not talk like God on insubstantial foundations" (3).

55. Morgan, quoted in Bringhurst, "Fawn M. Brodie, 'Mormondom's Lost Generation,'" 16.

56. The fascinating chapter on Brodie's writing of *No Man Knows My History* in Bringhurst's forthcoming biography supplies two revealing pieces of data. First, when Brodie was with her father, he would try to convert her to his orthodox point of view, and she would try to convert him to her secular point of view. Second, she was shocked by Joseph Smith's polygamy, which she interpreted as promiscuity in essence, with polygamy as a mere disguise. So she strikes one as a very monogamist twentieth-century Mormon, entirely unsympathetic to the nineteenth-century Mormon idea of polygamy as authentic marriage. She even felt that polygamous women were promiscuous. So *No Man Knows My History* has something of Harriet Beecher Stowe in it and something of the missionary tract.

57. Josephine Fisher affidavit, February 24, 1915 (Vault Folder, LDS Archives, as cited in Bachman, "A Study," 141, 354.) See also Angus M. Cannon, statement of interview with Joseph Smith III, pp. 25–26, LDS Archives. On p. 141, Bachman collects general evidence for Joseph Smith's children by polygamous wives. Mary Elizabeth Lightner Smith Young, for instance, said that she knew of three of his children who grew up under other names. (See "Remarks, Apr. 14, 1905," p. 5 in the Mary Elizabeth Lightner Collection, Lee Library.)

58. See Newell and Avery, *Mormon Enigma: Emma Hale Smith*, 136.

59. Chauncey Webb, in Wyl, *Mormon Portraits*, 57.

60. *No Man Knows My History*, xii.

61. Cf. Stanley Kimball, *Heber C. Kimball*, 315, 307. So the practice of relying on authorities can perpetuate an error *ad infinitum*, especially since many scholars cite Brodie as an authority.

62. See Wyl, *Mormon Portraits*, 65–66; *No Man Knows My History*, 485.

63. Cordelia Morley, Autobiography, Lee Library.

64. Full documentation for the following women is impossible here. See a forthcoming work by myself and cf. documentation in Bachman, "A Study"; Van Wagoner, *Mormon Polygamy*; and Brodie.

65. Lerner, *The Creation of Patriarchy*.

7

―――♦♦♦♦♦♦――

From Old to New Mormon History
Fawn Brodie and the Legacy of Scholarly Analysis of Mormonism

Roger D. Launius

If there had been no Fawn Brodie, Mormon historians would have had to invent her. Ever since she published *No Man Knows My History: The Life of Joseph Smith, the Mormon Prophet* in 1945, calling into serious question most of the faith claims based on Mormonism's early history, an enormous amount of energy has been expended by Mormon historians, apologists, and critics of all backgrounds and persuasions either to defend or to deny her conclusions.[1] The themes explored by Mormon historians since that time have too often responded to and sought to refute or substantiate Brodie's arguments. The degree to which Mormon historiography has been shaped by the long shadow of Fawn Brodie since 1945 is both disturbing and unnecessary, but it has been and remains a persistent tradition in the study of Mormonism's first generation.

When Brodie first published *No Man Knows My History* in 1945, she analyzed Mormonism's founder using the standards of secular scholarship. She interpreted him as a charlatan at first motivated by self-serving desires but gradually coming to believe in his own prophetic mission. She also acknowledged his very real accomplishments in forming an important religious movement in the United States. In many ways it was a seminal study that served as a transition point between what has been inaccurately called

195

the old and the new Mormon history, the "old" generally viewed as polemical while the "new" was considered less concerned with questions of religious truth and more interested in understanding why events unfolded as they did.[2] In the words of Paul M. Edwards, this newer approach to Mormon history represented

> a decided shift away from polemics designed as either attacks on or defense of the Mormon movement. . . . This [type of history] is not to be understood as lacking faith, being unfaithful, or going beyond faith. Rather it is an affirmation that one moves through reason and understanding to a larger faith. It suggests that doubt and unanswered questions are not issues of weak faith but the consideration of faithful persons seeking to know that which they do not understand. This assumption arises within historians and is based on their understanding of humans, and their own personal relationship with God. Thus they work fully aware that their faith is personal, not historical.[3]

It is a measure of the success of her biography of Smith that it is still considered fifty years later the standard work on the subject and the starting point for all analyses of Mormonism. A second edition of this book, published in 1971, revised some of her earlier conclusions, especially her contention that Smith had been a charlatan, and incorporated recent trends from psychohistory to explain him more as an imposter who grew in his own self-belief in his religious mission as a prophet.[4]

But the importance of Brodie's *No Man Knows My History* should be measured also by the amount of effort made in the post–World War II era by Mormon historians to take exception to her conclusions. Unfortunately, later historians have too often taken as their most important work responding to the questions she framed rather than pushing into other areas of investigation. Specifically, Brodie set the agenda for much of the historical research conducted since that time; concentrating on the first generation of Mormons, on the question of character and the church's origins, on the conflict between theocracy and democracy, and on polygamy and other theological innovations. The result, unfortunately, has been a stunting of Mormon studies. While the ghost of Brodie prompted other students of Mormon culture to wrestle with issues in ways that might not have arisen until much later had she not been present, a generally positive development, too often later Mormon historians have chased her shadow rather than researching in other areas that might have been more profitably explored. While these historians have been preoccupied with the issues raised in *No Man Knows My History*, they have ignored many of the important themes being investigated in the broader tapestry of American history; these range from issues of demography to institution building to power and the question of who controls it to social life. A fully rounded portrait of Mormon culture has been slow to appear, in part because Brodie's powerful book channeled later research into directions that would respond to it. Like so many trends in historiography, it at first seemed fresh and alive with insights about early Mormonism only to eventually become a straight-jacket for investigators of the Mormon past.

In part because of this, much serious Mormon historical writing of the recent past has been consumed by what Charles S. Peterson has appropriately called a "cult of the Prophet."[5] While there had been a fair amount of historical work on Joseph Smith and early Mormonism before 1945, this was balanced by a series of excellent monographs on later periods and broader subjects.[6] Indeed, I would suggest the very sophisticated set of challenges raised by Brodie about Joseph Smith and Mormon origins has been overly responsible for the concentration of Mormon historiography on questions of origin. The questions, issues, and perspectives of many historical explorations in Mormon history have too frequently provided narrowly defined responses to Brodie's arguments without incorporating larger contexts that have informed contemporary developments in other historical disciplines.[7] Over time because of this, at least in part, Mormon historians found themselves talking and writing for each other and for a small community of people who were mostly interested in the subject because they shared some aspect of Mormonism's religious heritage. While more Mormon historical articles were being produced, few outside the immediate sphere of Mormonism took much notice of it.[8]

The reasons for this myopic concern with Mormon origins and Brodie's spin on it is that the Latter-day Saints do not so much have a theology as they have a history. Confusing theology with history, therefore, requires that believing Saints accept a specified set of affirmations that are grounded in the "pure" thoughts and actions of past individuals, especially those of Joseph Smith. One sophisticated exposition of this position boiled the issue down to the answers that had to be given of two related questions: "Was Joseph Smith a genuine seer and prophet, and is the Book of Mormon true? If either one or the other is true, because both are linked, the truth of the other is thereby warranted."[9] Without acceptance of these truths, advocates of this position would argue, Mormonism could and probably should fall of its own weight. The perception of truth or falsity about the religion, therefore, rests on what historians say about those who have gone before. Brodie, perhaps intentionally, dealt a damaging blow to this variety of belief system when she questioned most of the basic assumptions about Mormon origins in her biography of Joseph Smith.

In *No Man Knows My History* Brodie systematically dealt with five basic issues that have challenged Mormon historians ever since. One of the most important was Joseph Smith's "first vision," for which she emphatically denied that there was any valid evidence until Smith fabricated it in 1838, when he began dictating his history to provide a starting point for his prophetic career that would counter charges that he was involved in treasure seeking. A second was the whole issue of treasure seeking itself and its relationship both to Smith and Mormon origins. Third, Brodie questioned the origins and content of the Book of Mormon, asserting that it was a product of Joseph Smith's vivid imagination and not an actual history of any group of people who came from Palestine to America. Fourth, she explored in depth the origins of plural marriage and the duplicity Smith registered in originating it to justify what she thought was his licentious nature. Finally, Brodie interpreted Smith as a would-be tyrant seeking to take over some or all of the territory of the United States to create his own theocratic state with himself in charge. I will discuss each of these major themes in turn and describe how Mormon historiography has been configured by an obsession with responding to Brodie's contentions.

The first major controversy over Joseph Smith in Brodie's book is her skeptical recounting of the first vision of Moroni to the teenage Smith about 1820, in which he was told of his sacred mission to bring forth the Book of Mormon and re-establish the gospel in its ancient purity. The first vision has been a linchpin of Mormon faith since at least the 1850s. Historian James B. Allen concluded that "next to the resurrection of Christ, nothing holds a more central place in modern Mormon thought than that sacred event of 1820."[10] Challenging the legitimacy of this event, Brodie wrote matter-of-factly that "when in later years Joseph Smith had become the revered prophet of thousands of Mormons, he began writing an official autobiography, in which his account of his adolescent years differed surprisingly from the brief sketch he had written in 1834 in answer to his critics."[11] While this 1838 autobiography contained a detailed account of a first vision, she noted, an 1834 autobiography did not mention the incident. Brodie then went on to comment that the Palmyra newspapers failed to note anything about this incident in spite of the fact that Smith described persecution when he told others of it. "The awesome vision he described in later years was probably the elaboration of some half-remembered dream stimulated by the early revival of excitement and reinforced by the rich folklore of visions circulating in the neighborhood," she concluded. "Or it may have been sheer invention."[12]

Brodie's contention that the beloved first vision was the result of a bad pickle or outright lies could not be left ignored by those accepting the Mormon faith. Soon historians were scurrying about the New York countryside trying to find evidence refuting Brodie's allegations. They found proof that Joseph Smith did indeed record this event prior to 1838 and that it was not a significant religious issue for the Latter-day Saints of the 1830s. Only later did it reach its central place in the history/theology of the movement. They contended, however, that it did happen.[13] But they also found that the eight different accounts of the first vision that are extant have numerous discrepancies and they have, accordingly, had to deal with conflicting testimony coming from Joseph Smith.[14]

Numerous articles have been dedicated to dealing with the problem of the divergent accounts of the first vision and what that might mean for the Saints, specifically trying to refute any possibility of duplicity on the part of Joseph Smith in providing different accounts.[15] In *The Mormon Experience*, historians Leonard J. Arrington and Davis Bitton summarize the problems and reconciliation of the various accounts in a way that would be acceptable to most Mormons: "If the later version was different, this was not a result of inventing an experience out of whole cloth, as an unscrupulous person might readily have done, but rather of reexamining an earlier experience and seeing it in a different light."[16] Unstated but implied was the conclusion that Brodie's assessment of Smith having made the whole thing up to lend credibility to his prophetic claims was unfounded.

A new twist was placed on the first vision controversy in 1967 when the Presbyterian minister and anti-Mormon Wesley P. Walters questioned whether there had been a Palmyra revival in the 1819–1821 time period. The sectarian revivals, Smith said, had been the catalyst for his own questioning and his trip to the grove where he experienced his first vision. Walters could not find, however, evidence of revivals in Palmyra during this period, once again suggesting—â la Brodie—that Joseph Smith might have invented the event to legitimize his prophetic role.[17] Coincident with this renewal of concerns about the first vision's veracity in 1967, five Mormon historians met in Salt Lake City to organize a research effort on "Mormon Origins in New York." Headed by Truman G. Madsen, director of the Institute of Mormon Studies at

Brigham Young University, it helped fund literally hundreds of researchers looking for, among other things, evidence to repel the challenge.[18] The papers resulting from this effort were published in a special issue of *Brigham Young University Studies* in the spring of 1969,[19] and *Dialogue: A Journal of Mormon Thought* published the Walters article along with a reply by Richard L. Bushman.[20] Others have sought to deal with the same issue since that time, always trying to pull the first vision out of the ash heap to which Brodie had assigned it.[21]

One of the great problems with following the course charted by Brodie on the first vision, indeed it is the problem with all the questions she raises about Joseph Smith, is that it focuses historical research into an "either/or" mode. Mormon historiography has enough problems with this anyway—the churches of Mormondom are always seeking to buttress their validity as religious institutions through their history—but in this instance it crippled historical inquiry for more than forty years by forcing the answering of questions that are inappropriate for history to begin with and distorted beyond validity. Did Joseph Smith actually see God and Jesus Christ in a first vision or did he invent the story after the fact to legitimate his religious work? That question is ill-suited to analysis by historians who are by definition concerned with the human condition. In addition, the question, it seems to me, is both far less interesting and significant than a related one: What kind of religion is it that Smith brought into being and how did the first vision relate to it? A comment by Marvin S. Hill is suggestive on this score. He emphasizes the fact that Joseph Smith was anti-pluralistic and that a firm belief in right and wrong in religion is validated in the first vision. God tells Smith to "join none of them" (the other religions in the world) and that while all have a form of godliness, they deny the power thereof. He was told to restore the "true" gospel of Jesus Christ to the Earth and to demand repentance of all peoples.[22] Equally suggestive is a fact emphasized by non-Mormon scholar Jan Shipps, that the first vision was a means of keeping Joseph Smith, the founding prophet, center stage in the movement when it would have been quite easy to emphasize other aspects of the religion. This symbolic emphasis has shaped the direction of Mormonism to the present.[23] Such issues are more interesting, and ultimately more illuminating, than the narrow "either/or" dichotomy framed by Fawn Brodie.

A second great question raised by Fawn Brodie is the nature of treasure seeking in the early republic and Joseph Smith's role in it. She dredged up some early affidavits and found some additional information that implicated Joseph Smith in efforts to use folk magic to recover buried treasure. Specifically she found an 1826 account of a court case filed against Joseph Smith for defrauding a Josiah Stowel of money in a treasure hunting scheme. It accused him of being a "glass looker" and a money digger. Brodie concluded that the story of the Book of Mormon's "golden plates," buried in the earth and presumably recovered by Smith in 1827, had originated out of that tradition of folk magic and money-digging. This, too, she thought was an example of Smith's non-legitimate origins as a religious leader. He was, she asserted, a frontier scryer who found a way to make money-digging pay in the only way it could, as a scam.[24]

For many years Mormon historians denied Smith's connection with these types of activities, asserting that the affidavits had been prepared as anti-Mormon statements designed to drum up opposition to Smith in the 1830s and that the 1826 court record was possibly a forgery and at best questionable as a historic document.[25] But other records emerged in the 1970s and 1980s that confirmed the fact that Smith had been involved in money digging and Mormon historians felt the need to answer the charges. At first hesitantly but later with more openness they began to construct an interpretation of Mormon origins that allowed for Smith to have been involved in treasure seeking.[26] One particularly adventurous essay suggested that Smith was imbued with a magical world view and that evidence of magic could be found in all manner of Mormon theology and institutions.[27]

Like the case of the first vision, the money-digging issue got a much needed boost from some additional challenges following

Brodie's original line of inquiry, in this case in the form of new documents that appeared to tie Joseph Smith closely to folk magic and treasure seeking in the 1820s. Two letters, one supposedly from Joseph Smith to Josiah Stowel in 1825 and a second supposedly from Martin Harris to W. W. Phelps in 1830 placed treasure seeking squarely in the middle of the origins of the Book of Mormon and the birth of the church. Both of these documents later turned out to be modern forgeries by Latter-day Saint documents dealer Mark W. Hofmann, but they opened a pandora's box of concern about the subject.[28] As a result Richard L. Bushman—perhaps the quintessential practitioner of what he once titled "faithful history," an approach that emphasizes the sacred nature of the history of Mormonism—felt the need to try to cohere the folk magic tradition of Joseph Smith with his later career in his award-winning book *Joseph Smith and the Beginnings of Mormonism*.[29] The icing on the cake of this subject was the book by D. Michael Quinn on Mormonism and magic, in which the two were interpreted as being inextricably intertwined throughout the first generation of the church's history.[30]

Once again, the either/or dialectic set out by Brodie wrapped up some very talented historians who might have explored other aspects of this subject had they not been consumed with the desire to refute and later explain away her arguments. The folk magic context in early Mormonism is truly an interesting area of exploration, but a broad-based analysis divorced from the question of Mormon legitimacy would have been more useful. An investigation that employed the Kuhnian argument of paradigm shift and *weltanschauung* across a broad spectrum of social issues, the rational/irrational world only one part of a much larger avenue of exploration, would be especially rewarding.[31] Moreover, the problem of money-digging took historians away from their other worthwhile studies and like the "dutch boy" plugging the dike sacrificed their services to a perceived immediate public relations and theological/historical problem. An example of what might be accomplished by historians who move beyond the initial framework of the question is the recent analysis of Mormon cosmology by John L. Brooke. Bringing together an analysis of Mormonism's occult origins in folk magic and money-digging with its later expression in unique theological ideals, Brooke goes beyond these earlier concerns with Brodie's dialectical approach to show how Smith unified Mormon thought using the opposing forces of European hermetic purity and danger.[32]

The Book of Mormon, of course, has been a controversial publication since it first appeared in 1830. There have been numerous studies since 1945, therefore, that either defend or condemn the book. In some way or another, almost all of these reflect the fingerprints of Brodie and her erudite handling of the subject. The first and most central part of this issue was the determination as to whether the book was an authentic history of a group of religious pilgrims who came to America, what Joseph Smith said it was, or whether it was a product of frontier mythology written either by Smith or some other author. Fawn Brodie eloquently challenged the conventional Mormon perception of the coming forth of the Book of Mormon and in the process undermined the legitimacy of the work as scripture. She charged that Smith had originally intended the book as a secular history of ancient America, but his own treasure seeking opportunism led to its transformation into a religious history with attendant angelic visitations, "golden plates," and translation of ancient records through the "Urim and Thummim" by the "gift and power of God."[33]

Specifically, she argued that frontier America was consumed with interest in the origins of the Indians and that a favorite theory was that they were remnants of the lost tribes of ancient Israel. Smith was as curious as anyone else and enjoyed speculations about the development and eventual extinction of the mound builders, a perceived ancient and extinct aboriginal people.[34] The Book of Mormon, Brodie charged, was basically the history of two rival mound builder groups, one a "fair and delightsome people" of refinement, the other a "wild and ferocious, and a bloodthirsty people; full of idolatry and wandering about in the wilderness, with a short skin girded about their loins, and their heads shaven; and their skill . . . in the bow, and the cimeter and the axe."[35]

Smith started out wanting to write a history of the mound builders, Brodie concluded, but gradually came to the decision to describe only the "peregrinations of two Hebrew families, headed by Lehi and Ishmael, who became the founders of the American race. He began by focusing upon a single hero, Nephi, who like himself was peculiarly gifted of the Lord. This device launched him smoothly into his narrative and saved him from having bitten off more than he could chew."[36] Joseph Smith drew his information on the Native Americans from Ethan Smith's 1825 edition of *View of the Hebrews*, which argued that the Indians were descendants of Hebraic peoples.[37] The whole religious angle, she speculated, was dreamed up sometime after 1828 when Smith had gathered around him a small group of believers who accepted him as a prophet of God.[38] To support her contentions, Brodie cited statements of Palmyra editor Abner Cole, who wrote under the pseudonym Obadiah Dogberry, and affidavits by neighbors of the Smith family.[39]

Not long after the organization of the church, and especially because of the attraction of the Book of Mormon to members of the Disciples of Christ, Alexander Campbell published the first genuine criticism of the book. In it he commented that the Book of Mormon dealt with "every error and almost every truth discussed in New York for the last ten years."[40] Brodie latched upon this analysis of the scripture as *the* explanation of the message of the book as Smith fully grasped his role as a prophet, suggesting that he was extraordinarily responsive "to the provincial opinions of the time." For this to be possible, of course, the Book of Mormon could not have been a sacred translation of ancient scripture but was a modern work written by Joseph Smith.[41] Taking as her departure point Campbell's observation and Brodie's championing of it, Susan Curtis Mernitz concluded in a 1982 article that the "Book of Mormon offered ideas that were familiar to New Yorkers in 1830 when distribution of the book began. Though the Book of Mormon tells us much about its author, it also illuminates ideas and social phenomena that characterized the generation of 1830."[42]

Richard L. Bushman has taken issue with this position and argues that the republican tendencies that were everywhere present in the early American nation were absent from the Book of Mormon. Indeed he suggests that the scripture was strangely distant from the social and political milieu of the United States in 1830. He sees more "Old World" perspectives than early American thought in the book.[43] Marvin S. Hill offers a slightly different perspective by concluding that the Book of Mormon presents a non-democratic position with government by judges and kings, a tone suggesting the inability of individuals to govern themselves and a sense of hierarchical structure that inhibited pluralism. "The Book of Mormon," he writes, "is thus an ambivalent spokesman for republicanism." Hill then describes the anti-pluralistic, non-democratic approach toward life by Joseph Smith and the quest to retreat from the Jacksonian era to one of more order.[44]

Mormon and non-Mormon scholars have debated the points raised by Brodie about the origins of the Book of Mormon back and forth *ad nauseam* for a half century without resolution.[45] To a very real extent, the conclusion reached is based on whether one is a believing member of the church and not on evidence. Like attorneys arguing a case, each side amasses evidence to either buttress or destroy the foundations of the Book of Mormon as ancient scripture, convincing only those who already hold pre-conceptions in that direction. All this is so much sound and fury signifying nothing, as non-Mormon scholar Mario S. De Pillis has astutely observed, "since Mormonism as a religion developed mostly after 1830 in Smith's revelations, Campbell—and the historians who so avidly quote him instead of the Mormon sources—was premature and wrong in equating the Book of Mormon with Mormonism."[46]

While Campbell's challenge to the ancient origin and divinity of the Book of Mormon motivated much of Brodie's analysis of the scripture, she also exploded a century old myth about the origins of the Book of Mormon that no one before her had been able to destroy despite its deserving death. In a conspiracy theory of outlandish proportions, Eber D. Howe, a newspaper editor in nearby Painesville, Ohio, suggested that Solomon Spaulding, a minister and would-be novelist from Conneaut, Ohio, had written the manuscript for the Book of Mormon, sent it to a publisher in Pittsburgh, where Sidney Rigdon had discovered and stolen it, passed it on to co-conspirator Joseph Smith, who brought in additional conspirators as witnesses to the book's divinity, published it, and began to masquerade as a prophet.[47] This theory held sway for nearly a century among non-Latter-day Saints. Unfortunately, Spaulding was long since dead and the manuscript could not be found that he had supposedly written, therefore the account was mostly hearsay and recollection and had all the veracity of the tabloids. It was not until the 1880s when Spaulding's papers were discovered in Hawaii and his manuscript compared to the Book of Mormon that it became apparent that there was no relationship between the two books.[48]

Other aspects of the Book of Mormon story as discussed by Brodie have also sent Mormon historians since then off in search of evidence and ideas. These have included the story of the so-called Anthon transcript, supposedly a sheet of paper on which Smith copied some of the "reformed Egyptian" characters of the golden plates that Martin Harris took to an accomplished linguist for verification and which Brodie suggests may have given Smith an inkling of insight into his role as a prophet;[49] the method of translation of the book, which Brodie argued bore more relationship to treasure seeking than to Christian religious activity;[50] and the nature, development, and disposition of the texts of the Book of Mormon.[51] But the most interesting area explored here is the role of the witnesses to the divinity of the Book of Mormon. The three key figures—Martin Harris, Oliver Cowdery, and David Whitmer—all were excommunicated from the church in 1838, but none ever denied their testimony to the divinity of the scripture. This is remarkable, and Brodie offers the suggestion that Smith became adept at hypnosis to convince the three that they had seen what she fully believed were non-existent golden plates.[52] The reaffirmation of this testimony has been important for Mormons and led to all manner of historical exploration into the question as a means of shoring up the question of the book's sacred origin and message.[53] Unfortunately the amassing of a mountain of information about these individuals, aimed as it is solely toward buttressing the wall of support for the divinity of the Book of Mormon, has been a blind alley down which Brodie led Mormon historians. The central question needs to be asked about how and why these three dominant characters in the formation of the church were removed from the power center of church governance in the mid-1830s and what role that fact might have played in their dissent in the latter part of the decade, important questions Brodie did not raise and that have gone begging.[54]

Recently, a few Mormon historians have begun to get away from the either/or type of questions about the Book of Mormon that Brodie was so wont to raise. For instance, while the historicity of the Book of Mormon has been under attack from without since nearly the beginning of the church and within Mormonism for most of this century in some form or another, concern for finding a way to deal with the book as a non-historical sacred text has become increasingly visible. There is evidence that B. H. Roberts, perhaps the greatest Mormon intellectual, in the early part of this century questioned the book's historicity as an actual document portraying the record of people calling themselves Nephites, but this was not widely circulated until the 1980s.[55] More recently, a book edited by Brent Lee Metcalfe seriously questioned the historicity of the Book of Mormon. One essayist bluntly summarized the central issue tackled in this book: "Members of the Church of Jesus Christ of Latter-day Saints should confess in faith that the Book of Mormon is the word of God but also abandon claims that it is a historical record of the ancient peoples of the Americas."[56]

There has been considerable concern about such statements, and the forces of traditional truth claims about the book are now engaged in a struggle for how Latter-day Saints should interpret the scripture. While some of those questioning the book's historical origins have suggested that the church should formally repudiate the Book of Mormon, many people wisely have suggested that this is throwing out the baby with the bath water. Contrary to the position of Fawn Brodie and traditional Latter-day Saints that the Book of Mormon must be an authentic history of a central group of ancient peoples in America or it must be a hoax, a more "catholic" middle position can be adopted that emphasizes the powerful message for the present-day LDS church and the world as a whole.[57] If there is one central theme in the book, it is the continual covenanting together of God and humanity in a cyclical pattern of covenant-righteousness-turning from the gospel-falling away-covenanting anew. This pattern, coupled with the strong Christology of the Book of Mormon, makes a powerful statement of humanity's worth in a world where human worth is everywhere questioned. The conclusion of non-Mormon William P. Collins seems to be appropriate here, "When I examine the Book of Mormon for truth rather that facticity, my reading reveals powerful, eternal, and relevant truths which are capable of changing and guiding men's lives."[58]

Fawn Brodie had a fascination for the violation of normal sexual mores by all of her biographical subjects, and these inclinations have been some of the most hotly contested issues in her work.[59] As a result, Joseph Smith's polygamous practices with some forty-eight women, by Brodie's count, occupied much of her attention in *No Man Knows My History*. Her approach to this subject was melodramatic and judgmental from the beginning. Her first chapter given over to this subject was called "If a Man Entice a Maid," and that chapter title said much about the approach she took toward handling the subject.[60] In the words of Marvin Hill, she concluded that Smith was "a sensualist and a libertine who hid his excessive sexual needs behind the protective cloak of religion."[61] A sense of moral indignation permeates her discussion of polygamy, which was, of course, a sexual institution just as surely as it was a religious, political, economic, and social one. From the "dirty nasty, filthy affair of his and Fanny Alger's" in 1835 to the marriage to several women just before his death in 1844, Brodie almost gleefully recounts what she never lets the reader forget is sexual misconduct by one of almost total power and influence over his followers.[62]

Plural marriage was responsible for the last dramatic act of Joseph Smith's life, the destruction of the *Expositor*, which led directly to his assassination by a mob in Carthage, Illinois, on June 27, 1844. In the spring of 1844 many influential Latter-day Saints, led by William Law, a counselor to Joseph Smith in the first presidency for a time in the early 1840s, left the movement because they were convinced that the organization had departed from the true principles of the gospel. The dissenters also included Wilson Law, William's brother and a brigadier general in the Nauvoo legion; Austin Cowles, a member of the Nauvoo stake's high council; and James Blakeslee, Robert D. Foster, Chauncey Higbee, and Charles Ivins, all prominent church members.[63]

These dissidents worked to expose what they considered the evils of the church in a newspaper called the *Nauvoo Expositor*. On June 7, 1844, they issued the paper's only number, and it contained a number of affidavits about the practice of plural marriage by church officials. The publication of the *Expositor* raised a furor in the community, and Smith, acting as mayor of Nauvoo, ordered that the press be silenced by city authorities. William Law immediately went to Carthage, the seat of Hancock County, to swear out a complaint against Smith for inciting a riot and unlawfully destroying property. State authorities arrested Smith on this charge, as well as some others drummed up later, and while incarcerated in the county jail, a mob lynched him and his brother on June 27, 1844. In an irony of the foremost magnitude, whether one believes any of the charges levied by William Law against Smith matters not; the prophet was vulnerable to the mob because he had been arrested for exercising injudiciously the very power Law accused him of exercising injudiciously.[64] Brodie lays all of this out in great detail, coming close to saying that

Smith's inability to control his sexual proclivities led directly to his death.

The discussion of plural marriage in the early history of the Mormon church has been an important topic of discussion ever since the publication of *No Man Knows My History*. It has also been one of the most contentious. Assignment of responsibility for the origination of the doctrine, with all of its sexual impropriety overtones, has been hotly contested. For instance, responding directly to the challenges raised by Brodie, in addition to those by the Utah Latter-day Saint church, until the early 1980s the Reorganized church, the second largest of the Mormon factions, officially denied that Smith had been the author of plural marriage and asserted that it had been started by Brigham Young and was evidence of apostasy.[65] Indeed, Robert B. Flanders was virtually shunned from the church after his 1965 book on Nauvoo appeared because he accepted the Brodie line of argument on polygamy's origins and offered some of her same moral judgments about Smith's character.[66] This began to change in a fundamental way only after the 1983 publication of an article by RLDS Church Historian Richard P. Howard that viewed plural marriage as something that arose in Nauvoo as a historical accident which grew like Topsy near and immediately after the death of Joseph Smith Jr.[67] As misguided as this interpretation was because of its conservatism and inability to deal with Smith's earlier indiscretions, it opened the door for the acceptance of more critical appraisals, ones in which Brodie's arguments have been largely accepted.[68]

Latter-day Saint historians never denied Smith's responsibility for originating plural marriage but tried to explain his sexual antics as religious in origin. Hugh Nibley, in one of the first responses to Brodie, defends all of Joseph Smith's actions as noble in character. He then comments, in one of the most asinine statements ever written about Mormon history, that Smith's "teachings are so well-knit and perfectly logical that they have never had to undergo the slightest change or alteration during a century in which every other church in Christendom has continually revamped its doctrines." Nibley must have somehow forgotten that the church was forced by the federal government officially to abandon the practice of plural marriage in 1890 despite its supposedly eternal nature as a doctrine of God.[69] Other Mormon historians have also emphasized the pious dimension of the development of plural marriage, in the process downplaying the sexual aspects of the doctrine.[70] Biographies of Brigham Young, Heber C. Kimball, and Wilford Woodruff, all prolific polygamists, describe the practice's burden and implicitly argue that they took additional wives not because of any drive of the libido but because of their commitment to the Mormon religion.[71]

Marvin Hill explicitly took on Brodie's sexual misconduct explanation for plural marriage and concluded that it was probably the result of Smith's seriousness about his prophetic role. Hill wrote that "Brodie failed to appreciate the degree to which the prophetic role liberated Smith from the social restraints which customarily control sexual behavior." He noted that Smith was not charged with any sexual misconduct until 1832, well after his emergence as a prophetic leader, and that if he was such a libertine, it should have been present in the 1820s. Hill also comments that Smith seems to have been greatly influenced in his thinking about plural marriage by his reading of the Old Testament, providing "further proof of Smith's early and complete absorption in his prophetic role." Smith also, according to Hill, did not have sexual relations with many of his wives, again parrying the sexual drive as the reason for the practice. In all, Smith emerges as a more authentic and legitimate religious leader than Brodie makes him out to be.[72]

It is this desire for an answer to Brodie's charges of Smith's misconduct and illegitimacy that helps explain the great acceptance of non-Mormon historian Lawrence Foster's collective studies of sexual practices among the Mormons, the Shakers, and the Oneida Perfectionists.[73] A very fine body of work, Foster was drawn to this subject by the desire to understand the experimentation in the marriage relationship that took place in a broad spectrum of antebellum America. In this comparative effort, Foster interpreted Joseph Smith as only one of several highly creative and restless souls who were seeking a more perfect relationship of individuals. He was not, therefore, the licentious womanizer that Brodie made of him. He also was not, and this seems to have been largely missed by most Mormons who embraced Foster's work, the prophet of the living God who restored the true gospel in its ancient purity to the earth.[74]

One aspect of the effort to clothe the origins of plural marriage in religious reverence resulted in specifically trying to push the date of the revelation on the subject back to 1831. Brodie had pointed out the inconsistency in the official date, July 12, 1843, of the recording of the revelation of plural marriage, Section 132 in the Latter-day Saints Doctrine and Covenants, with the de facto practice of plural marriage from at least 1836. Using an 1861 recollection of W. W. Phelps, at best a questionable source since polygamy had been firmly established in Utah by then and it was under attack both by the federal government and the Reorganized church as an illegitimate institution, historian Danel W. Bachman made a case that on July 17, 1831, Smith had told five followers in a revelation in Jackson County, Missouri, "It is my will, that in time, ye should take unto you wives of the Lamanites and Nephites, that their posterity may become white, delightsome and just." Phelps asked Joseph Smith later how this could be since the men to whom the revelation was given already had wives. Smith had told him that it would be done as it was in the Old Testament with Abraham and Jacob, "by *Revelation*."[75] Accordingly, if one accepts this argument, the practice was commanded as early as 1831 and put into place at least by 1836, with the formal recording of an earlier revelation completing the process only in 1843.[76]

The efforts to explore Mormon plural marriage practices have led to some valuable observations. But, as in other instances, the either/or nature framing Brodie's arguments on the subject have prompted Mormon historians to take limiting approaches. The comparative approach of Lawrence Foster has been illuminating, for instance, but I would suggest that without his approaching it as a non-Mormon with multi-religious interests, it never would have evolved as usefully as it did. Additionally, studies of plural marriage on its own terms, without moral judgments as to sexual deviance of those involved, have been stunted. And a whole raft of questions never suggested by Brodie await exploration. For instance, the whole gender issue and its relationship in plural marriage is ripe for exploration. Also, what role did plural marriage play in efforts by insecure males to secure traditional gender roles in a society in flux in Jacksonian America? Did the all male priesthood headed by Joseph Smith embrace these practices because of status anxiety?[77] Historian Mark C. Carnes has argued that Victorian males desired to restore order and to resecure the patriarchal authority lost in the Industrial Revolution and its attendant social upheavals. Could plural marriage have been a part of this effort?[78] Joseph Smith's preoccupation with Old Testament images, especially those associated with the biblical patriarchs, and the elaborate rites of plural marriage and other temple concepts share linkages to actions taking place in broader American society.[79] Could similar concerns for status and security have prompted the development of plural marriage as a religious rite? We await future studies that will develop these and other issues.

Finally, the place of the Mormon religion in the world was raised by Brodie, and she condemned Joseph Smith as a power-hungry manipulator who sought to create a theocratic government with him in complete control. Although she noted this tendency from the beginning of the movement, Brodie especially focused on it during the Mormon church's sojourn in Nauvoo, 1839–1846, when Smith and the church truly came to dominate the political, economic, and social as well as the religious aspects of life in the region. She saw in Nauvoo a highly unified, separatist community that did not cooperate with outsiders, and agreed with the non-Mormons who lived near the Saints that the theocratic tendencies of Smith represented a threat to democratic government.

Brodie emphasized Smith's participation in politics, especially his involvement in bloc voting in the congressional election of 1843 and his candidacy for the U.S. presidency in the 1844 election. She also highlighted the creation of the Council of Fifty in the spring of 1844. This secret organization was a body charged with the responsibility of setting up a political kingdom of God on earth, with Smith as its chancellor. She thought Smith was "intoxicated with power and drunk with visions of empire and apocalyptic glory" and that his political adventures were so much evidence of this. An especially warped act along these lines, according to Brodie, came when Smith had himself crowned king of this political kingdom just a few weeks before his murder.[80]

Not surprisingly, Brodie found, the vigorous movement of Mormonism into politics in Nauvoo, as well as the city's economic and military power, prompted opposition from settlers as far away as Macomb, Quincy, Alton, and other Illinois communities, but it was centered in Hancock County, where the Mormons dominated local politics by 1842. These communities, something of a microcosm of pluralistic America, had welcomed the Saints at first and their openness to this religious group had made Nauvoo's theocracy possible. As a result, it was not surprising that residents around the Mormon stronghold objected to Smith's theocratic domination of government at Nauvoo, his encouragement of bloc voting for candidates he supported, his use of the Nauvoo charter to avoid prosecution, and, eventually, his violation of the civil rights of his critics. That he also headed a huge militia, the Nauvoo legion, made the threat of despotism seem all the more real. A conspiracy to take over the government appeared in the offing from the Mormon prophet.[81]

Brodie's portrait of a rapacious prophet in complete control of people, land, and other resources did not square with Mormon conceptions about the history of the church. Ever since the 1840s Mormons have viewed Nauvoo as a pivotal episode in the development of their religion, important for the growth, organization, and doctrines of the Latter-day Saint faith.[82] As one of the best general histories of Mormonism indicates, the community's significance centers around what the Mormon prophet accomplished there:

At Nauvoo Joseph Smith reached the zenith of both his temporal and spiritual influence. As a secular leader he became mayor of one of the two largest cities in Illinois, editor of its newspaper, a leading entrepreneur, and a candidate for the presidency of the United States. As a spiritual leader he announced important new doctrinal ideas, began the erection of a magnificent temple, introduced a sacred temple ceremony that helped increase brotherhood and spirituality among the Saints, and laid the foundation for expanding the Kingdom worldwide. His tragic martyrdom in 1844 became a rallying point for a greater spiritual unity among the Saints and strengthened the Kingdom instead of destroying it as his antagonists had hoped.[83]

Furthermore, Smith was regarded within the church not as a martyr to the theocracy that Brodie was so interested in, but as a martyr to freedom of religion. And Nauvoo for them represents the sacred context of that martyrdom.

Because of this dichotomy of what Brodie said about Smith's theocratic tendencies, historical writing about Mormon Nauvoo has been voluminous. Much of it seeks to refute the Brodie thesis and argues that the Saints were innocent victims of religious persecution by anti-Mormons in western Illinois. While most might admit that some of the actions of individual members could occasionally have been unwise or indiscreet, collectively they never seriously question the actions of the church hierarchy and never seriously consider the perspective of those outside the faith, a strength of Brodie's work. Indeed, some of them overtly trace their questions to Brodie's biography.[84]

There have been a handful of truly significant historical studies explicitly looking at the questions Brodie raised about Smith's political and theocratic life. Probably the most significant was Robert Bruce Flanders's *Nauvoo: Kingdom on the Mississippi.* Interested in government, politics, economics, and the development of Mormon institutions, Flanders in his 1965

book—incomplete as it is because of its intentional disregard of
social and religious issues—stood the sacred history approach on
its head and opened an avenue of exploration that extended
beyond Roberts. Flanders, who is not a member of the Utah
Latter-day Saint church, said that he wrote of Joseph Smith not
as a religious leader but exactly as Brodie had, as a "man of
affairs—planner, promoter, architect, entrepreneur, executive,
politician, filibusterer—matters of which he was sometimes less
sure than he was those of the spirit." He also wrote of Mormon
Nauvoo as a western boom town and not as a religious "city on a
hill" and about Smith as a theocratic leader bent on fashioning
"the Kingdom of Heaven into a kingdom of this world."[85]
Flanders "secularized and humanized Nauvoo's story to remove it
from the celebratory aura of sanctioned interpretations," according to Glen M. Leonard, and in the process charted a path that
most historians inside the Mormon church have been unwilling
to follow since that time.[86]

Historian Klaus J. Hansen has suggested that while they
admit that there is much to admire in Flanders's secular emphasis, scholars who are members of the Latter-day Saint faith
community could not have written it because they have an
especially difficult time overcoming their predispositions to
view the church, its leaders, and its institutions as always righteous and just. Unlike Flanders, wrote Hansen, "Utah Mormons cannot admit a major flaw in Nauvoo, for these were the
very practices and doctrines [Brigham] Young transplanted to
the Rocky Mountain kingdom."[87] For inheritors of the Mormon legacy, Nauvoo was the first major explication of their
vision of the world, and they tended to see this significance
first. Most historians who are also Mormons have accepted traditional interpretations (or perhaps have never even considered going beyond them because of their religious convictions).
As Ronald K. Esplin commented in a recent essay, "Nauvoo
was, and is, and will be important to Latter-day Saints because
it was the City of Joseph. It was the city he built, where he lived
and acted, where he died. Above all, it was the city where he

fulfilled his religious mission. . . . In a very real sense, his other labors were prologue."[88]

More ominous than the overarching abstract principle of theocracy was the Council of Fifty that Brodie described in *No Man Knows My History*. Organized at Nauvoo in the spring of 1844 to bring about the political kingdom of God, presided over by the coronated Joseph Smith Jr. as the ruler of God's kingdom on earth, for years Mormon leaders had denied the organization's existence. Then in 1967, after several preliminary essays on the subject, Klaus J. Hansen published his pathbreaking *Quest for Empire:The Kingdom of God and the Council of Fifty in Mormon History*.[89] Although Hansen took pains to present his case in a non-judgmental manner, in *Quest for Empire* he presented a compelling interpretation of the empire-building designs of Joseph Smith that exhaustively documented many of the interpretations of Fawn Brodie about Mormon theocracy.

Other Mormon historians emerged to challenge the interpretation of a conspiratorial Council of Fifty as a shadow theocratic government seeking to overthrow the United States.[90] In particular, Marvin S. Hill offered a thesis that argued that all of the "empire-building efforts by Joseph Smith should be viewed as an attempt to escape from American pluralism and secularism." According to Hill, the early Mormon attempt to develop a communal utopia under theocratic control during the 1830s and 1840s was partially a reaction against the increasing importance of democratic, competitive, secular tendencies and the overall decline of religion in American life. The Mormon church, therefore, "sought to revitalize this magical world view [such as had been present in medieval society], combine it with elements of more traditional Christianity, and establish a theocratic society where the unconverted, the poor, and the socially and religiously alienated could gather and find a refuge from the competing sects and the uncertainties they engendered. His efforts to do so would bring him into conflict with leaders and others of the established order who were otherwise-minded."[91] The emerging emphasis on personal freedom, as expressed in Jacksonian democracy, then, was an unnerving ingredient in this, as was a general sense of alienation from other religious denominations, especially those that embraced the tendencies of larger society.[92]

The erection of a strong theocratic organization to counter these external pressures, Hill asserted, was imperative in this environment and social milieu. Consolidation of authority, therefore, became an early and persistent goal of the Mormon leadership. Far from being a conspiracy, the actions that Brodie was so critical of emerged relatively benignly from the religious concerns of the movement about the problems of larger society.

Since first appearing in 1945, *No Man Knows My History* has exerted a tremendous influence on the Mormon historical community, for both good and ill. It has forced other historians to come to grips with several themes that had been largely ignored beforehand or, when considered, had been dealt with in a decidedly faith-promoting manner. Brodie's heavy-handed either/or approach to interpreting Joseph Smith compelled historians to confront evidence for the purpose of refuting or revising her assessments. Looking at the historical records in a new way, opening new insights. and stretching interpretations are the meat and potatoes of historical inquiry. These are positive developments. At the same time, and Brodie is just as responsible for this as anyone else, the historical inquiry has wrapped historians into a tightly wound set of considerations about Smith. It has contributed to the insular nature of the field, and that helped ensure that it did not thrive as it might have, had new and different and challenging questions been asked that had application and interest beyond the narrow Mormon community.[93] In part because of this, the Mormon historical community seems to be in more of a holding pattern than in the past. In spite of the amount of historical research and writing being done, and there remains a prodigious output in the 1990s, there seems to be little that is new or exciting in Mormon history.

The dust jacket for the 1971 edition of *No Man Knows My History* contained a quote from the *Saturday Review* about the

1945 edition. According to the quotation, that edition was distinguished by, among other things, "the richness and suppleness of its prose, and its narrative power." I would suggest that those attributes have made the book the legend that it is among historians and a work that had to be answered for the past fifty years. The virtuosity of Brodie's marshalling of evidence, which was admittedly not particularly new, the potency of her vision of Smith, the power of her prose, and the sheer opulence of her interpretation made *No Man Knows My History* the significant book that it became. Virtually everyone working in Mormon history still must contend with it in some way in their own work. It has not been supplanted by additional biographies of Joseph Smith, although several have been written, and it will not be until an author steps forward who can create as compelling a portrait of the Mormon founder that effectively moves beyond the Brodie tradition. It is time, fifty years later, to get on with that task.

Notes

1. Fawn M. Brodie, *No Man Knows My History: The Life of Joseph Smith, the Mormon Prophet* (New York: Alfred A. Knopf, 1945). A revised and expanded second edition appeared in 1971. All citations in this essay are to the 1971 edition.

2. I would suggest that these are inaccurate labels. There is no clear demarcation between the "old" and the "new" Mormon history. It has come to mean any number of things to any number of Mormon observers, a means of lumping together a diverse array of scholars with diverse sets of interests and approaches. What I believe has happened is not so much a transition from an "old" to a "new" approach toward Mormon history as the rapid and sustained professionalization of the field. The characteristics of both trends have been present to a greater or lesser degree for quite a long time, but a non-belligerent position either for or against the movement became dominant during the latter 1950s. For a fuller discussion of my ideas on this subject see Roger D. Launius, "Whither Reorganization History?" *John Whitmer Historical Association Journal* 10 (1990): 24–37.

3. Paul M. Edwards, "The New Mormon History," *Saints Herald* 133 (November 1986): 13. See also Richard P. Howard, "New Currents in Mormon History," *Saints Herald* 135 (November 1988): 483.

4. Brodie, *No Man Knows My History,* 418–21.

5. Charles S. Peterson, "Beyond the Problems of Exceptionalist History," in Thomas G. Alexander, ed., *Great Basin Kingdom Revisited: Contemporary Perspectives* (Logan: Utah State University Press, 1991), 133–51, quote from p. 146.

6. Ibid. As examples see E. E. Erickson, *The Psychological and Ethical Aspects of Mormon Group Life* (Chicago: University of Chicago Press, 1922); Joseph A. Geddes, *The United Order Among The Mormons (Missouri Phase)* (New York: Columbia University Press, 1922); Nels Anderson, *Desert Saints: The Mormon Frontier in Utah* (Chicago: University of Chicago Press, 1942).

7. There have been several overall critiques of *No Man Knows My History* by Mormon scholars. The earliest, and by far the most flippant and easily dismissed is Hugh Nibley, *No Ma'am, That's Not History* (Salt Lake City: Bookcraft, 1946). For many years this work was made available in many Utah libraries and bookstores side by side with Brodie's, poison and antidote. The most sophisticated overall critique is still Marvin S. Hill, "Secular or Sectarian History? A Critique of 'No Man Knows My History'," *Church History* 43 (March 1974): 78–96, reprinted in this volume. See also Marvin S. Hill, "Survey: The Historiography of Mormonism," *Church History* 28 (1959): 418–26; and Marvin S. Hill, "Brodie Revisited: A Reappraisal," *Dialogue: A Journal of Mormon Thought* 7 (winter 1972): 72–87.

8. The insular nature of Mormon historiography has been criticized in several publications. See Peterson, "Beyond the Problems of Exceptionalist History;" Thomas G. Alexander, "Historiography and the New Mormon History," *Dialogue: A Journal of Mormon Thought* 19 (fall 1986): 25–49, especially 39; Roger D. Launius, "The 'New Social History' and the 'New Mormon History': Reflection on Recent Trends," *Dialogue: A Journal of Mormon Thought* 27 (spring 1994): 109–27.

9. Louis Midgley, "The Challenge of Historical Consciousness: Mormon History and the Encounter with Secular Modernity," in *By Study and Also by Faith,* vol. 2, ed. John M. Lundquist and Stephen D. Ricks (Salt Lake City: Deseret Book Co., and Provo, Utah: Foundation for Ancient Research and Mormon Studies, 1990), 503–51, quote from p. 510.

10. James B. Allen, "Emergence of a Fundamental: The Expanding Role of Joseph Smith's First Vision in Mormon Thought," *Journal of Mormon History* 7 (1980): 43–61, quote from p. 43.

11. Brodie, *No Man Knows My History,* 21.

12. Ibid., 25.

13. James B. Allen, "The Significance of Joseph Smith's First Vision in Mormon Thought," *Dialogue: A Journal of Mormon Thought* 1 (autumn 1966): 29–46; Allen, "Emergence of A Fundamental;" Milton V. Backman Jr., *American Religions and the Rise of Mormonism* (Salt Lake City: Deseret Book Co., 1965); Richard Lloyd Anderson, "Circumstantial Confirmation of the First Vision through Reminiscences," *BYU Studies* 9 (spring 1969): 373–404; Richard P. Howard, "Joseph Smith's First Vision: The RLDS Tradition," *Journal of Mormon History* 7 (1980): 23–29; Richard Lloyd Anderson, "Confirming Records of Moroni's Coming," *Improvement Era*, September 1970, 4–9.

14. The first to develop this problem was Paul R. Cheesman, "An Analysis of the Accounts Relating Joseph Smith's Early Visions," (M.A. thesis, Brigham Young University, 1965), but this was not a published account and only after the divergent accounts were ballyhooed as evidence of Smith's fraudulent claims did Mormon scholars really get busy trying to cohere the differences. See Jerold and Sandra Tanner, *Joseph Smith's Strange Account of the First Vision* (Salt Lake City: Modern Microfilm Co., 1965).

15. See James B. Allen, "Eight Contemporary Accounts of Joseph Smith's First Vision—What Do We Learn from Them?" *Improvement Era*, April 1970, 4–13; Dean C. Jessee, "The Early Accounts of Joseph Smith's First Vision," *BYU Studies* 9 (spring 1969): 275–94; Richard P. Howard, "An Analysis of Six Contemporary Accounts of Joseph Smith's First Vision," in *Restoration Studies 1*, ed. Maurice L. Draper and Clare D. Vlahos (Independence, Mo.: Herald Publishing House, 1980), 95–117; Neal E. Lambert and Richard H. Cracroft, "Literary Form and Historical Understanding: Joseph Smith's First Vision," *Journal of Mormon History* 7 (1980): 31–42.

16. Leonard J. Arrington and Davis Bitton, *The Mormon Experience: A History of the Latter-day Saints* (New York: Alfred A. Knopf, 1979), 8.

17. Wesley P. Walters, "New Light on Mormon Origins from the Palmyra (N.Y.) Revival," *Bulletin of the Evangelical Theological Society* 10 (fall 1967): 227–44. This publication did not receive much circulation in the Mormon community, so Walters also submitted the paper for publication to *Dialogue: A Journal of Mormon Thought*, but it did not appear until the spring of 1969. The journal held up publication on it until a sympathetic historian could write a reply.

18. James B. Allen and Leonard J. Arrington, "Mormon Origins in New York: An Introductory Analysis," *BYU Studies* 9 (spring 1969): 241–74; "Roundtable: The Question of the Palmyra Revival," *Dialogue: A Journal of Mormon Thought* 4 (spring 1969): 59–60; Truman G. Madsen, "Guest Editor's Prologue," *BYU Studies* 9 (spring 1969): 235–40.

19. The articles include Allen and Arrington, "Mormon Origins in New York," 241–74; Dean C. Jessee, "The Early Accounts of Joseph Smith's

First Vision," *BYU Studies* 9 (spring 1969): 275–94; Milton V. Backman Jr., "Awakenings in the Burned-Over District: New Light on the Historical Setting of the First Vision," *BYU Studies* 9 (spring 1969): 301–20; Larry C. Porter, "Reverend George Lane—Good 'Gifts,' Much 'Grace,' and Marked 'Usefulness'," *BYU Studies* 9 (spring 1969): 321–40; T. Edgar Lyon, "How Authentic are Mormon Historic Sites in Vermont and New York?" *BYU Studies* 9 (spring 1969): 341–50; Marvin S. Hill, "The Shaping of the Mormon Mind in New England and New York," *BYU Studies* 9 (spring 1969): 351–72; Anderson, "Circumstantial Confirmation of the First Vision through Reminiscences," 373–404.

20. See "Roundtable: The Question of the Palmyra Revival," *Dialogue: A Journal of Mormon Thought* 4 (spring 1969): 59–100. It included these articles: Wesley P. Walters, "New Light on Mormon Origins from the Palmyra Revival," *Dialogue: A Journal of Mormon Thought* 4 (spring 1969): 60–81; Richard L. Bushman, "The First Vision Story Revived," *Dialogue: A Journal of Mormon Thought* 4 (spring 1969): 82–93; Wesley P. Walters, "A Reply to Dr. Bushman," *Dialogue: A Journal of Mormon Thought* 4 (spring 1969): 94–100.

21. Milton V. Backman Jr., *Joseph Smith's First Vision: The First Vision in Historical Context* (Salt Lake City: Bookcraft, 1971, 2nd. ed. 1980); Peter Crawley, "A Comment on Joseph Smith's Account of His First Vision and the 1820 Revival," *Dialogue: A Journal of Mormon Thought* 6 (spring 1971): 106–109; Marvin S. Hill, "A Note on the First Vision and Its Import in the Shaping of Early Mormonism," *Dialogue: A Journal of Mormon Thought* 12 (spring 1979): 90–99; Richard L. Bushman, *Joseph Smith and the Beginnings of Mormonism* (Urbana: University of Illinois Press, 1984), 53–59; Donna Hill, *Joseph Smith: The First Mormon* (Garden City, N.Y.: Doubleday and Co., 1977), 41–54; Marvin S. Hill, "The First Vision Controversy: A Critique and Reconciliation," *Dialogue: A Journal of Mormon Thought* 15 (summer 1982): 31–46.

22. Hill, "A Note on the First Vision," 95–96; Hill, "The First Vision Controversy," 31–46. Smith's anti-pluralism is exhaustively documented in Marvin S. Hill, "Counter-Revolution: The Mormon Reaction to the Coming of American Democracy," *Sunstone* 13 (June 1989): 24–33, and Marvin S. Hill, *Quest for Refuge: The Mormon Flight from American Pluralism* (Salt Lake City: Signature Books, 1989). See also, Richard T. Hughes and C. Leonard Allen, *Illusions of Innocence: Protestant Primitivism in American, 1630–1875* (Chicago: University of Chicago Press, 1988), see chapter "Early Mormons and the Eclipse of Religious Pluralism;" Dan Vogel, *Religious Seekers and the Advent of Mormonism* (Salt Lake City: Signature Books, 1988).

23. Jan Shipps, *Mormonism: The Story of a New Religious Tradition* (Urbana: University of Illinois Press, 1985), 30–33.

24. Brodie, No Man Knows My History, 16–33.
25. Deseret News, Church Section, May 11, 1946; John A. Widtsoe, Joseph Smith—Seeker After Truth (Salt Lake City: Deseret Book Co., 1951), 78, 267; Hugh Nibley, The Myth Makers (Salt Lake City: Bookcraft, 1961), 142.
26. Perhaps the first serious attempt to wrestle with Brodie's challenge can be found in Marvin S. Hill, "Joseph Smith and the 1826 Trial: New Evidence and New Difficulties," BYU Studies 12 (winter 1972): 223–33. See also Richard Lloyd Anderson, "Joseph Smith's New York Reputation Reappraised," BYU Studies 10 (spring 1970): 283–314; Wesley P. Walters, "From Occult to Cult with Joseph Smith, Jr.," Journal of Pastoral Practice 1 (summer 1977): 121–31; Wesley P. Walters, "Joseph Smith's Bainbridge, N.Y., Court Trials," Westminster Theological Journal 36 (winter 1974): 123–55; James B. Allen and Glen M. Leonard, The Story of the Latter-day Saints (Salt Lake City: Deseret Book Co., 1976), 35–36; Arrington and Bitton, The Mormon Experience, 10–11.
27. See Reed C. Durham Jr., "Is There No Help for the Widow's Son," in Joseph Smith and Masonry: No Help for the Widow's Son: Two Papers on the Influence of the Masonic Movement on Joseph Smith and his Mormon Church, by Jack Adamson and Reed C. Durham Jr. (Nauvoo, Ill.: Martin Publishing Co., 1980), 15–28. This was the 1974 presidential address of the Mormon History Association, and Durham was disciplined because of his statements. Three years later Paul M. Edwards, in "The Secular Smiths," Journal of Mormon History 4 (1977): 3–17, suggested that Joseph Smith was a mystic in the eastern pattern and did not separate magic from the broader world.
28. A special issue of BYU Studies was dedicated to trying to defend the challenge. See Dean C. Jessee, "New Documents and Mormon Beginnings," BYU Studies 24 (fall 1984): 397–428; Ronald W. Walker, "The Persistent Idea of American Treasure Hunting," BYU Studies 24 (fall 1984): 429–59; Ronald W. Walker, "Joseph Smith: The Palmyra Seer," BYU Studies 24 (fall 1984): 461–72; Marvin S. Hill, "Money-Digging Folklore and the Beginnings of Mormonism," BYU Studies 24 (fall 1984): 473–88; Richard Lloyd Anderson, "The Mature Joseph Smith and Treasure Searching," BYU Studies 24 (fall 1984): 489–560. On the Hofmann affair see Linda Sillitoe and Allen Roberts, Salamander: The Story of the Mormon Forgery Murders (Salt Lake City: Signature Books, 1988); Steven Naifeh and Gregory White Smith, The Mormon Murders: A True Story of Greed, Forgery, Deceit, and Death (New York: Weidenfeld and Nicolson, 1988); Robert Lindsey, A Gathering of Saints: A True Story of Money, Murder, and Deceit (New York: Simon and Schuster, 1988); Richard E. Turley Jr., Victims: The LDS Church and the Mark Hofmann Case (Urbana: University of Illinois Press, 1992).

29. Bushman, *Joseph Smith and the Beginnings of Mormonism*, 64–76. On the "faithful history" approach see Richard L. Bushman, "Faithful History," *Dialogue: A Journal of Mormon Thought* 4 (winter 1969): 11–28.

30. D. Michael Quinn, *Early Mormonism and the Magic World View* (Salt Lake City: Signature Books, 1987). See also Alan Taylor, "Rediscovering the Context of Joseph Smith's Treasure Seeking," *Dialogue: A Journal of Mormon Thought* 19 (winter 1986): 18–28.

31. Thomas S. Kuhn, *The Structure of Scientific Revolutions* (New Haven, Conn.: Yale University Press, 1957).

32. John L. Brooke, *The Refiner's Fire: The Making of Mormon Cosmology, 1644–1844* (New York: Cambridge University Press, 1994).

33. Brodie, *No Man Knows My History*, 50–66.

34. See Curtis Dahl, "Mound Builders, Mormons, and William Cullen Bryant," *New England Quarterly* 34 (1961): 178–90; Dan Vogel, *Indian Origins and the Book of Mormon: Religious Solutions from Columbus to Joseph Smith* (Salt Lake City: Signature Books, 1986); Robert N. Hullinger, "The Lost Tribes of Israel and the Book of Mormon," *Lutheran Quarterly* 22 (August 1970): 319–29.

35. These quotations are from Book of Mormon (Palmyra, N.Y.: E. B. Grandin, 1830), 72, 144–45. The Brodie analysis is presented in *No Man Knows My History*, 34–49.

36. Brodie, *No Man Knows My History*, 49.

37. On the subject of defenses of Joseph Smith's contention that it was a sacred record and not a product of frontier mythology as expressed in *View of the Hebrews*, see Spencer J. Palmer and William L. Knecht, "View of the Hebrews: Substitute for Inspiration?" *BYU Studies* 5 (winter 1964): 105–15; Roy E. Weldon, "Masonry and Ethan Smith's 'View of the Hebrews'," *Saints Herald* 119 (September 1972): 26–28.

38. Brodie, *No Man Knows My History*, 35–55.

39. See Richard Lloyd Anderson, "Joseph Smith's New York Reputation Reappraised," *BYU Studies* 10 (spring 1970): 283–314, which challenges the Brodie contention of the reliability of the statements of neighbors in Palmyra. He further but indirectly elaborates on the good character of Joseph Smith by analyzing his ancestry in Richard Lloyd Anderson, *Joseph Smith's New England Heritage: Influences of Grandfathers Solomon Mack and Asael Smith* (Salt Lake City: Deseret Book Co., 1971). These contentions were specifically challenged by Rodger I. Anderson, *Joseph Smith's New York Reputation Reexamined* (Salt Lake City: Signature Books, 1990), who argues that the neighbors were reliable and that the Brodie conclusions were justified. On Obadiah Dogberry see Joseph W. Barnes, "Obadiah Dogberry: Rochester Free-Thinker," *Rochester History* 36 (July 1974): 1–24; Russell R.

Rich, "The Dogberry Papers and the Book of Mormon," *BYU Studies* 10 (spring 1970): 315–20.

40. Alexander Campbell, *Delusions: An Analysis of the Book of Mormon* (Boston: Benjamin H. Greene, 1832), 13. For a discussion of the harmful nature of this quote on Mormon history see Mario S. De Pillis, "The Quest for Religious Authority and the Rise of Mormonism," *Dialogue: A Journal of Mormon Thought* 1 (spring 1966): 68–88, especially p. 79.

41. Brodie, *No Man Knows My History*, 69, 86.

42. Susan Curtis Mernitz, "Palmyra Revisited: A Look at Early Nineteenth Century America and the Book of Mormon," *John Whitmer Historical Association Journal* 2 (1982): 30–37. See Grant Underwood, "Book of Mormon Usage in Early LDS Theology," *Dialogue: A Journal of Mormon Thought* 17 (autumn 1984): 35–74 for a discussion of the centrality of the scripture in the life of the church. A new collection challenges the historicity of the *Book of Mormon*. See Brent Lee Metcalfe, ed., *New Approaches to the Book of Mormon* (Salt Lake City: Signature Books, 1993).

43. Richard L. Bushman, "The Book of Mormon and the American Revolution," *BYU Studies* 17 (fall 1976): 3–20, reprinted in Noel B. Reynolds, ed., *Book of Mormon Authorship: New Light on Ancient Origins* (Provo, Utah: Brigham Young University Religious Studies Center, 1982), 189–211; Richard L. Bushman, "The Book of Mormon in Early Mormon History," in *New Views of Mormon History: A Collection of Essays in Honor of Leonard J. Arrington*, ed. Davis Bitton and Maureen Ursenbach Beecher (Salt Lake City: University of Utah Press, 1987), 3–18; Richard L. Bushman, "The Character of Joseph Smith: Insights from his Holographs," *Ensign* (April 1977): 11–13; Bushman, *Joseph Smith and the Beginnings of Mormonism*, 115–42. See also Hyrum L. Andrus, "The Second American Revolution: Era of Preparation," *BYU Studies* 1–2 (autumn 1959–winter 1960): 71–100.

44. Hill, "Counter-Revolution, 24–33.

45. See as examples Wayne Larson, Alvin C. Rencher, and Tim Layton, "Who Wrote the Book of Mormon? An Analysis of Wordprints," *BYU Studies* 20 (spring 1980): 229; Hugh Nibley, *Since Cumorah: The Book of Mormon in the Modern World* (Salt Lake City: Deseret Book Co., 1967); Gayle Goble Ord, "The Book of Mormon Goes to Press," *Ensign* (December 1972): 66–70; David Brion Davis, "Some Themes of Counter-Subversion: An Analysis of Anti-Masonic, Anti-Catholic, and Anti-Mormon Literature," *Mississippi Valley Historical Review* 47 (September 1960): 205–24; Blake Ostler, "The Book of Mormon as a Modern Expansion of an Ancient Source," *Dialogue: A Journal of Mormon Thought* 20 (spring 1987): 66–124; Robert Paul, "Joseph Smith and the Manchester (New York) Library," *BYU Studies* 22 (summer 1982): 333–56; Larry C. Porter, "The Colesville Branch and the

Coming Forth of the Book of Mormon," *BYU Studies* 10 (spring 1970): 365–85; Larry C. Porter, "William E. McLellin's Testimony of the Book of Mormon," *BYU Studies* 10 (summer 1970): 485–87; Noel B. Reynolds, ed., *Book of Mormon Authorship: New Light on Ancient Origins* (Provo, Utah: Religious Studies Center, Brigham Young University, 1982); Noel B. Reynolds, "Nephi's Outline," *BYU Studies* 20 (winter 1980): 131–49; Russell R. Rich, "Where Were the Moroni Visits?" *BYU Studies* 10 (spring 1970): 255–58; B.H. Roberts, *Studies of the Book of Mormon*, ed. Brigham D. Madsen (Urbana: University of Illinois Press, 1985); Timothy L. Smith, "The Book of Mormon in a Biblical Culture," *Journal of Mormon History* 7 (1980): 3–21; John L. Sorenson, "The 'Brass Plates' and Biblical Scholarship," *Dialogue: A Journal of Mormon Thought* 10 (autumn 1977): 31–39; Geoffrey F. Spencer, "Anxious Saints: The Early Mormons, Social Reform, and Status Anxiety," *John Whitmer Historical Association Journal* 1 (1981): 43–53; Geoffrey F. Spencer, *The Burning Bush: Revelation and Scripture in the Life of the Church* (Independence, Mo.: Herald Publishing House, 1975); Geoffrey F. Spencer, "Mormonism in the Historical Setting of 19th Century America," *Commission*, September 1979, 12–19; Ernest H. Taves, *Trouble Enough: Joseph Smith and the Book of Mormon* (Buffalo, N.Y.: Prometheus Books, 1984); John A. Tvedtnes, "Composition and History of the Book of Mormon," *New Era*, September 1974, 41–43; John A. Tvedtnes, "Hebraisms in the Book of Mormon: A Preliminary Survey," *Sunstone* 12 (January 1988): 8–13; Grant Underwood, "Book of Mormon Usage in Early LDS Theology," *Dialogue: A Journal of Mormon Thought*, 17 (Autumn 1984): 35–74; Steven C. Walker, "More Than Meets the Eye: Concentration in the Book of Mormon," *BYU Studies* 20 (winter 1980): 199–205; John W. Welch, "Chiasmas in the Book of Mormon," *BYU Studies* 10 (autumn 1969): 69–84; Douglas Wilson, "Prospects for the Study of the Book of Mormon as a Work of American Literature," *Dialogue: A Journal of Mormon Thought* 3 (spring 1969): 29–41.

46. Mario S. De Pillis, "The Social Sources of Mormonism," *Church History* 37 (March 1968): 50–79, quote from p. 62. For a discussion of Mormon scripture see the essays in Dan Vogel, ed., *The Word of God: Essays on Mormon Scripture* (Salt Lake City: Signature Books, 1990).

47. Eber D. Howe, *Mormonism Unvailed* (Painesville, Ohio: n.p., 1834), 278–89. Brodie's discussion is in *No Man Knows My History*, 442–56. See also Hans Rollmann, "The Early Baptist Career of Sidney Rigdon in Warren, Ohio," *BYU Studies* 21 (winter 1981): 37–50; F. Mark McKiernan, *The Voice of One Crying in the Wilderness: Sidney Rigdon, Religious Reformer, 1793–1876* (Lawrence, Kans.: Coronado Press, 1971), 36–40.

48. This story has been ably documented in Lester E. Bush Jr., "The Spaulding Theory: Then and Now," *Dialogue: A Journal of Mormon Thought* 10

(autumn 1977): 40–69 and Charles H. Whittier and Stephen W. Stathis, "The Enigma of Solomon Spaulding," *Dialogue: A Journal of Mormon Thought* 10 (autumn 1977): 70–73.

49. See Danel W. Bachman, "Sealed in a Book: Preliminary Observations on the Newly Found Anthon Transcript," *BYU Studies* 20 (spring 1980): 321–45; Ariel L. Crowley, "The Anthon Transcript: An Evidence for the Truth of the Prophet's Account of the Origin of the Book of Mormon," *Improvement Era* 45 (1945): 14–15, 58–60, 76–80, 124–25, 150–51, 182–83; Stanley B. Kimball, "The Anthon Transcript: People, Primary Sources, and Problems," *BYU Studies* 10 (spring 1970): 325–52; Edward H. Ashment, "The Book of Mormon and the Anthon Transcript: An Interim Report," *Sunstone* 5 (May–June 1980): 29–31.

50. James E. Lancaster, "By the Gift and Power of God," *Saint's Herald* 109 (November 15, 1962): 798–802, 806, 817; reprinted with minor revisions in the *John Whitmer Historical Association Journal* 3 (1983): 51–61; Ronald W. Walker, "Joseph Smith: The Palmyra Seer," *BYU Studies* 24 (fall 1984): 461–88; Richard S. Van Wagoner and Steven C. Walker, "Joseph Smith: The Gift of Seeing," *Dialogue: A Journal of Mormon Thought* 22 (summer 1982): 48–68; Dean C. Jessee, "Lucy Mack Smith's 1829 Letter to Mary Smith Pierce," *BYU Studies* 22 (fall 1982): 457–58; Clair E. Weldon, "Two Transparent Stones: The Story of the Urim and Thummim," *Saints' Herald* 109 (September 1, 1962): 616–620, 623.

51. Dean C. Jessee, "The Original Book of Mormon Manuscripts," *BYU Studies* 10 (spring 1970): 259–78; Stan Larson, "Textual Variants in Book of Mormon Manuscripts," *Dialogue: A Journal of Mormon Thought* 10 (autumn 1977): 8–30; Richard P. Howard, "Latter Day Saint Scriptures and the Doctrine of Propositional Revelation," *Courage: A Journal of History, Thought, and Action* 1 (June 1971): 209–25; Richard P. Howard, *Restoration Scriptures: A Study of Their Textual Development* (Independence, Mo.: Herald Publishing House, 1969, rev. ed. 1994).

52. Brodie, *No Man Knows My History,* 67–82.

53. The key publication in this vein is Richard Lloyd Anderson, *Investigating the Book of Mormon Witnesses* (Salt Lake City: Deseret Book Co., 1981). See also Richard Lloyd Anderson, "Martin Harris, The Honorable New York Farmer," *Improvement Era,* February 1969, 18–21; Richard Lloyd Anderson, "Reuben Miller: Recorder of Oliver Cowdery's Reaffirmations," *BYU Studies* 8 (spring 1968): 277–85; Wayne Cutler Gunnell, "Martin Harris, Witness and Benefactor to the Book of Mormon" (M.A. thesis, Brigham Young University, 1971); Preston Nibley, comp., *The Witnesses of the Book of Mormon* (Salt Lake City: Deseret Book Co., 1973 ed.); Ronald W. Walker, "Martin Harris: Mormonism's Early Convert," *Dialogue: A Journal of Mormon Thought* 19 (winter 1986): 29–43; Stanley R. Gunn, *Oliver Cowdery: Second Elder and Scribe* (Salt Lake City: Bookcraft, 1962).

54. There has been some recent work in this category, nearly fifty years after Brodie. See Phillip R. Legg, *Oliver Cowdery: The Elusive Second Elder of the Restoration* (Independence, Mo.: Herald Publishing House, 1989); Ronald E. Romig, "David Whitmer: Faithful Dissenter, Witness Apart," in *Differing Visions: Dissenters in Mormon History*, ed. Roger D. Launius and Linda Thatcher (Urbana: University of Illinois Press, 1994), 23–44.

55. See B.H. Roberts, *Studies of the Book of Mormon*, ed. Brigham D. Madsen (Urbana: University of Illinois Press, 1985); Truman G. Madsen, "B. H. Roberts and the Book of Mormon," *BYU Studies* 19 (summer 1979): 427–45; "New B. H. Roberts Book Lacks Insight of his Testimony," *Deseret News*, December 15, 1985; John W. Welch, "B. H. Roberts, Seeker after Truth," *Ensign* 16 (March 1986): 56–62; Brigham D. Madsen, "B. H. Roberts's Studies of the Book of Mormon," *Dialogue: A Journal of Mormon Thought* 26 (fall 1993): 76–86.

56. Anthony A. Hutchinson, "The Word of God Is Enough: The Book of Mormon as Nineteenth-Century Scripture," in *New Approaches to the Book of Mormon: Explorations in Critical Methodology*, ed. Brent Lee Metcalfe (Salt Lake City: Signature Books, 1993), 1.

57. See as a way of interpreting it, Wayne Ham, "Problems in Interpreting the Book of Mormon as History," *Courage: A Journal of History, Thought, and Action* 1 (September 1970): 15–22; William D. Russell, "History and the Mormon Scriptures," *Journal of Mormon History* 10 (1983): 53–63.

58. William P. Collins, "Thoughts on the Mormon Scriptures: An Outsider's View of the Inspiration of Joseph Smith," *Dialogue: A Journal of Mormon Thought* 15 (autumn 1982): 53.

59. The most famous of these controversies was over Brodie's contention that Thomas Jefferson had enjoyed a longstanding affair with a slave, Sally Hemings, and that the couple had several children together. See Fawn M. Brodie, *Thomas Jefferson: An Intimate History* (New York: Alfred A. Knopf, 1974). This contention set off a debate that incensed the established Jeffersonian scholars and several rebuttals were issued, any one of which were more able and effective than those about Joseph Smith prepared by Mormon historians. See John C. Miller, *The Wolf by the Ears: Thomas Jefferson and Slavery* (New York: Free Press, 1977); Virginius Dabney, *The Jefferson Scandals: A Rebuttal* (New York: Dodd, Mead, 1981); Dumas Malone and Steven H. Hochman, "A Note on Evidence: The Personal History of Madison Hemings," *Journal of Southern History* 41 (November 1975): 523–28; T. Harry Williams, "On the Couch at Monticello," *Reviews in American History* 2 (December 1974): 523–29. Brodie was also fascinated by the sexual escapades of Sir Richard Burton, who himself was fascinated by unusual sexual practices, translating the highly erotic stories of the Arabian nights into English, engaging in Muslim polygamy, and investigating eastern sexual techniques such as the Kama Sutra. See Fawn M. Brodie, *The Devil*

Drives: A Life of Sir Richard Burton (New York: Alfred A. Knopf, 1967). She even explored a possible homosexual relationship in her work on Richard Nixon, but this failed to pan out. See Fawn M. Brodie, *Richard Nixon: The Shaping of his Character* (New York: W. W. Norton, 1981).

60. Brodie, *No Man Knows My History*, 297–308. She had earlier discussed the affair in Kirtland with Fanny Alger, 181–85.

61. Hill, "Secular or Sectarian History?" 93.

62. The quote is from Oliver Cowdery to Warren A. Cowdery, January 21, 1838, Oliver Cowdery Papers, Huntington Library, San Marino, Calif.

63. On these men see Lyndon W. Cook, "William Law, Nauvoo Dissenter," *BYU Studies* 22 (winter 1982): 47–62; Robert Bruce Flanders, *Nauvoo: Kingdom on the Mississippi* (Urbana: University of Illinois Press, 1965), 305–10; John Frederick Glaser, "The Disaffection of William Law," in *Restoration Studies III*, ed. Maurice L. Draper and Debra Combs (Independence, Mo.: Herald Publishing House, 1986), 163–75.

64. *Nauvoo* (Ill.) *Expositor*, June 7, 1844; Dallin H. Oaks, "The Suppression of the *Nauvoo Expositor*," *Utah Law Review* 9 (winter 1966): 862–903; Dean C. Jessee, "Return to Carthage: Writing the History of Joseph Smith's Martyrdom," *Journal of Mormon History* 8 (1981): 3–21.

65. Elbert A. Smith, *Differences that Persist: Between the Reorganized Church of Jesus Christ of Latter Day Saints and the Utah Mormon Church* (Independence, Mo.: Herald Publishing House, 1943); Roy A. Cheville, *Joseph and Emma Companions: For Seventeen and a Half Years, 1827–1844* (Independence, Mo.: Herald Publishing House, 1977); Maurice L. Draper, *Marriage in the Restoration* (Independence, Mo.: Herald Publishing House, 1969); Russell A. Ralston, *Fundamental Differences* (Independence, Mo.: Herald Publishing House, 1963); George Njeim, "Joseph Smith: Prophet and Theologian," *Saints' Herald* 117 (January 1970): 18-19, 48; 117 (February 1970): 24-26; 117 (March 1970): 34–36, 66; Francis W. Holm Sr., *The Mormon Churches: A Comparison from Within* (Independence, Mo.: Midwest Press, 1970); Aleah J. Koury, *The Truth and the Evidence* (Independence, Mo.: Herald Publishing House, 1965).

66. See Flanders, *Nauvoo*, 264–74.

67. Richard P. Howard, "The Changing RLDS Response to Mormon Polygamy: A Preliminary Analysis," *John Whitmer Historical Association Journal* 3 (1983): 14–29.

68. See Linda King Newell and Valeen Tippets Avery, *Mormon Enigma: Emma Hale Smith, Prophet's Wife, "Elect Lady," Polygamy's Foe* (Garden City, N.Y.: Doubleday, 1984); Alma R. Blair, "RLDS Views of Polygamy: Some Historiographical Notes," *John Whitmer Historical Association Journal* 5 (1985): 16–28; Paul M. Edwards, "William B. Smith: The Persistent 'Pretender'," *Dialogue: A Journal of Mormon Thought* 18 (summer 1985):

128–39; Don H. Compier, "The Faith of Emma Smith," *John Whitmer Historical Association Journal* 6 (1986): 64–72; Roger D. Launius, *Joseph Smith III: Pragmatic Prophet* (Urbana: University of Illinois Press, 1988), 190–217; Paul M. Edwards, "William B. Smith: 'A Wart on the Ecclesiastical Tree'," in *Differing Visions: Dissenters in Mormon History*, ed. Roger D. Launius and Linda Thatcher (Urbana University of Illinois Press, 1994), 140–57.

69. Nibley, *No Ma'am, That's Not History*, 57–58. Similar statements are made on pp. 46 and 62.

70. See, as examples, Hyrum L. Andrus, *Joseph Smith: The Man and the Seer* (Salt Lake City: Deseret Book Co., 1976); Lyndon W. Cook, *The Revelations of the Prophet Joseph Smith* (Provo, Utah: Seventy's Mission Bookstore, 1981), 293–95; Francis M. Gibbons, *Joseph Smith: Martyr, Prophet of God* (Salt Lake City: Deseret Book Co., 1977); John A. Widtsoe, *Joseph Smith: Seeker after Truth, Prophet of God* (Salt Lake City: Deseret Book Co., 1951); Richard S. Van Wagoner, *Mormon Polygamy: A History* (Salt Lake City: Signature Books, 1985); Thomas G. Alexander, "'A New and Everlasting Covenant': An Approach to the Theology of Joseph Smith," in *New Views of Mormon History*, ed. Bitton and Beecher, 43–62; Ivan J. Barrett, *Joseph Smith and the Restoration: A History of the Church to 1846* (Provo, Utah: Brigham Young University Press, 1973); Larry C. Porter and Susan Easton Black, eds., *The Prophet Joseph Smith: Essays on the Life and Mission of Joseph Smith* (Salt Lake City: Deseret Book Co., 1988).

71. Leonard J. Arrington, *Brigham Young: American Moses* (New York: Alfred A. Knopf, 1985), 5–6, 100–102, 117–18; Stanley B. Kimball, *Heber C. Kimball: Mormon Patriarch and Pioneer* (Urbana: University of Illinois Press, 1981), 93–103, 122–23, 227–41, 245–56, 290–98; Thomas G. Alexander, *Things in Heaven and Earth: The Life and Times of Wilford Woodruff, a Mormon Prophet* (Salt Lake City: Signature Books, 1991), 128, 167, 186, 234–56; 308–26.

72. Hill, "Secular or Sectarian History?" 94–95.

73. Lawrence Foster, *Religion and Sexuality: Three American Communal Experiments of the Nineteenth Century* (New York: Oxford University Press, 1981); Lawrence Foster, *Women, Family, and Utopia: Communal Experiments of the Shakers, the Oneida Community, and the Mormons* (Syracuse, N.Y.: Syracuse University Press, 1991). In spite of other deficiencies, it also helps explain the rejection of a similar book that also appeared in 1981. Louis J. Kern, *An Ordered Love: Sex Roles and Sexuality in Victorian Utopias—the Shakers, the Mormons, and the Oneida Community* (Chapel Hill: University of North Carolina Press, 1981), took an approach that warmed over Brodie's ideas about Smith's sexual misconduct and his basically dishonest approach to religion.

74. As creative as Smith admittedly was and Foster acknowledged, he does not see him as a legitimate prophet. As an example of his beliefs about Smith see Lawrence Foster, "The Psychology of Religious Genius: Joseph Smith and the Origins of New Religious Movements," *Dialogue: A Journal of Mormon Thought* 26 (winter 1993): 1–22.

75. See, Danel W. Bachman, "New Light on an Old Hypothesis: The Ohio Origins of the Revelation on Eternal Marriage," *Journal of Mormon History* 5 (1978): 19–31.

76. Danel W. Bachman, "A Study of the Mormon Practice of Plural Marriage before the Death of Joseph Smith" (M.A. thesis, Purdue University, 1975); Richard S. Van Wagoner, *Mormon Polygamy: A History* (Salt Lake City: Signature Books, 1986), 3–69; Hill, "Secular or Sectarian History?" 94.

77. This theme has been explored in Joseph R. Gusfield, *Symbolic Crusade: Status Politics and the American Temperance Movement* (Urbana: University of Illinois Press, 1963); Rowland Berthoff, *An Unsettled People: Social Order and Disorder in American History* (New York: Free Press, 1971).

78. Mark C. Carnes, *Secret Ritual and Manhood in Victorian America* (New Haven, Conn.: Yale University Press, 1989).

79. The explicit connection between the Mormon temple ceremonies and lodges, especially Masonry, has been made in numerous publications. See David John Buerger, "The Development of the Mormon Temple Endowment Ceremony," *Dialogue: A Journal of Mormon Thought* 20 (winter 1987): 33–76; Reed C. Durham Jr., "'Is There No Help For the Widow's Son?'" Presidential address to the Mormon History Association, April 20, 1974, Nauvoo, Ill.; Mervin B. Hogan, *Mormonism and Freemasonry: The Illinois Episode* (Salt Lake City: Campus Graphics, 1980); Carnes, *Secret Ritual and Manhood in Victorian America*, 6–7, Roger D. Launius and F. Mark McKiernan, *Joseph Smith, Jr.'s Red Brick Store* (Macomb: Western Illinois University Monograph Series, 1985), 28–32.

80. Brodie, *No Man Knows My History*, 348–66, quote from p. 354.

81. Ibid., 367–95.

82. James B. Allen and Glen M. Leonard, *The Story of the Latter-day Saints* (Salt Lake City: Deseret Book Co., 1976), 171.

83. Ibid., 137.

84. See, Richard D. Poll, "Nauvoo and the New Mormon History: A Bibliographical Survey," *Journal of Mormon History* 5 (1978): 105–23.

85. Flanders, *Nauvoo*, vi.

86. Glen M. Leonard, "Remembering Nauvoo: Historiographical Considerations," *Journal of Mormon History* 16 (1990): 25–39, quote from p. 33.

87. Klaus J. Hansen, "The World and the Prophet," *Dialogue: A Journal of Mormon Thought* 1 (summer 1966): 103–107, quote from p. 106.

88. Ronald K. Esplin, "The Significance of Nauvoo for Latter-day Saints," *Journal of Mormon History* 16 (1990): 71–88, quote from p. 72.

89. Klaus J. Hansen, *Quest for Empire: The Kingdom of God and the Council of Fifty in Mormon History* (East Lansing: Michigan State University Press, 1967). See also Klaus J. Hansen, "The Metamorphosis of the Kingdom of God," *Dialogue: A Journal of Mormon Thought* 1 (autumn 1966): 63–83 and Klaus J. Hansen, *Mormonism and the American Experience* (Chicago: University of Chicago Press, 1981), especially 113–46.

90. See especially D. Michael Quinn, "The Council of Fifty and its Members," *BYU Studies* 20 (winter 1980): 163–97; Marvin S. Hill, "Quest for Refuge: An Hypothesis as to the Social Origins and Nature of the Mormon Political Kingdom," *Journal of Mormon History* 2 (1975): 3–20; and Andrew F. Ehat, "'It Seems Like Heaven Began on Earth': Joseph Smith and the Constitution of the Kingdom of God," *BYU Studies* 20 (spring 1980): 253–79.

91. Hill, *Quest for Refuge: The Mormon Flight from American Pluralism* (Salt Lake City: Signature Books, 1989), 17.

92. See the argument in Peter L. Berger, *The Sacred Canopy* (New York: Doubleday Anchor, 1969), 111–12.

93. Perhaps I make too much of this, certainly the questions that Brodie raised were important and deserving of investigation and reinterpretation and perhaps that is enough. Clearly, she placed her finger on several compelling factors that contributed to Smith's development and informed his direction of the movement. A careful reading of the historical literature, however, convinces me that chasing the shadow of Brodie's Joseph Smith has been in many ways unnecessary and counterproductive. This is especially true of later historians' propensity for combatting Brodie's interpretation on her terms, either seeing Smith as an authentic prophet or as a charlatan. The elucidation of exactly how far each of her interpretations merits further discussion I gladly leave to others.

Notes on the Contributors

Lavina Fielding Anderson is president of Editing, Inc. She is editor of the *Journal of Mormon History*, a member of the Board of Editors of Signature Books, co-associate editor of *Dialogue: A Journal of Mormon Thought*, former associate editor of *Ensign*, and past president of the Association for Mormon Letters. She is the editor of numerous articles and essays on various aspects of Mormon studies and has been published in a number of journals, including *Dialogue* and *Sunstone*.

Newell G. Bringhurst is an instructor in history and political science at College of the Sequoias in Visalia, California. He is the author of *Saints, Slaves, and Blacks: The Changing Place of Black People Within Mormonism* and *Brigham Young and the Expanding American Frontier*. He is completing a book-length biography of Fawn McKay Brodie.

Todd Compton is an independent researcher who holds a Ph.D. in classics from the University of California, Los Angeles. He is the author of numerous articles dealing with polygamy in the early Mormon church, which have been published in various journals, including *Dialogue* and the *Journal of Mormon History*. He is also the author of *In Sacred Loneliness: The Plural Wives of Joseph Smith*.

Mario S. De Pillis is professor emeritus in social and religious history at the University of Massachusetts at Amherst. He was the founding editor of *Communal Societies* and a founding editor of

The Journal of Social History. He is a past president of the Mormon History Association and the author of numerous articles on Mormons, Shakers, and Norwegian immigration.

Marvin S. Hill is professor emeritus of American history at Brigham Young University. He is the author of *Quest for Refuge: The Mormon Flight from American Pluralism;* co-author, with Dallin H. Oaks, of *Carthage Conspiracy: The Trial of the Accused Assassins of Joseph Smith;* and, with Larry T. Wimmer, of *The Kirtland Economy Revisited: A Market Critique of Sectarian Economics.* He is a past president of the Mormon History Association.

Roger D. Launius is chief historian with the NASA History Office in Washington, D.C. and the author of numerous books and monographs in the field of Mormon studies, including *Invisible Saints: A History of Black Americans in the Reorganized Church; Joseph Smith III: Pragmatic Prophet;* and, with John E. Hallwas, *Cultures in Conflict: A Documentary History of the Mormon War in Illinois.* He is a past president of the Mormon History Association.

William Mulder is professor emeritus of English at the University of Utah. He is the author of various works dealing with the Mormon experience, including *Homeward to Zion: The Scandinavian Mormon Migration,* and co-editor, with the late A. Russell Mortensen, of *Among the Mormons: Historic Accounts by Contemporary Observers.*

Index